P9-AQV-794

BILL W.

BILL W.

Robert Thomsen

Harper & Row, Publishers
New York, Evanston, San Francisco, London

Grateful acknowledgment is made for permission to reprint the following:

Excerpts from *Twelve Steps and Twelve Traditions*. Copyright 1953 by Alcoholics Anonymous World Services, Inc. Reprinted by permission of Alcoholics Anonymous World Services, Inc.

Letter to William Wilson from C. G. Jung, January 30, 1961. Copyright © 1963 by the A A Grapevine, Inc. Reprinted by permission.

BILL W. Copyright © 1975 by Robert Thomsen. All rights reserved. Printed in the United States of America. No part of this book may be used or reproduced in any manner whatsoever without written permission except in the case of brief quotations embodied in critical articles and reviews. For information address Harper & Row, Publishers, Inc., 10 East 53rd Street, New York, N.Y. 10022. Published simultaneously in Canada by Fitzhenry & Whiteside Limited, Toronto.

FIRST EDITION

LIBRARY OF CONGRESS CATALOG CARD NUMBER: 74–1861

ISBN: 0–06–014267–7

Designed by C. Linda Dingler

75 76 77 78 79 10 9 8 7 6 5 4 3 2 1

HV5293
.W75T5
1975
GET5

AUTHOR'S NOTE

It is an act of presumption for any man to write the life of another—
how can any of us be so sure of our own perceptions to say in print
"this is what so-and-so was really like"? When the subject of a biography is a man whose life has had a revolutionary effect on hundreds of
thousands of others, that presumption may seem a kind of impertinence.

Bill W. told his own story many times; he also wrote about it. Possibly because of New England reticence, the emphasis was always on
the second half of his life. He gave few details of his childhood, his
youth or the early years of his marriage. However, it was my privilege
—my blessing, if you will—to have known and worked beside Bill during
the last twelve years of his life, when he had begun to understand that
his biography would be written one day, and he made many attempts
in notes, in letters, and on tape recordings "to set the record somewhere
near straight."

Bill Wilson was an alcoholic and believed his alcoholism a three-
pronged illness, physical, mental and spiritual. Because of this he knew
that a drunk's true story must be told subjectively; otherwise it would
be only an endless series of ridiculous, unmotivated episodes. I agreed.
(I was younger then, and many things seemed easier and less pre-
sumptuous.)

Also Bill wanted his story aimed at the general reader, not at the
academician or professional worker in the field.

Apart from Bill's letters and the notes and transcriptions of recordings which he left, the primary source of material has been the first-

hand recollections of relatives—notably his sister Dorothy and her husband, Dr. Leonard Strong, Jr.—friends and colleagues. But because of a peculiar circumstance—the AA tradition of anonymity—most of these must remain unacknowledged here.

Such a book must inevitably contain quotations from Bill's published works: *Alcoholics Anonymous, Twelve Steps and Twelve Traditions, AA Comes of Age,* and random articles that appeared above his initials in *The Grapevine.* He was a man who cared about words and on occasion possessed a kind of Yankee genius for finding the apt phrase. It would have been not only arrogant on my part but foolhardy to have searched for substitutes. At times his words have been juxtaposed here, sometimes they have been blended, but none of them has been misquoted. And to cite chapter and verse would simply have cluttered his story.

Make no mistake about it; any truth that appears in these pages about the AA way of life comes not from me, but from Bill Wilson, and here I want to thank Alcoholics Anonymous World Services, Inc., for permission to quote from his works so freely.

There is one person I must thank by name—Lois Burnham Wilson. Her journey back through her memories has often been painful, but it has always been courageous, always loving . . . and invaluable.

I should also like to thank the AA archivist, whose kindness and extraordinary knowledge of AA's history has been a constant help. Most especially, I want to mention the managing editor of *The Grapevine.* Her endless generosity and concern step by step have been the mainstay of this biography, and through her I have been given many incisive glimpses into the character and development of Bill Wilson. Also I want to thank the General Service Board and all the staff members. In fact, my heartfelt thanks go to each and every member of the Fellowship I have met for making four years of research and writing an experience I can never forget and for which I shall never be able to express my gratitude.

If there were to be a dedication to this book, I think Bill would like it to be addressed to the Fellowship. I think, too, that he would join me in repeating a phrase from his last message to the members:

"I salute you. And I thank you for your lives."

BILL W.

BOOK ONE

1

When he stood beside his father Bill Wilson never felt too tall. He never felt skinny then or thought his ears stuck out too far and he was never afraid that he was going to do something awkward that would make people laugh and call him Beanpole. And now he was realizing this had been true whether they were walking in town, playing catch or—he turned to glance back at the little light shining from the shed at the quarry's entrance— whether he was just standing, waiting. If his father was nearby there was nothing to fear. But tonight—he couldn't help it—to- night everything was different, wild and dangerous and what- ever his father was doing, he wished he'd hurry, come out and join him.

It had to be midnight now, possibly even twelve-thirty, be- cause it had been after eleven when they'd passed the church, and once again the thought of the old clock high above the silent town filled him with a sense of wonder. Never in his life had he been awake and out riding through the night when everyone else was sleeping. And he had been warned—he tried to smile now, remembering—many times he had been warned by his mother that God did not approve of nine-year-old boys being up past bedtime. But his mother and God had no connection with what was happening here.

It was one of those clear September nights when a three-quarter moon slips slowly into the west against a sky so ablaze with stars it makes the earth doubly dark. Fir trees of every variety grew above the quarry, then sloped gradually down to frame the clearing where he waited, and all the trees were ink black now, with no shading anywhere. Indeed, the only color, the only spot of light on the mountainside, was this one open shelf, and here everything glistened. At his back, rinsed in pure white light, stood piles of marble, slabs ten, some of them twenty feet high, towering above him, one on top of the other like ramparts of a prehistoric fort. And it might have been this, the eerie whiteness all around—for now even the ground beneath his feet glittered as though covered with snow—that made the place feel so remote. The snow, of course, was only tiny marble chips, debris left by men who for generations had been chiseling and blasting out the mountain, way back even before his father's time. Still the whiteness added to the peculiar hush that was settling over the world.

Without moving, he slid his eyes back to the window, and he listened for some indication that his father was still there. But there was no breeze to carry a sound and when finally all he could make out was the distant jangle of a harness as the mare shifted about, he turned and took several slow, tentative steps toward the shed. As he did, both his hands reached up and out before him—this almost automatic movement, with fingers spread wide, his family said, he'd been making ever since he was an infant—trying to feel and grab hold of moonlight. Tonight, however, the light had no warmth and the fingers relaxed, his hands fell to his sides. He wasn't afraid, that wasn't the word, yet as he drew near the shed he could feel a new shiver of excitement gripping his body. The little shed with its window half open, its sign, G. WILSON, MANAGER, hanging above the door, seemed to be waiting too, and it too seemed to be peering across the valley.

He did not understand his feeling, but as he went on, a curious sense of expectation crept over him. Something was going to happen and it had to do with him, with his father, and with the fact that no one in the world knew that they were here.

In the last few hours he had moved so far from the ordinary, so far into danger, there had been no time to review the steps that had brought him here. Still he knew the moment it had begun. He and his sister had been waiting at the supper table. Out in the kitchen they had heard voices; no words, just voices. First his mother's voice, high and frightening, then his father, calmer, not arguing, just quietly stating some fact. On and on it had gone, but he couldn't make out the words. Then there had been the shocking silence, and when finally he had been able to bear it no longer he'd pushed back his chair and run into the kitchen. And there he had found them, his parents confronting each other: his mother, her head high, shoulders squared, with one hand grasping the side of the table, and his father, not three feet away, looking straight into her eyes, searching her eyes.

In an instant he knew what was happening. His father had told her something, but—he could read this in the tilt of her head, the rigid stance of her body—she would not believe what she'd been told. Then, when he looked back at his father, he saw what he had never seen before. His father nodded his head, accepting her terrible judgment, and without a word, turned, went through the door and started across the yard. And Billy watched him go, and he knew, although neither of them spoke, that his mother was watching too.

At supper and afterward when they'd sat silently in the little front room, until his mother said she felt one of her headaches coming on and asked if he would put his little sister to bed, his mind had shot off in all directions, searching for an explanation. There had been arguments before and often, but this time there had been something in his mother's tone that had made him know tonight was unlike other nights. Before when there'd been quarrels, it was usually because of something he,

Billy, had done, or something he and his father had been involved in together; then his father had always spoken out in his behalf. Tonight he had stood there, he had not argued.

Long ago Billy had come to understand that his father also had to be on guard, just as Billy had to be, or he too could be placed on probation, then he too would have to think up some method of winning his way back into her affection. And somehow, knowing this had made all sorts of things easier. But now his father must have committed a wrong Billy knew nothing about.

Up in his own room he had flung himself across the bed, but he had known that he would not sleep because now there were other questions. Now he was asking not only what but why. Why hadn't his father answered? Why had he allowed her her moment of triumph? More and more he found it difficult to concentrate; one thought that had been hovering in the corners of his mind was demanding attention. If his father could walk away and not return even for supper, then wasn't it possible that he might one day walk away and never come back?

On the bureau by the window his alarm clock ticked off the minutes and he watched the long hand creep on an inch. Ten minutes to. Five to. Nine o'clock, and there it seemed to halt, to stand perfectly still as if he'd touched it with a finger. Then it slowly went on and started down again. When it was almost a quarter past, he heard his mother's footsteps in the hall. She passed his door and for one moment he thought of calling out, but he checked himself and she moved on.

He hadn't looked back at the clock, but he was sure it must have been almost ten-thirty when the front door opened. The sudden wave of relief that poured through him then was so vast and profound it seemed to take with it every particle of his strength.

Other boys had told him you could tell when a man was drunk by the heavy way he walked and stumbled around. The opposite was true of Gilman Wilson. Billy could always tell about him by the lightness of his step. Now he sat on the side of the bed and listened to the footsteps coming carefully, quietly up the stairs. At the head of the stairs they paused, but only for a second, then they moved across the hall into Billy's room and there his father stood at the foot of the bed, swaying slightly, looking down at him.

Neither of them spoke. Their eyes met and held, then, still saying nothing, his father made a gesture, a slight jerk of the head, turned and started away, and Billy knew he was to follow.

Downstairs, he was sure they'd go out back, where they could talk without being overheard, but when instead of going through the kitchen his father opened the door and stepped onto the porch, everything, the whole world, changed. A silvery blue light flooded the yard and he could see, standing in front of the house, a horse and buggy from O'Reilly's livery stable.

When his father had got in and had patted the seat beside him, Billy crawled up—was drawn up like someone in a dream—and together they started off through the silent town. Billy didn't try to say anything; neither did his father. A jug of whiskey was on the baseboard by their feet and occasionally he saw his father reach down, pick up the jug and take a swig, but their eyes were always focused straight ahead.

He never knew how long the trip had taken, he never cared, for as they trotted along, then slowed to a walk, he was seeing it all—the moon, the road ahead as bright as day, the fields at the side enameled over with tiny white flowers—and he was seeing it with such awareness, such clarity of vision, that he knew, even as it happened, that it was being recorded and that he would remember it all the days of his life. Even when they reached the quarry gate, turned, and the old mare strained slowly up the mountain road, even when his father stopped, got out and, unclipping the reins, tied them together to form a halter which he fastened to a tree, even then Billy had not worried.

7

But after his father had disappeared into the shed and he'd been left to wait, he could no longer tell what had happened and what was part of a dream. Superimposed over the picture of his father walking away was the memory of the two of them facing each other and his father nodding, admitting she was right.

He dug his hands into his pockets, squinted and stared at the sky. How could his father give in to her and just walk away? He felt deserted, betrayed, and the thoughts he tried not to think shook the foundations of everything he'd always taken for granted.

Once when he was about to push the door open and run into the shed, he stopped himself. He was supposed to wait, that was what his father had said. In time he'd come out. Then they would talk. His father would put his hand on his shoulder the way he did and he would explain. And in that explaining everything would be made right again.

But when his father finally stepped from the shed he did none of these things. For a time they stood, side by side, looking across the valley, then he moved off a step and leaned back, his shoulders resting against a tree, and when he spoke it was not at all what Billy had expected.

"You'll take care of her, won't you, Billy?" he said. "You'll be good to your mother, and to little Dotty too." And before he could answer his father reached out a hand and mussed the back of his hair. "Sure you will," he said. "Sure. You're okay, Billy." Then he withdrew his hand and Billy knew that this was it.

In his right hand his father was still carrying the jug and Billy watched him lift it to his lips and take a long, slow drink. *This was it,* and watching him lean down and place the jug on the ground, Billy knew that the explanation he was waiting for would not be given.

And, watching, he knew one other thing, knew it instantly

and with complete certainty: this was as it had to be. His father was silent now as he had been before his mother, and Billy could see his silence was not weakness, it was strength. If he talked, if he'd felt he must put it all into words, it would have stirred up the ugliness, made it live again. Women and little children put everything into words. They had to. Men didn't. What was more, this silence, this acceptance, in no way changed his father or made him less. And suddenly, looking at the plain bony face in the moonlight, Billy was filled with a huge and beautiful emotion. He felt closer to his father than he'd ever felt to anyone; he felt a part of him.

When Gilman Wilson began to speak again, not about what had occurred, but about what they always talked about when they were outside at night: about stars and the moon, about the wind he felt rising and about the mountains, the great Taconic range and the Green, and how they had been here even before there were men to call them mountains . . . as he went on now, behind the words—or was it because of them, because of the things he chose to talk about and the things he chose to ignore?—somewhere in there Billy was beginning to feel another, a deeper, meaning, and he knew he was just on the edge of grasping it but couldn't quite understand. He knew that it was serious, that it related to him, to his body, but it was like a problem in arithmetic: as soon as he thought he had it, it would dissolve and fall apart.

Now his father was speaking about the moon again, how it changed every night, every hour, but had been here always and always the same, and now, looking up into his face, listening to the voice he knew better than any other voice, Billy made still another discovery. It came to him that he didn't only feel a part of his father, he *was* a part of him—just as he was part of his grandfather and he in turn of his father. And in that same instant he understood why when they walked together through town and would meet someone and his father would

9

say, "This is my son," he always had that same solemn feeling inside.

He had the feeling now and as his father moved from the tree, walked over and sat on a low square of marble and, tilting his head, began to study the sky, Billy watched him with a sense of awe, aware of something—he had no other word for it—of something *ancestral* in himself.

And Billy listened to everything his father said now about the night, the heavens, the vast galaxies sailing through space. His father could locate and identify each constellation, each star and planet. He knew how long it took a speck of light to come down and reach the two of them on their mountain and he was speaking now of distances in trillions of miles, of age in billions of years, and he told Billy that they weren't just citizens of Vermont or even just the United States; they were citizens of this whole tremendous universe.

Such talk, he said, could sometimes make a man despair. Against the immensity of the cosmos his own insignificance could make him feel lost and no account. But now, in this instant, Billy Wilson knew he was feeling the exact opposite. The thing he'd learned, the hard awareness of his descent and all that meant, was still with him and he knew this was actual and perfect, while everything else—the whole past of people laughing at him, of arguments and fights with his mother—was trivial and unimportant.

In time his father rose and, placing his great hand on Billy's shoulder, he led him back toward the buggy.

Driving down the mountainside there may have been more talk, there may even have been some questions, but by the time they reached the pike Billy could feel his eyelids growing heavy and when they turned and started east toward home he shifted his weight and let his head fall back against the rough prickly tweed of his father's sleeve. Then he slept.

Years later, after his life had been given over to the business of growing up and earning a living, when the confusion of other memories had blocked out details of this night, Bill Wilson could still remember the stars and the feel of his father's coat.

When he awakened in the morning, his sister, Dorothy, was waiting to tell him that their father had gone away.

This was in the autumn of 1905. Billy didn't see his father again until the summer of 1914, and by then they had discovered they had nothing at all to say to one another.

2

In the town of East Dorset word of the final separation of Gilman and Emily Griffith Wilson came as a shock, but it was not really a surprise.

In fact, from the beginning there had been little that was surprising in the story of this handsome, healthy young couple who'd been born in the same year, 1870, in the same township, had attended the same schools, the same church. It was true they had been separated briefly when Gilly had gone off to attend Albany College in New York State and Emily had studied to be a teacher at the normal school in Castleton, but even then they were together for the holidays and it was not too long before they fell in love and finally married.

Even their backgrounds appeared curiously similar. The Griffiths had come to America from Wales, while the Wilsons had emigrated from Scotland to Ireland and then on to the States. Wilsons were recorded among the original settlers of Manchester Center, some nine miles south of East Dorset, and Emily's family was in the environs of Danby long before the Revolution—one great-grandfather had marched south in the spring of 1779 to join mad Anthony Wayne and lend a hand in the taking of the garrison at Stony Point. No, there was no question that these young lovers from the oldest Yankee stock seemed in some special way meant for one another. Yet from the start—and everyone who knew them sensed this—these were two very definite and strong individuals with marked and potentially troublesome differences.

Yeats has written of "the folly that man does or must suffer if he woos a proud woman not kindred of his soul," and herein may lie a clue. For Emily Griffith was a proud woman, and for all the apparent similarities of background and environment these two were of extremely dissimilar temperaments.

And if this was true of Emily and Gilly, it was no less true of their families. To begin with, the Griffiths were loners. When they arrived in Vermont they did not, as did the Wilsons, settle close by others, but instead chose a rugged piece of farmland just below the timberline and at a considerable distance from any town. The Wilsons, on the other hand, seem to have felt some deep need to work with and surround themselves with the warmth of others. Years later Bill was to describe the Griffiths as people of extremely high native intelligence, high-minded and hard-driving as well, with immense will, immense valor and fortitude. For the most part self-educated, they became lawyers, teachers and judges. Highly respected, they were not ever popular, nor dearly loved.

By comparison the Wilsons seem to have developed at an opposite pole. Tall, raw-boned, they were warm, likable men of tremendous geniality who laughed easily, and all of them were superb storytellers. For generations they had been quarrymen, often moving rapidly up from worker to foreman to manager of a project. Perhaps on occasion they would stay too late in the taverns spinning their yarns, matching drinks with their neighbors, and sometimes they may have arrived home slightly under the weather, but with the Wilsons such little failings were understandable and easily forgiven.

When at the close of the Civil War William C. Wilson, Gilly's father, had chosen a bride, he had wisely chosen Helen Barrows, one of whose ancestors had built the largest house in

East Dorset, a great rambling structure that stood just across from the churchyard on a plot of ground that had been granted still another ancestor by George IV. For years this had been run as an inn, the old Barrows House, but soon after the wedding William discovered that along with his work in the quarries he quite enjoyed managing an inn and the name was changed to the Wilson House.

The Wilson House may not have been the most elegant, and it certainly was not the most successful inn in the county—East Dorset was after all no more than a village with only one industry, the polishing of marble that mule teams hauled down from the hills—but it was the people who lived there and the constant stream of guests, commercial travelers for the most part, who lent it excitement and made it seem the concentrated center of all that was happening. Then, too, there was always Willie Wilson to spin a tale and offer one on the house after every third round.

Always, that is, until Willie gave up the drink. The rumor was that he'd been deeply impressed by the words of an itinerant preacher who'd passed through Dorset during a series of revival meetings, and somehow Willie had been persuaded to hit the sawdust trail. Whatever the true story, he was never known to have another drop of alcohol until his death, in the summer of 1885.

His widow, Helen, decided to continue to run the inn with the aid of her two growing sons, George and Gilman. It was congenial work, she said, making strangers comfortable.

Griffiths and Wilsons. For all the doughty New England virtues they shared, it would be difficult to imagine two more disparate ways of living, of thinking or—what was to prove even more telling—of feeling. But none of this appears to have worried either Gilly Wilson or Emily Griffith when in 1894 Gilly asked Gardener Fayette Griffith for his daughter's hand in marriage.

Fayette had by this time given up farming. Some years be-

14

fore, he'd got the notion of lumbering, had bought up land above his farm, imported a group of French woodchoppers and finally had moved his family into East Dorset. His eldest daughter, Emily, was a tall, extremely handsome young woman with masses of dark chestnut hair and deep-set thoughtful eyes. In every respect a true Griffith, she had grown up an avid reader of the classics and of the high-flown inspirational literature of her day, a woman one would have thought marked off for a career of teaching and a genteel, quiet domestic life. But by one of those quirks of nature so frequent in the lives of women drawn to Wilson men, Emily found herself in love with a fellow she never truly understood. If, during their brief engagement, certain things troubled her, she was quite able to rationalize them. If, for example, Gilly seemed to be a spendthrift, she could tell herself that a young bachelor had no incentive to save; with the responsibilities of marriage all that would change. If their personalities occasionally clashed, she was still hopeful; she'd read a great deal about temperaments finally balancing. Perhaps what she was seeing in Gilly was material, raw, attractive material which she would shape, for there was no doubt that throughout her life Emily fancied herself a shaper of men. And whatever worries might have presented themselves, they were all ignored in the beautiful spring of '94. Fayette gave his consent and in September they were married in the white Congregational church.

At the start all apparently went well. The newlyweds set up housekeeping in the rear of the Wilson House and here—fittingly enough—in a small room behind the bar, William G. Wilson was born on November 26, 1895.

The first indication that the marriage was in some trouble may have appeared during Emily's pregnancy. She knew that she was nervous and not the best of company and knew that it was only natural for men to be restless at such a time, so it was Emily who suggested that Gilly go out alone, and quite often Gilly did go out. Later, a small room dominated by an

15

infant's schedule couldn't have been much of a home, not to a man of Gilly's energies, and he seemed more and more to be away in the evenings. By the time their second child, Dorothy, was born and they had moved to a home of their own, a neat clapboard house just a few doors south of the inn, Gilly's advice was being sought about the feasibility of various quarry sites, and sometimes he had to make his reports up in Boston, sometimes even down in New York, which of course meant he'd be away for several nights running.

In 1902, while still overseeing two quarries at Munson's Falls, Gilly was offered the management of the entire Rutland-Florence operation. Perhaps he hoped that life in a larger town like Rutland would be more interesting and prove more of a stimulus for Emily, perhaps it was such a splendid business opportunity he simply couldn't resist it. Billy was seven at the time, in the second grade at the little two-room schoolhouse in East Dorset, Dorothy just entering kindergarten. Surely the Rutland public school, only two blocks from the house Gilly found on Chestnut Street, would provide a much better education. Whatever his reasoning, the move promised a change in a marriage that had begun to bog down in the stifling details of domesticity.

Emily's life at this juncture appears to have been devoted to an effort to analyze and then in some way dominate her circumstances. It was almost as though she had begun to see others from above, as though their behavior formed part of a complex pattern which she believed her superior knowledge and training should enable her to interpret. On the other hand, Gilly's life (or so it appeared to Emily) seemed constantly acted upon by events and experiences which he approached with no theories or preconceived attitudes. And this may have been true, for as keen as Gilly was in assaying the quality of a quarry, he admitted there was always something mysterious to him about the motives of others. He had no confidence in himself as an

16

intellectual being, he approached the world as a healthy, contented animal with his arms outstretched, and if he were ever to understand others and what motivated them, he was sure he'd find them admirable, even lovable.

By the time they were living in Rutland these two outlooks were firmly established, and they had begun to create in Gilly a kind of disturbance he'd never known before and which he had no way of handling. And Emily did—or could do—nothing about it. She had loved Gilly, but she could not like him. She was perhaps constitutionally incapable of giving the unquestioning adulation he and all Wilson men needed from their women, and that indeed may have been all they needed.

By 1904 others had begun to notice that something was wrong with the marriage. From the start they had suspected it wouldn't turn out too well. The responsibility of raising children might help, they said, and for a time it did seem it might not turn out too badly. But then in 1905 an incident occurred, probably while Gilly was off in New York. There was talk—an affront to dignity—and that was more than the proud Emily could stand.

Gilly left town.

Emily's behavior remained impeccable. We were still a young country in 1905, with many inviting frontiers, and she let it be known that her husband had gone west. Everything she did, everything she said, was above reproach. In time she sent word to her father in East Dorset and asked him to drive up and collect his family. She was calm and completely herself, completely a Griffith.

In her short time alone in the house on Chestnut Street she had examined her world and plotted the future. She was thirty-five years old, a woman with a son and a daughter to look after. She would, of course, have to consult with her father about certain financial matters, but there was no reason the children could not stay in East Dorset with her parents, no reason she

17

could not move into Boston. She was exceptionally intelligent, she could study, start over again and launch herself on a brand-new career.

Arrangements for a divorce—as shocking as that word might be to many old Vermonters—would be handled by a lawyer down in Bennington. And it would all be done discreetly, with a minimum of publicity. She would be careful to hide, even from herself, any of the scars that had been inflicted by an impossible marriage, and if for any reason Billy or Dorothy should ever have to examine the Records of Divorce, they would find nothing to upset them. There would be only a slight reference, couched in the legal terminology of the day, to Gilman Wilson's utter irresponsibility.

3

It would be like going home, his mother had said. After all, he and Dorothy had been born in East Dorset, they'd started school there and they knew everyone in town, everyone knew them. And this was true, of course, but there was a difference now and sometimes Billy wondered if his mother understood but just didn't care to talk about it.

In Rutland they'd had a home all their own. In Rutland he'd been part of a family with a mother, a sister and a father. Now, no matter how kind and loving his grandparents might be, he was a guest. Children, he imagined, were always forced to be somebody's guest when they had no fathers, and now it was as though his father were dead. It was worse really, because people talked to you about the dead, but no one ever spoke of Gilman Wilson. Even late at night when they thought he was sleeping and he would sneak out to listen from the top of the stairs, even then they talked about Lawyer Barber in Bennington and what he thought of the case, but they never once mentioned Gilly's name.

In fact, it wasn't until the day before his mother was to leave —her skirts and shirtwaists had all been washed and ironed, her suitcase packed and the steamer trunk already shipped— not until then did she tell them they were to go on a picnic

19

just the three of them, because there was something they had to discuss, and with a terrible tightening in the stomach he knew what she was going to say.

It was a crisp, clear October afternoon and they drove up to Dorset Pond—the summer folks had renamed this Emerald Lake, but the natives still called it Dorset Pond—and it was there, while his mother and Dot spread out the Indian blanket and started to unwrap the sandwiches, that he came to understand that there are many different kinds of shock. There was the totally unexpected kind that could catch you off guard, but there was also the kind that a part of you had been expecting, but for some reason you hadn't made any preparations for, and he guessed he didn't know enough to tell which kind was worse.

As his mother started to talk Billy sat a little apart on a long, flat rock that jutted out into the water, his arms wrapped around his knees, hugging them to him, and his eyes studying the little patterns of ripples on the pond. But he tried hard to listen. Their father, she said, was out in British Columbia now and she'd just learned that some of the men from his old Rutland gang were going west to join him. He'd found work there, and he wouldn't be coming back—ever.

He heard the words but—he couldn't help it: it was as though his mind had gone numb—he was unable to focus his thoughts. He could hear but he literally could not accept what she was saying. Once when she rose to hand him a sandwich he turned and looked up at her, but now—it was the strangest thing—he wasn't seeing her as she was, standing above him, tall, handsome, with the afternoon sun shining on her hair; he was seeing her as she had been that evening when she'd taken him out behind the shed and had thrashed him with her hairbrush, when she had made him drop his trousers down so his bare bottom was exposed before her. He couldn't ever remember what he'd done to provoke that thrashing, but he remembered the wild anger in her eyes and his own impotent terror as he

20

was forced to stretch his body out, awkward, naked and ashamed, across his mother's lap.

It was wrong, and he knew it, to be thinking about this. He should speak up. ("You'll take care of her, won't you, Billy? You'll be good to your mother, and to little Dotty too. . . .") Maybe it was right that he'd kept silent in the beginning, but now in his role of son and big brother more was expected of him. Yet aside from such phrases as "Don't worry," or "Things will work out," which had no meaning, he could think of nothing to say.

Later, when they went for a walk around the edge of the lake and he remembered to brush aside the low-hanging branches and hold them away from his mother and Dot, he was still unable to speak and—what was much worse, he knew—he wasn't even feeling what he should be feeling. Even driving back to East Dorset the words would not come, and after a time he stopped trying to find them and concentrated his attention on holding the reins "loosely yet firmly," as he'd been taught.

When finally they were back before his grandfather's house, the sun was already sinking behind the mountains. Dot and his mother went inside and he loosened the halter and secured the old mare to the hitching post. He'd even started to follow them into the house, but halfway up the path he twisted around, darted back down the road, across the churchyard and partway up the hill toward an ancient oak tree, the oldest and tallest tree he knew about in all East Dorset. There he paused, resting his shoulders against the trunk; then suddenly he started to climb—higher and higher until he reached the topmost branch that would hold his weight. Here he was sure he would not be seen by anyone, here he would not have to search his mind for words; he was gasping, panting for breath, but he knew now he was going to be all right.

In this valley between the Taconic and the Green, October

days do not end as August and September days end, with evening gradually easing into night. In no time now the darkness solidified and he could no longer make out, even from so great a height, where the sky stopped and where the mountains began. Soon yellow lights were coming on in the inn and he could see lanterns being lit in kitchens all up and down the road. He could hear mothers calling children in and old Mr. Landers whistling for his dog.

Billy had never climbed this particular tree before and as a matter of fact he was never to climb it again, but from that night on the feeling of the ancient oak, the sense of being sheltered in its arms, was seldom completely absent from his mind. It became a sort of symbol: it wasn't a hideaway or a secret private room such as he knew some boys had—it was more an escape hatch, a place he knew he could run to if and when this might be necessary.

It was during that same winter, his first year of staying with Grandpa Griffith, that he made one other simple but important discovery. He discovered that he was living on what seemed to be two separate planes, in what seemed to be two different worlds. Sometimes he thought there might even be three worlds, but the third one was made up of feelings that came and went away and he couldn't yet explain it. First there was the world of men and of animals, of getting up and going to bed at night, of going to school and coming home, talking to people, milking the cow, doing chores. Then there was the world in which he thought, dreamed and imagined things. The third world, the one he couldn't pin down, had to do with the things his father had talked about, with what had been here before he was born and would go on long after he was dead. But the strangest part of this discovery was that whichever world he happened to be in, a shadow from the other world, like the shadow of a cloud crossing a field on a summer day, could fall over him.

Sometimes he would look at others, especially at grownups, and wonder if they too were aware of different worlds and if this was another of those secrets they wouldn't talk about. He was sure that one day when he was older he would understand more about it. Now he spake as a child, understood as a child, and saw, as the Bible said, through a glass darkly. But there would be a time—and these days he thought a good deal about this—when he would *know* as also he was known. It was as though there were a specific date somewhere ahead when he would meet the rest of himself. This was moving toward him now just as he was moving toward it.

Meanwhile he was sure it was best not to talk about it. Until he fully understood, he had a responsibility to shield it, so it couldn't be twisted all out of shape. But even if he had wanted to talk, he didn't know exactly whom he'd tell. Certainly not the boys in school. They were not friends, they were rivals. With them it was always a question of who was stronger, taller, who could throw a baseball with the greatest skill or swim the farthest, fastest.

In place of a confidant he guessed he still used his father—in the beginning, anyway—a character he was making up half out of memory, half of imagining, and sometimes during those first months alone in the little attic room he would carry on long conversations with this wondrous man who did perhaps drink a little too much, but who *had* to drink now because of the perilous nature of his work, which involved blasting with dynamite and constantly dealing with savage natives out in the wild Northwest. Some nights his father would even confide in him, telling Billy he wanted him to leave Vermont, run away and hitch a ride west because he needed him now. But for some reason instead of feeling better after these conversations, he often felt much worse. He knew that they were becoming what his father in reality would call "indulgence," something babies or little girls might do, and in time he grew self-conscious and gave them up.

Of course he knew he might talk to Rose or Bill Landon, who were just next door, or even with old Frank Jacobs, Rose's father, who had come to stay with them now that he had given up working.

Old Frank had been the town's shoemaker. A short, grizzled, not very talkative old codger, he always seemed to be waiting whenever Billy stopped by. Frank hadn't had much education, but he knew just about everything there was to know about nature, and it was from him that Billy learned how to track down honeybees to their stores and the name of every flower, every shrub and tree. They would sit sometimes for hours on end without speaking, and together they would wait for special birds that could be seen only on certain days of the year and only at certain hours of those days.

Bill Landon, Frank's son-in-law, was as voluble as Frank was still, but somehow he too could always find time for Billy and he soon took it upon himself to train and make a crack shot out of the boy—even persuading the Griffiths to invest in a 25–20 Remington, a rifle Billy was to keep and love all his life.

The supreme moment of Bill Landon's life had occurred some forty years before when he was a sergeant on the staff of General Philip H. Sheridan down in the Shenandoah valley. Since then Landon had become an incorrigible monologist and often seemed compelled by some inner passion to share every instant of his famous afternoon at Cedar Creek. The rebel forces had crushed all Union resistance until the meadows and lanes around the creek had become a chaos of wagons, stragglers and fleeing men. Then, shortly after one o'clock—Bill knew every detail—down the broad highway from Winchester, a beautiful jet-black charger had appeared, bearing his master. The road was so totally blocked the general had been forced to take to the fields to appraise the situation, but suddenly above the din they heard Sheridan cry out, "Back. We will go back and retake our camps!" and sweeping off his hat and vaulting his horse over a low stone

24

wall, he galloped to the crest of the field. "We will go back. . . ."
Bill Landon would repeat these words as if they were some holy
incantation, his voice reverberating like organ music. In a matter
of minutes, he declared, no more, the men broke into a cheer,
a line of regimental flags arose as if coming up from the earth
itself and new lines began to form.

With Sergeant Landon that afternoon had stood two future
presidents of the United States: on the left of the road Colonel
Rutherford B. Hayes, on the right, Major William McKinley, and
together they watched Sheridan, hat still in hand, still barking
out orders, move to the front of his men. When, a short time
later, the rebs opened another attack, our troops were ready.
Union infantry moved forward, the cavalry swept in behind.

Ignominious defeat had been turned into victory and all
through the action of one man, Philip H. Sheridan. Never again
would our national capital be threatened by rebel hordes. And—
think of it—Bill Landon had been there. At the start of the attack a Minie ball had struck his musket, passed clear through
and had stuck in his skull just above one eye. The sergeant had
simply plucked it out and continued with the charge. Now he
had one rather drooping eye, occasional poor vision and a deep
scar across his forehead to back up his story. But no Minie ball
had affected his recall. As Billy listened, drinking in every word,
he could see the gray columns retreating, stampeding horse-
men, the foam that flecked Sheridan's noble black stallion; he
could hear the roar of musketry and smell the gunpowder.

That winter and on into the spring, ambling home from school,
Billy was no longer moving along an old Vermont dirt road. He
was on a wide valley highway near Cedar Creek, Virginia, and
in the evening, when his grandparents would look out to see him
charging up a hillock behind the house, his Remington at the
ready, he wasn't after a rabbit or a squirrel; he was responding
to a sacred admonition. "Back. We will go back and retake our
camps!"

If old Bill Landon with his beautiful wild rhetoric was the first to feed Billy's second world of dreams and imaginings, still there were others who contributed, and not the least of these was Landon's wife, Rose.

Barefoot Rose, as she was called, was no ordinary next-door neighbor. The rumor—and it was true—was that Rose had not only been a great beauty, but had in her day possessed a remarkable voice, so remarkable that a man in Albany had wanted to finance her with the idea that she might sing at the opera house in New York. But things had not worked out for Rose. Instead of going to New York she'd married Landon and they'd had a great number of children, all of whom were grown now and seldom came around.

Billy got to know Rose through a series of errands she sent him on. "You, Willie," she'd call out. "The well's 'most dry again," and he knew this meant he must make the run down to the drugstore. There he'd be handed a small packet wrapped in tinfoil. Her "surcease," Rose called it, and once on his way back to the house he unfolded the tinfoil and examined its contents. It was a chunk of something that looked like beeswax with a lot of white dust all around and it smelled—at first he couldn't place it, but then he recognized the odor—it smelled exactly like a bunch of poppies. Rose always kept one of these in her apron and occasionally as they talked she'd nibble at it. Sometimes in the evening, when they'd be sitting on the porch, she would suddenly moan, rock back in her chair and lift her head in such a way that the blue of her eyes would completely disappear and he'd be looking only at the whites. Then, it was true, Billy would be a little frightened.

But he kept going back to visit Rose because she was the only person who might tell him about his father. Rose, of course, knew all about the divorce and, not surprisingly, tended to side with Gilly. But she was always careful not to speak unkindly of Billy's mother. Gilly's fault, she declared, if fault it was, was that he couldn't love just one special woman; Gilly Wilson loved all people, all men, all women. And she would say this as though she spoke of a rare and most admirable quality.

Yet strangely, no matter how late they talked on the porch, Rose never expressed any sympathy for Billy's loss. She had had troubles too and she was enough of a New Englander to assume that any person of stamina would not wish to dwell on such subjects.

Then suddenly, and possibly without realizing she was doing it, one summer afternoon she was able to offer Billy a way out, an escape every bit as exhilarating and as hallucinatory as her opium.

A gentleman from Manchester riding in a fine buckboard arrived in East Dorset looking for a place to open a traveling library. Rose, hearing of this, suggested her father's empty cobbler's shop, and the following Saturday five hundred books were in the shop and Barefoot Rose Landon was the town's librarian.

Until now Billy had been a casual reader. He'd done his homework and he'd written book reports with occasional excursions into *Heidi* and the Alger series. But now suddenly all manner of new and indescribable excitements entered his world. Rose would lend him any book he wanted, often letting him take five or six at a time, and, alone in his room or wandering home from school, it was no longer a matter of being a recruit with the Union forces in Virginia. With Ulysses he was viewing the carnage of Troy, with Sydney Carton he looked down at Paris.

There was one other peculiar sensation he didn't understand and that was that many of the novels Rose lent him seemed not only written especially for him, but about him too. The settings and some of the lesser characters might be alien, but he felt so close to what the hero was going through, it was as though he were reading a part of his own story.

But after a time, while he realized that reading could offer a perspective, a clarity, this wasn't always the case. When he'd

27

close certain books he'd find himself with questions. And often these were the most tremendous questions—about justice and truth and sometimes even about the wisdom of God Himself. And again he had no one to turn to with such problems. He thought of writing his mother—letters from her were coming regularly from Boston—but he knew she had her troubles and it didn't seem right to burden her further. Moreover, he wasn't sure she'd approve of his asking; one still had to be on guard with her. So often, as he'd close a book, he again turned to his father.

Only now, whenever he spent any time thinking of Gilly, there always seemed one overall question that could change the whole climate of whatever world he was in. Dimming the lantern, he would lie back in bed and stare at the ceiling, his sense of aloneness, of being a guest at its most acute. It still seemed incredible to him that his father would want to be away, that he wouldn't even write a letter.

He searched for explanations. It was something in him, he was sure, that had caused this to happen. But what? Was it something he had done—or something that he lacked—that had made his father leave and stay away? For this was the fact of his life now. Gilman Wilson, unlike any father he saw or knew about, had walked away—walked away not only from his mother but from him.

If only his parents had loved him more they wouldn't have separated. And this meant if he had been more lovable, it never would have happened. It always came around to that. It was, it *had* to be, his fault. He was the guilty one.

After a while these late-night questionings invariably ended in the same way. Finding no answer on the ceiling, unable to absorb the feelings of rejection, the nameless guilts he could never honestly pin down, he would get out of bed, walk across to the bureau and stand for a while studying himself in the mirror. Then his bony face would set its jaw, his eyes would flash back into his own. So his father wanted no part of him;

he wanted to cut him off from his life. . . . Very well. Very well, he could do some cutting off himself. He would show him. *He'd show them all.*

And as though he'd found the answer he'd been seeking, as though this put a period to the subject, he'd repeat the words: "I'll show them all," get into bed, turn up the lantern and begin to read again. Though at first the words mightn't make sense, he'd read stubbornly on and on. He was training himself to focus all his thoughts on what he was doing. If he didn't, he knew he'd be completely lost.

4

There was nothing in any way eerie about Fayette Griffith. But there were times—and Bill was to become increasingly aware of this—when the old man seemed able to read his thoughts.

One evening in the late summer of 1907, Fayette looked at the boy and it was as though he sensed the immense determination that was beginning to form, and as though he understood that such a passion must be given some direction.

"It's an odd thing," he said, and he said this casually as if it were no more than a passing thought. "I've been reading a good deal about Australia lately and no one seems to know why Australians are the only people in the world who are able to make a boomerang."

There was a pause, then Bill looked up into his eyes. "The only people?"

That was all that was said. But the next day Bill borrowed two books from the library, both about Australia, and that night he carried the second volume of the Encyclopaedia Britannica up to his bed; the second volume contained several columns on the history, uses and design of a boomerang.

On Saturday he crossed the highway to visit a French woodcutter and spent the entire afternoon talking with him. Then there were more books, other conferences with other Frenchmen, all having to do with grades of lumber and which would be best for shaping a weapon three feet long and weighing no more than eight ounces.

As summer began to shift into fall, every scrap of paper in the house seemed to be covered with diagrams and figures and the boy was spending more and more time shut up in the shed beside the house, where there was a constant sound of wood being sawed, carved, whittled. What had started as an interest was developing into an obsession. Chores were neglected, the cow was never milked on time, eggs were seldom collected, and in November a note came from Miss Milot, his teacher. She did not understand. Bill was failing all his subjects.

Now his grandmother grew concerned. It was plain silliness, it was unnatural and, what was more, she had read some of his books and a return boomerang was no plaything. It was a deadly weapon that could prove as dangerous to the thrower as to the subject at which it was thrown. She spoke to Willie severely. And to his grandfather.

Fayette nodded and said he'd have words with the boy. But this wasn't quite the time. The time for worry would be when Willie gave up, when he would have to admit failure.

Fayette Griffith, a man of honor and a man of quiet faith, was to become the most important person in Bill Wilson's young life.

But at sixty-four he was also a deeply troubled man. He had taken on the responsibility of rearing two children at a time of psychological and spiritual crisis—though he would have been slow to admit that such words could apply to him. In fact, great reader that he always was, Fayette Griffith found it difficult to express any of his feelings about himself, his family or his country.

He'd been only a young infantryman in '62 when he heard Lincoln's message: "We shall nobly save or meanly lose the last, best hope of earth." And that pretty well summed it up, defined his place. If the Union could be saved, then he believed—and believed it with complete certainty—that other nations would follow our example and someday the world would be one great republic with free men everywhere. And after the war he knew that he was not alone in this idea. Like a great wind down from the mountains, this feeling was sweeping across the land and he was a part of it, it was a part of him. To some, democracy might seem almost mystical in its concepts, but to Fayette it was as plain and practical as the kitchen table.

He always thought of those years after the war as his confident, glad years. Glad, not easy, for they had been years of endless work—up before daylight and never to bed before ten, plowing, hoeing, planting in stubborn rock soil on a side hill farm, then watching and doing battle with every kind of pest. Fortunately he had married a strong woman—by some standards you could say his Ella was stronger than he—who bore him three children, two daughters and his boy, Clarence. She was never ill a day in her life, or never let him know it, and was up with him each morning, seeing to the dairy, in winter fixing breakfast for twenty choppers and often as not driving them over snowbound roads in zero weather so work on the mountaintop could begin at first light.

There had been little money in those days but they had had what they needed. Ella made their clothes, every stitch the children wore, and they were both mindful of the small amenities that make a family a family. No matter how late supper had been, there was always time for reading aloud, and then a time for Fayette to be alone with his books, his Gibbon and his Blackstone.

Then, as things had eased and he was able to buy up more timber land and so farm less, they had moved to the house in East Dorset. But nothing of importance had changed. Indeed, if a life can ever be divided into moments, Fayette thought that his most satisfying moments might have been during those intervals at night when his boy would move into the next room and take out his violin. Fayette would sometimes sit for an hour, listening to him play or listening to him practice, Clarence knowing that certain passages were difficult, but knowing too that there was only one right way to play them. Clarence was a good boy; his father was proud of him, believed he would go far. And alone at night, hearing the comfortable sounds of daughters upstairs preparing for bed and in the next room the sounds of a young man's vigorous, hopeful striving, he knew this was part of the whole, his link with the future.

And this place where he had chosen to live was peculiarly right for him. To a traveler riding up the highway, East Dorset might have seemed a not very prepossessing town tucked away in the valley, but to the Griffiths it was a place of beauty with its vast purple mountains towering on either side and, best of all, a place of good people with a reputation for good law. Fayette knew the Lincoln theories about democracy were not only taken for granted here; he saw them in practice every day. And that belief in self and in the future gave warmth and meaning to his days and was part of the legacy he would hand on to his son.

Then, in 1894, came the tragedy. Clarence had not been well for two years. It was his lungs, Dr. Bemas said, and the doctor in Rutland agreed. The Vermont winters were too severe for him, but he'd surely improve in a milder climate. So they sent him out to Colorado. In December a telegram came. Clarence was dead. His body was shipped east to be buried in the family plot.

Fayette had gone on. One does, he wrote later, not because one wills to, but because one must. In time he had prospered. In the late eighties and early nineties he had been buying up mountainside acres, usually at tax sales, then holding them until someone wanted to order, say, a certain amount of spruce; he would drive up, take a look at what he had and make a deal; he tried to be honorable in all his affairs.

In time Emily married Gilman Wilson and had her children.

Millie married Perry Fairfield and went to live in New Hampshire. With more free hours now, Fayette read more, even sending off to the city for special books. His beliefs were still there, but now they were no more than intellectual, all theory. And he noticed that he felt cold so much of the time. When he pulled his chair close to the fire and stared down at the flames, it seemed he could never clear his mind of one picture, of Ella putting the violin away in the trunk in the attic or of the sound of her locking the trunk.

He went on, read his Bible, supported the church, but there was a verse from Matthew that would return to torment him when he finished his reading: "If the salt have lost its savour . . ."

Then Emily brought her children and left them while she moved on to take up her studies. They were bright children and they were kind. And Fayette tried. He knew, in theory, what they needed. But there is a difference, and it is not simply a matter of age, between a grandfather and a father. There were many things he felt he should be saying, but even as he tried to form the words in his mind they sounded hollow and he left them unspoken. He had heard a cynic say that it was the duty of old men to lie to the young, and there was doubtless some truth in this. The young, he knew, need to believe.

Sometimes he would stand by the door of the shed and watch Bill working, so concentrated on his three-foot slabs of wood he'd not even realize he was being watched, or he'd walk with him out to an open field and listen to his description of the proper stance a man must take to throw a boomerang. "You must pivot on your spine, that's the trick, then make a half turn before you let go." And he would stand and watch the boy, his long legs spread wide, the weapon in his right hand as he'd eye the field. Then, slowly stretching his arm into position, he'd whirl round on his left foot and let the missile spin out. It would go curving off thirty, forty, sometimes fifty feet, Bill's eyes following its every inch, his body hanging in the air; he'd forget even to draw back his arm. Then after a perfect half circle—and the same thing always happened—as if the missile had spent itself, it would fall with an ugly crack. Bill's arm would drop, he'd shake his head and move out to retrieve his weapon and the whole procedure would begin again; back to the shed he'd go to start work on another kind of wood.

Why, Fayette wondered, why did the arm always stay in the same position even after he'd thrown the weapon? Did he believe he was actually helping, willing it along? And what was it that fed this dogged industry? On many occasions he'd looked deep into the boy's eyes and he had always found the same thing there, intense determination and intense self-doubt. He had tried to do something about the self-doubt by suggesting little projects, and, in part, the boy had responded. The first winter there'd been skis and sleds; Bill had made an iceboat, which they'd sailed up and down the icy roads. But whatever he did easily or well he immediately lost interest in. Fayette knew Bill hated to do things that were difficult, but it was as if the boy sensed he had to go at them, as if he understood he would find no peace until he conquered them.

But where could this lead now? How would that extraordinary drive accept its failures? The boy seemed goaded by some dark and mysterious desire that his grandfather could not understand. And the projects were no answer. They were diversions, interesting perhaps, and good for a growing body, but they had no connection with a man's true nature, or where that nature might be tending.

Finally Fayette saw that the problem he was facing had nothing to do with Bill. It was in himself and it grew out of the bitterness in his own soul, because the boy he was rearing now was not his Clarence.

Late on a cold February afternoon the change occurred.

That afternoon Bill led him not out to the open field, but to the graveyard beside the church. Fayette would always remember the day because that morning Ella had discovered that a three-foot plank had been cut from the headboard of Bill's bed

35

and it had taken some doing to quiet her. It was almost six months since his remark about the Australians and their boomerangs. That had been in hot summer; now it was midwinter.

They stopped by a tombstone at the edge of the churchyard. Bill took his stance, legs spread, the weapon in his hand. Then, after a moment in which neither of them spoke, the boy stretched out his arm, spun his body round and the boomerang flew out, curving farther and farther over the graves. But this time it kept on. Instead of spending itself, it seemed even to be taking on momentum as it kept going in a perfect circle until—there was no question about it—it was definitely returning, coming back, right back toward them. With the long, low whistling sound of a giant beetle shooting through the air, it was circling back nearer and nearer and straight toward them. Suddenly Bill let out a yell and they threw themselves forward, flat out on the ground, as the boomerang dipped and cracked against a headstone close beside them.

For a full minute they lay side by side on the frozen earth, panting, hardly able to take in the magnitude of what they had witnessed. If they had not ducked, if they had remained standing, they might well have been decapitated. Then very slowly they both sat up, turned and looked at one another. Still neither of them smiled. "I did it," Bill whispered. "I did it." Then with a wild leap he was on his feet and the banshee cry he let loose could have been heard in Manchester. "*I did it. . . .*"

That evening little else was talked about at supper, but the thing that struck Ella was not the account of the triumph, nor even their close call with injury or death; it was the miracle of change, the quickening of old Fayette Griffith. Her husband never stopped talking. "The very first American to do it. Our Willie. The number-one man."

After the meal Fayette calmed down a little as the young folks babbled on, and for a time he stood by the window looking out at the cold, empty road. But even with his back to the room, even standing still, there was a new look about him, a new aliveness in his body.

When finally he turned back, his voice was quieter, but there was no mistaking what he said. He said he would like her please to give him the key to the trunk in the attic.

As she fetched the key, as Fayette gestured to Bill and then led him up the stairs, he began telling him about his uncle Clarence, and how he used to play for them in the evenings and it did seem a pity to have a violin locked away, not doing anyone any good.

5

The creation of the boomerang marked a turning point for both Bill and his grandfather. In Fayette it seemed to bring forth a kind of joyous opening out. He'd found someone he wanted to be with, to talk to, someone for whom he could feel a deep, wholehearted respect.

And respect, of course, was what Bill needed most. He had been born with a bright, healthy and naturally curious disposition and he'd been born into a family where, despite the disorder of parents separating and a gnawing sense of isolation, there had still been nothing to curb or in any way block his curiosity. Now a new stimulus was added to this young, inquisitive nature.

Bill said later that there is no true learning without a need to know, and at this point his need was urgent. It had come about through a startling insight that night at the supper table. While his grandfather had been praising him, Bill heard himself called a "number-one man." And at that moment all the lights in the room seemed to come up brighter. He was filled with a kind of power, and when they went on about his accomplishment he could feel it growing, spreading, through his body, as if some potent drug had been released.

Yet strangely there was nothing unexpected about it. It was

what he'd always wanted. In Rutland, when his father had taken him to the circus, he'd wanted to outride and outshoot Buffalo Bill. He wanted to outbat Ty Cobb. This yearning to be foremost was not new; his grandfather had simply given him the name for it. And to achieve that, to be number one and keep this feeling, would be worth any investment of energy, any amount of time.

And at that same moment, still at the supper table, he made one other discovery. Six months before, he had known nothing about a boomerang, but he had worked, he'd asked the woodcutters and he'd listened. He watched and each time he'd failed he'd not gotten excited but had carefully appraised what had gone amiss. Seeing the perfect return this afternoon and seeing the look in his grandfather's eyes now had to prove one thing: he was capable of learning. And with that it happened— his future was mapped. The next day and in the days, weeks and months that followed, Bill became a learner, a listener, a watcher.

Primarily, of course, he was learning from his grandfather, who at this point was having to do some appraising himself. Through a singular twist of fate he had been given a second chance—and dear God, he didn't want to fumble this time. Perhaps if his beliefs had taken a more religious turn, he might have prayed for Billy now, but he knew that if one day this boy could stand on a hillside and look out, as once years before he himself had looked out, if Billy could know then that he was a part of his land, his country, and of where it was heading, then he would not need prayers.

But Fayette also knew he must move slowly here, never try to give more than a boy could accept, and, above all, never try to fob off secondhand beliefs.

One evening after they had completed an errand down in Manchester, Bill watched his grandfather draw their buggy up beside the battle monument that stood on the green in front of the church. The monument, made of granite, was surmounted by a statue of a continental soldier and on its sides were listed the names of all the local men who'd served in American wars. Darkness was settling over the town—only a thin finger-shaped streak of yellow above the western hills showed where the sun had been and where it was setting—and Bill wondered if his grandfather could even make out the names.

From the expression on his face Bill was sure he wanted to tell him something, probably some story about his war, but the old man kept silent and not until they'd moved on down the hill, past the lights of Factory Point, and were heading north again did he finally speak. But it was not a war story he wanted to tell; he was trying to say what the war had been about.

And now, just as old Landon had made him see the romantic side of battle, his grandfather was making him understand why a group of Vermont boys who'd seen no more of the country than their own little county had gone traipsing off to fight and be killed for an idea.

The idea of democracy, he said—and Billy was not to forget it —was that all men are equal and that the things they have in common, that hold them together, are stronger than anything that tries to separate them. Everything depended on this, and on people knowing and remembering it, always. For this was the basis of the tremendous experiment our young country was launched upon, and the whole world was watching to see if it could work.

Put this way as they rode north on a crisp spring night, the idea of an experiment that would affect the entire world was suddenly more exciting, more of a challenge, than the battles that had been fought to preserve it. But Fayette did not push too far; he kept his thoughts concise. Then, one night when they talked again, just as Landon had made him feel the thrill of Cedar Creek, his grandfather made him feel the meaning of Appomattox, of that unique forgiveness of millions toward millions, "with malice toward none. . . ."

Fayette felt he must also be clear about the difference between law and justice. Laws could make mistakes, he knew, but justice never. So reach out for justice, he said, and remember that the noblest thing any man could ever do was add his bit to the world's tiny store of knowledge, then join his weight to our unending battle for justice.

These were heady words to pass on to a thirteen-year-old and many a night Bill went to his room with his mind so giddy with new ideas there was no hope of sleep. His picture of the man he was going to be was constantly changing now. His fantasies were changing too. Instead of Quixote, he saw himself as a lone attorney arguing his case for the people in the Supreme Court building in Washington, D.C., and some nights he could even make out an elderly gentleman, Mr. Fayette Griffith, sitting in the spectators' gallery, nodding respectfully.

Their neighbors soon grew accustomed to seeing the two of them walking together down to the depot of an evening or just leaning back against a rail fence, sometimes talking, sometimes not. For now Bill found he was learning not only from words, but from what was being left unsaid.

And here again there was something familiar. That night on the mountaintop when he had realized why his father had kept silent, he knew he'd been close to understanding some vital fact about his life. Now, although he knew his grandfather and Gilly to be very different men, he could feel the same sense of power in their silence. And as the months and seasons raced by—in summer working in the fields, in fall starting back to school—he had to find out about every kind of power a man might have.

The winter months were of course punctuated by the holidays and visits from his mother, and always, before she would arrive, he would make long lists of the questions he planned to ask her. She would appear laden with gifts and the latest news about her classes, and since she was now enrolled in the Boston Academy of Osteopathy and since very few women had ever attempted this, Billy wondered if she too understood the need to be number one. But before they knew it, New Year's would arrive, she'd be gone and none of his questions asked.

He was also learning from all sorts of other people, from the whole incongruous mixture of individuals who make up a small New England town. He discovered that there were those among them who seemed to crave and to need someone with whom they could share their experience. There were also those who did not. But the majority, he learned, were talkers, and if he was careful and approached them with the right sort of questions, they were eager to share.

Perhaps they sensed the determined reaching out in this tall boy who'd stop at their gate to wish them good evening, because now, as his young body began to change and take on its final shape and form, as his long arms found their comfortable hang, these people told him many things and their lives and their stories traced deep lines in his mind. In a way, they talked their memories into his memories.

Years later, when he tried to list their names he had to give up; there were too many. There was Mary Milot, who would talk long after her classes were finished, and old Uncle Marley sitting sphinxlike behind his counter at the general store; there was dear old Frank Jacobs, and crazy Charlie Ritchie with his huge brood of children; and Bill Landon and Barefoot Rose.

And then there was Mark.

6

Mark Whalon came meandering into Bill's life in the spring or early summer of 1908. Neither of them could remember a first meeting—they were neighbors, they just naturally knew each other—and although Mark was ten years older than Bill and in the beginning they saw each other only when he was on vacation from the state university, he became Bill's first friend.

Mark seems to have been a man so uniquely fashioned by nature to serve Bill's needs it would be hard to imagine what the boy's life would have been if Mark had not been there to make him laugh and not, as Bill put it, take himself so damn serious. Mark was a tall, thin, slow-moving fellow, with a great crop of unruly brown hair, one lock of which always fell over his forehead. He was also a jack of many trades, for along with his university classes, which were the bright center of his life, he had worked the quarries, been a lumberjack, a lineman for the phone company, and in the summer of 1908 he had some vague employment in the general store. There were many advantages to this job, among them access to a delivery wagon, which meant he and Bill could go driving off and visit neighboring towns. Early in their relationship Bill discovered that Mark too was a people-watcher and no day was totally lost for them if they were allowed a few free hours to draw up on a main street, sit back, laugh and watch the world moving by. Bill also discovered that he and Mark laughed at the exact same things.

In the beginning it was true Mark did kid Bill unmercifully, but Bill was never offended. There was too much to be learned, and Mark had brought back from his college a great store of information. Much of this was green, fermenting information and still unrelated, but he possessed a prodigious memory and as they'd go rattling along in the delivery wagon, he would recite long passages from Shakespeare and Burns and from writers Bill had never heard about, Robert Ingersoll, Karl Marx.

But above all Mark was a talker who loved to argue and expand on a subject in the hope that somehow a Socratic dialogue might develop. In contradiction to all Bill had been taught, Mark believed it had not taken six days to create the world, but that each of those days represented millions of years. He introduced Bill to the theory that man had ascended—Mark never used the word descended—from apes. And all his ideas were presented in such a buoyant manner that Bill was often left puzzled as to whether Mark was serious or just getting off another of his good ones.

That summer Mark Whalon was full of his new learning, his irrepressible good humor and a New Englander's distrust of all authority. In time he was to play many roles in Bill's life, but there was probably none he enjoyed more than that of devil's advocate. Years later Bill recalled in detail one particular afternoon when Mark had taken over this role with more than his usual relish.

They were in their wagon again, returning from a hunting expedition; their Remingtons and a half dozen squirrels lay on the floorboards at their feet. Bill had been going on about democracy and how the whole world was watching the American experiment. Mark had listened, he'd even nodded in what Bill thought was approval, but at last he cleared his throat and began to answer. The doctrine of democracy, he admitted, was a noble concept. But as to the proposition that men were equal, well, he thought Bill should give a little more thought to that.

The experiment, as he saw it, had to be based on the idea that all men were admirable and that they had been endowed by their Creator with the desire and the ability to improve themselves. And this, he said, was where the rub came in, because any miscalculation in this basic notion would not only rock the boat, it could play hell with the whole damned experiment.

Bill conceded that this might be true, and Mark went on to explain that as he viewed the world, it had become clear that only a blind-drunk optimist could fail to notice that people might be good, but they were also greedy, timid and often bone lazy, with no desire to improve anything. What was more, these defects of character were more pronounced the further down the social ladder you chose to look.

The expression "social ladder" was new to Bill. Sensing his confusion, Mark made a sudden turn when they reached the next crossing and headed the wagon down toward Manchester.

Approaching the town from the west, they passed the poor farm on their right, but Mark made no reference to this. He didn't have to. Every boy knew the poor farm represented the ultimate disgrace. To be taken here was more horrendous and more shaming than to be locked up in jail or in the crazy house in Brattleboro, and you just naturally rode past it in silence. Mark didn't even say very much as they entered the outskirts of town and trotted by the unpainted frame houses standing behind their straggly fences and unkempt little gardens. These, Bill knew, were the homes of immigrants, the Irish and Italians, and of people who'd been recruited from farms to service the town.

It wasn't until they moved onto the main street and were riding past the stately row of old homes that Mark began his lecture on Manchester's social structure. Using the butt end of his rifle as a pointer, he indicated certain architectural graces Bill had never noticed, delicate fanlights above doorways, cornices and neat white fences with carved pineapples on their posts. Then he pointed out some of the newer, less sedate homes along side streets and the walkways that edged the roads. These were broad slabs of marble that often were all out of line, having been pushed up by the roots of ancient elms. Not every American, Mark said, walked on marble sidewalks.

A few generations back, Manchester had begun to get a reputation as a summer resort and now each year, sometimes for a few weeks, sometimes for the full season, it was visited by "fashionable folks" from Boston, New York and Brooklyn. Indeed, until this afternoon Bill had thought of the town as divided into two groups, summer visitors and natives. He knew that some had considerably more money than others and he'd always accepted this, naturally and with no questions. But now Mark was introducing a new proposition. He was trying to make him see that there were differences among the natives and among the visitors too, and it wasn't only a matter of the amount of money a person had. Mark seemed to see a difference even in the money itself.

Old family money, he said, was one thing, but new money—and by that he meant the money a man earned or maybe made at the track—that was another matter. And in a town like Manchester new money had far less value than the old inherited capital. People didn't talk about it. If you asked, they'd just say they were comfortable or comfortably off. Still that fact and where their money came from was all-important, because it was what decided which rung a person belonged on.

Bill knew this was the most grown-up conversation he'd ever had and, because it was, he tried to follow everything Mark was saying, but the trouble was Mark kept talking about groups and levels. He saw all of life as a ladder on which people tried to climb, but the more he tried to explain, the more abstract and remote it seemed.

Then, as they were reaching the southernmost part of the town, he used still another phrase Bill had never heard. He was talking about the best people and a certain quality they all seemed to have that set them apart and this Mark called their great "x quality." Perhaps since making a living wasn't so all-fired important to them, they were freer to give themselves over to other interests, to what the rest of us would call hobbies.

But now as Bill studied his friend he knew it wasn't the confusion or just that he didn't know the meaning of certain words: the whole feeling of the conversation embarrassed him, everything in him resisted it, resented it. What Mark was saying might be right for some people in some places, in foreign countries maybe, with kings and noblemen, but it couldn't have anything to do with him. Didn't Mark know that here people had rights, that they could move ahead? Didn't he realize there were always exceptions, that a man could pull himself up?

Mark said he was glad Bill had mentioned this, because of course there were exceptions. There were some right here on Main Street, and with the butt of his rifle he pointed to a large, handsome white house. This, Bill knew, was the Burnham house; he'd often seen a family of golden-haired children playing in the garden. Dr. Clark Burnham, Mark explained, was a physician from Brooklyn and he had many wealthy patients who followed him anywhere—or he followed them; it didn't matter, because Bill was right—a doctor with his special skills could move up or down the ladder. But there weren't many who could; a minister perhaps, sometimes a lawyer. . . .

Then it *wasn't* all a question of family or money—Bill felt he'd scored a point—it was a man's education that mattered.

Mark agreed. That was part, but it wasn't the whole of it, because here it was not how much you knew, it was where you learned it. All the men of the old families had been to Yale or Harvard, or possibly Dartmouth, and before that they had gone to St. Paul's or Andover; the only locals who got invited to their

Saturday-night dances were the few boys who attended Burr and Burton.

Burr and Burton, Bill knew, was one of the oldest schools in Vermont, a gray stone edifice that stood on a hill overlooking Manchester. Its students were mostly boarders from out of town, with only a small number of natives among them. Bill could always spot these boys by the clothes they wore, tweed trousers and fashionable jackets with belts in the back. In East Dorset they considered them snobbish, but now—he wanted to be honest about this—he wondered if there wasn't something about them he'd secretly envied, their special "x quality"?

People were born into social groups and they stayed in those groups, Mark declared—oh, he was wound up this afternoon and Bill knew better than to interrupt again—and perhaps they wanted it this way, because only the rarest critter could ever summon the power to break from the mold. (There was that word "power" again, and for a moment Bill wondered if Mark was speaking in general here or directly to him.) And any man, Mark said, who wanted to get ahead had damned sight better understand what he was up against and the rigidity of social patterns.

Always before when Bill left Mark his spirits had been high. That night he was filled with doubts. If it had come from anyone except Mark, he could have dismissed it, but he knew that Mark loved and respected people as much if not more than his grandfather did.

Was this then some generational difference? Did Mark, being younger, see the world more clearly, with more shadings? And exactly how important were these shadings? If, as Mark seemed to believe, class distinctions meant so much, was this the real reason Bill had always felt a misfit, a guest? His mother was studying to be a doctor—did this mean that she understood what Mark was saying? Would her skills enable her to move up the ladder? But where and how would *he* acquire the power to climb? These were not questions that could be put aside. He knew it was just a matter of time: he'd be a man very soon, but who would this man be? Where would he belong?

On the Saturday following their Manchester trip—and Bill was never to know if this was intentional on Mark's part—just as he was settling down to do his homework he heard the delivery wagon drawing up. He had an examination first thing Monday morning and he'd promised his grandfather he would study. What was more, he wanted to study, but when he heard Mark's whistle, without thinking what he was doing he closed his books, went out and joined him.

They drove over to Danby to make a delivery and nothing in any way memorable happened on the ride over. But on the way back there was a decided chill in the air and as they passed an old tavern Mark said he thought he needed something to wet his whistle. Bill had ridden by the unpainted, nondescript building many times, but there'd been no reason to pay it any attention. A few wagons and buggies stood at the side and they pulled up next to them, got out and went in through a little back door.

Coming in from the sunshine, it took a minute to adjust to the dimness. The windows were painted over and the only light came from a series of spluttering oil lanterns. It took a minute to adjust to the noise too, because the room was filled with men—there must have been twenty or thirty of them—and everyone seemed to be talking at once, laughing at once. But something happened to Bill then, and it happened immediately although it took a while to figure it out. As they stepped through the door they were greeted by the warm, friendly smell of wet sawdust, spilled beer and whiskey, but that wasn't it.

Mark had a drink and, without his having to ask for it, somebody handed Bill a mug of cider. These men were hunters, he figured, down from the hills, and they were all bragging about their successes. After a time he and Mark got separated, but it didn't matter. From the very start, he knew, this was the friendliest gathering he'd ever been in. He could tell some of them had to be in their seventies and over by the wall there were a couple of fellows not much older than he, but everybody was talking together. Even when they began milling around and breaking up into little groups, they were together. And soon he began talking himself, swapping stories with two men who'd been out over a week after big deer.

But most of their stories now had to do with old Charlie Ritchie, who was sitting at the bar. Poor Charlie had become the butt of every joke. "I got me a cat at home and I swear he brings in bigger mice than anything you shot today." They went at him unmercifully, but the curious thing was, from the way they laughed, the way Charlie laughed too, you could tell there was nothing cruel and no hard feelings anywhere. Men who laughed this way couldn't be cruel.

Then after a little—he must have been on his second cider— as good a time as he was having, he let his mind wander back for a minute or two to the week he'd been through, to his grandfather and the work he'd promised he would do. He knew he should feel guilty. Yet here he was talking right up with a bunch of strangers and feeling he belonged with them and that everything was all right. He glanced around, looking for Mark, wondering if he would notice the change, and just at that moment Mark looked up and over at him, and in the short time they allowed their eyes to meet Mark winked at him; then they both grinned.

Everyone began circulating, carrying their drinks with them, and one old fellow Bill hadn't noticed before took out his fiddle and after plucking at it, trying to tune it, he broke into a song and a group of four or five at first, then a lot more, gathered behind him and began singing, harmonizing.

There weren't enough chairs at the tables and no stools along the bar, so Bill squatted down on the floor, leaning his long body back against the wall, listening to their slow, agonizing experiments with chords, watching them all and feeling they were all his friends and that they all liked him too. Sometimes the quintet would go intentionally sour, and everybody would yell or moan, but then they'd come up with a sweet one, unbearably sweet, and they would hold it longer than you'd think possible, and he could feel something in his throat, his eyes getting wet. It was beautiful, long and sweet and beautiful.

They stayed on in the tavern for maybe a couple of hours. It was already dark when they went outside, but Bill felt nothing but a crazy happy feeling of lightness. He had laughed so hard and so much, the muscles of his stomach ached, but his whole being was relaxed. Mark was a little drunk, he guessed, but that didn't matter; the horse knew the way and the night was crisp and clear and this new happiness inside lasted all the way back to East Dorset.

Just as a song may sometimes leave an echo and keep returning for no discernible reason, Bill kept remembering that afternoon and his feeling of being at home, his feeling for the men. Sometimes he could think of nothing else. He wanted it again. But he sensed this *had* to be wrong. What could any of this have to do with being a lawyer in the Supreme Court building, with his lifelong plan to be number one and bend everything to the accomplishment of that?

Something had to be wrong. With his mind he understood, but he could no longer *feel* it wrong. Those men in the bar were not only of different ages, they were from all rungs of the ladder, and yet the bond that existed among them, their camaraderie—he groped for the proper word—proved everything his grandfather had been saying. In a dark tavern, singing way off key, these men somehow made manifest the whole Lincolnesque idea about the things we have in common being stronger, more important. And finally, didn't they give the lie to Mark's theories about class and rigid social patterns? He wanted to go back, join them, go hunting with them, or just sit among them and listen to an old fellow playing his fiddle. And yet . . .

Yet if he did, how would he acquire the skills, the secret

power his whole life told him he must have? Now, as the days and then the weeks went by, it was as though he were two people and these two kept arguing. One was saying, "Go. Call Mark. Get him to take you back." And the other said, "No. Stay here. Work." And sometimes, alone late at night, he would clench his fists and stride around the room. Then, just as he had long ago, he would stop, look in the mirror and set his jaw. But now instead of repeating the words "I'll show them," his eyes would flash back at him and he would say, "I can. I can do it."

Once again he was trying to make a decision without taking into account the peculiar workings of fate and the simple fact that such decisions were often to be lifted out of his hands.

While he had been growing, wrestling with two sides of his nature, his grandparents had been watching and waiting. They approved of his friendship with Mark. Like everyone in town, they enjoyed Mark Whalon. It wasn't that. What concerned them now were the changes they couldn't help noticing in Bill himself. For each week the boy was coming to look more like Gilly Wilson, and this was now more than a matter of coloring or cheekbones, it was an attitude, a stance of strong shoulders, an independent tilt of head. They said nothing about this—and neither of them would have thought of mentioning it to anyone outside the family—but each knew the other had noticed.

Then, and without any reason being given, a decision was reached. In the late spring of 1909 his grandfather told him that after consulting with his mother, an application had been made for him to enter Burr and Burton Academy and the application had been accepted.

7

The years at Burr and Burton raced by. It was incredible, as if by the simple act of stepping from the confines of East Dorset all of life moved at a faster pace.

Afterward Bill remembered the times when he was happiest. But he also remembered days when he was filled with an overwhelming loneliness of the sort that perhaps only boys of fourteen or fifteen ever know.

The first such day began on the playing fields out behind the school. Until now, at his little two-room schoolhouse, he had been considered quite good at athletics, but there he'd been competing with farmer boys. Here he was up against young men from different parts of the country, young men who—as Mark would have pointed out—had had time to indulge their hobbies. All of them were highly knowledgeable about sports. Beside them Bill felt awkward and out of place. On his first appearance on the field someone threw a baseball at him. He put out his hand but missed, and it hit him in the head, knocking him down. Immediately he was surrounded by a crowd of boys, silent and deeply concerned, and all staring down at him. But the moment he moved, the moment he pulled himself up to a sitting position and they saw he wasn't hurt, they began to laugh, and they were laughing not with him but at him, at his clumsiness.

Suddenly his whole body was swept with a spasm of rage. He was on his feet screaming, and the words that poured forth were, "I'll show you. I'll show you all!"

The laughter only grew, and so did the insane, childish screaming: he'd do it, he would, he'd be the best goddamn player in the school, he'd show 'em, he'd be captain of their team.

And with that another obsession began. If he couldn't get anyone to play with him, he threw a ball up against the side of a building, any building. On weekends back in East Dorset he spent hours hurling rocks at telephone poles in an effort to perfect his aim, strengthen his arm, so that he might become not only the captain, but the acknowledged star of the team, the pitcher. In fact, he so overdid his practice that year that he injured the socket of his right arm and developed a condition which was described as rather like ringbone in a horse and which, to the end of his life, prevented the arm from ever being fully extended. But he also developed a deadly aim, speed and an ability to throw curves, spitballs, knuckleballs. In his second year he was a pitcher, in his third year captain of the team.

But baseball wasn't his only obsession. In the fall he played fullback and was soon recognized as the best punter on the team. By now a definite pattern was beginning to emerge. A remark would be made, often a casual, even a joking remark, and one that had not been meant unkindly, but Bill would take it amiss and immediately determine to right another situation.

Once, returning from a baseball trip, the team was singing together in the back of a wagon when someone next to Bill moaned, asked him for God's sake to take it easy and even suggested that he might be tone deaf. The following day Bill called on Mrs. Brooks, the headmaster's wife, and asked if she would consider giving him singing lessons. Mrs. Brooks was Italian. Before her marriage she'd sung at La Scala in Milan and since then had continued her career by giving occasional concerts in southern Vermont. Poor woman, she was perhaps flattered by the gangling student's turning to her for help. She accepted him as a voice student and only then discovered that Bill's voice had almost every fault that a young unsure baritone can have. It was husky and thin in the middle tones, but it was a voice and there was no denying that he loved to sing. The signora worked diligently and by the following spring Bill and a young tenor sang a duet with the Burr and Burton Glee Club.

The violin was another example. When his grandfather had taken the fiddle from the trunk in the attic, it was actually a battered and worthless instrument. It had only one string, a D string, but Bill had been able to tune this to a C, and getting his sister Dorothy to play "Work for the Night Is Coming" on the little melodeon in the parlor, he would saw out the tenor, conscientiously marking the spots where various notes fell. Eventually he got hold of a set of wire strings, of the sort used by country fiddlers, and an old jig book with a chart of a violin fingerboard. He made a new bridge from a chip of wood and he beavered away, playing scales, arpeggios, endless exercises. Finally he was not only performing for the family, he was playing with the school orchestra.

With each new triumph a new dimension seemed added to his life. More than that, he was slowly beginning to sense an unaccustomed ease with people. He still had no friend—Mark was away at the university most of the year—but he had acquaintances and among the younger boys some staunch admirers. All his classmates were from the "upper rungs" and this fact may well have colored his attitude; he joined in their late-night bull sessions and was even beginning to develop something of a reputation as a raconteur, but the stories these boys brought back from their holidays—lurid tales about girls who were willing to go all the way and about the incredible amounts of booze available in Albany and Boston—all this seemed alien to Bill, interesting, even exciting to think about, but belonging to another world.

He knew booze in particular could play no part in his scheme.

Indeed, at this time it represented an actual enemy, because it was so linked with Gilly, and Gilly's departure was something he would not think about.

Still, even if he couldn't feel intimate with his classmates, he was proving that if he adhered to his scheme—receiving a challenge, formulating a plan of action and then pursuing that plan —he'd not only be accepted, he would be admired, envied. For during these first years at Burr and Burton there was nothing accidental about Bill's behavior; it was all accurately planned.

But once again he was reckoning without taking two simple and inescapable facts into account. He was a young, extraordinarily healthy male, and Burr and Burton was a coeducational school.

Until the spring of his junior year girls had played no part in his life. Until now he'd considered his face too homely, his body too clumsy ever to attract a girl. Now he saw and was seen by Bertha Banford, the prettiest, brightest and surely the most charming girl in school. He fell in love, deeply, completely in love, and Bertha loved him,

There was a rare and special quality about Bill's loving, and there was a very special quality about Bertha herself, a quality which no one who was near her would ever forget. Hers was not the conventional prettiness of a sixteen-year-old, though she had her share of that—great dark eyes and a fine chin line softened by the gentle curve of her cheeks. But there was a glow about the girl, a promise. Everything, her young body, her manner, her eyes, spoke of the woman she was about to be.

Bill instantly forgot he'd ever been shy, and he never again thought of himself as a man who could plan only for himself. And that spring he made a miraculous discovery: when someone thinks you handsome, you are handsome.

In a way these two were blessed. For Bill had not fallen in love with an older woman who had to be worshiped from a distance. He loved in a much more explicit way a girl he saw at

56

chapel every morning. Each knew exactly where the other would be and their eyes would meet and they would stare at each other for one long moment. Then, with an effort, they'd withdraw their eyes, look down at a book, at someone nearby. And Bertha was there in classrooms, or she was there waiting when his classes were over. And in the evenings he was permitted to call at her home.

The simple fact of finding himself loved seemed unbelievable. Yet it was Bertha who led Bill into the "real world" and gave him a sense of importance in that world—as well as a sense of freedom. Now there appeared to be hundreds of new paths he might follow, nothing he couldn't do, and he began to cover himself with new honors: the glee club, the orchestra; he was head of the Y.M.C.A., captain of the ball team—and his team was winning every game. At the spring elections he was chosen president of the senior class. And all this was done easily and with a kind of tremendous, contagious joy. For above all, Bertha Banford was a girl who was delighted with life and shared her delight.

Earlier Bill had felt the two sides of his nature pulling in different directions. Now it was as though everything had united and he had become some happy combination of Gilly's good humor and Emily's earnestness. And he was convinced he would never again think of anything as dull.

All that spring and all during the summer there was a new aliveness everywhere, a sparkling haze over the world, and —this may have been part of their blessing—they both knew it.

One other important element—and they both realized this too —was Bertha's family. Most boys at sixteen or seventeen hate or fear their girl's family, but Bertha's parents were unlike any people Bill had known. Her mother came from Louisville and her father, who had been born in England, was rector of St. Luke's, and they both had a way of treating Bill as if he were a grown man, and a man whose ideas interested them.

Perhaps there was nothing remarkable in the things the Banfords talked about that summer, but their words as well as their attitudes were new to him. He could bring up an idea, any idea he'd been thinking about, and together they'd go ahead and develop it.

For example, none of Mark's theories about the great social changes that were needed in the world in any way upset the Banfords or disturbed the reverend's beliefs. In fact, he saw the desire for change, this instinct, as he put it, to break through into another dimension, as part of our heritage, something that went back through all history, possibly even before history, before men were even men. It might be, he believed, the factor that first set us apart from other animals, the vehicle of our evolution. Only men rebel. And he sometimes wondered if this might not be innate in man.

Bill and Bertha, he was sure, had enough, indeed seemed to have an abundance of this instinct, and he only hoped they'd work now and develop their minds so that when the time came and they reached out, struck out for change, it could be with some force, some meaning.

One night after such talk had led them into a discussion of Darwin and his theories about the survival of the fittest, and after the Banfords had said good night and retired upstairs, Bill and Bertha sat together side by side on the front porch steps. For a while neither of them spoke, but that was all right; Bill felt that she was with him, that she too was remembering what had been said, and that she was going over it all just as he was, trying to clarify and pin it down so she would not lose it.

Millions of years ago, her father had said, from the very earliest forms of life and all the way up to man, something had wanted to be more, to break through into a new dimension. And from that wanting had come the doing and from the doing—as he thought about this and accepted the thought into his mind, Bill slowly stretched out his hands before him—from that doing came the means with which to do.

Then suddenly he turned and looked at Bertha. Her arms

were across her knees but he saw that she too was looking at her hands, slowly moving her fingers one at a time, studying her fingers. "Then . . ." she said, and if there'd been any doubt about her being with him and thinking the same thoughts, her words would have answered his doubt: "Then what does it mean? It means we are not finished. It means man will always want to break through. We'll always want more. . . ."

And she said one other thing. Her voice was soft, no more than a whisper, but Bill heard and he remembered her words. "It's almost as though we owe them something, all those who went before, and"—she paused, looking up into his eyes—"if we don't want life to be more, if we aren't the most that we can be, then aren't we letting them down, going back on all that's happened, all their wanting?"

It was a question, but he knew there was no need to answer.

Some nights—and this was such a night—when the time came and he knew he must leave her, when the house behind them was dark and silent and the garden was filled with the scent of flowers, he wanted to take her in his arms, press her body close against his, his mouth hard against her mouth. It was hell being a man and just holding a girl by the hand and mumbling good night.

There were other nights in the late summer and early fall when, leaving her, he'd be filled with an overwhelming need to move, to walk, to run and keep on running. Then, instead of going by the highway and trying to hitch a ride, he'd cross over to the depot and follow the tracks all the way up to East Dorset. He loved throwing his head back and gazing at the stars. He loved the black trees edging up the hills, loved the mountains towering on either side and the glittering rails shining in moonlight, stretching on and on ahead.

When at last he would reach his grandfather's house and make his way up to his room it would not be to sleep. He would pull off his shirt, go across to the window and stare down at the sleeping town. He knew who lived in every house and some-

59

times it seemed he could look through their windows and actually see them sleeping. Most, he was sure, would be curled up on their sides like his grandmother and Dorothy downstairs. Some might be tossing, unable to sleep and getting up like him to peer out at an empty street. He knew them all and he loved them in a way he'd never known or loved before. For now, through a process that had nothing to do with thinking, he realized they were people who themselves had once loved, who like him were filled with hungers and desire.

And some nights his imaginings would lead him even beyond the town. He could see his mother in Boston, shut in her room, sitting at a table, poring over her books, and to the west, his father walking in the night, always walking, walking and wanting more. Now he could even picture people he didn't know: young men in cities studying, lost in the agonies of concentration, and some out on lonely farms and ranches, others crossing the continent on trains, riding through the night, all wanting more. . . .

He was in love, he could not sleep, and it seemed sometimes that he could feel all the wanting in the world pouring in on him. He was in love, and his love reached out to encompass all people, all men, all women everywhere.

It happened on a bright November morning, and although the events of that morning were to have so much to do with what came later, at the time they seemed unreal.

Bertha had gone down to New York with her family for three days. She had promised to write, and Bill was late that morning because he'd stopped at the post office, but there was no mail and he hurried on to chapel. They were already singing a hymn when he snuck into a place in the last row and even then, while they were still singing, something seemed strange.

At the close of the hymn Mr. Brooks, the headmaster, stood up to address the school. The sun was slanting in through the window beside him and it reflected off his glasses so Bill couldn't tell what his expression was. He saw him reach into his pocket and bring out a yellow piece of paper. Looking down at it, Mr. Brooks cleared his throat and said he had just received a telegram from New York City and someone very dear to all of them, Bertha Banford, had died the night before following surgery at the Fifth Avenue Hospital. That was all he said. Then he turned and sat down. A little murmur, like a wave, rose and moved across the students. A few heads turned and looked at Bill. Then there was silence, silence everywhere, until someone started playing another hymn and everyone got up and filed out of chapel.

Bill went to his first class; he went to his second and third. Girls came up to him and mumbled things, but they were all teary and he didn't hear them. Boys just looked at him and shook their heads, but it didn't matter because none of it was really happening.

At recess he had to get away. He walked up in the hills, walked all afternoon until it was dark. He could see Mr. Brooks, he could hear what he said; still it had no reality.

Three days later there was a memorial service at the church. He attended. He put on his blue suit and a dark tie and he sat way over at the side and again he was seeing and he was hearing everything. There would be no burial now, they said, because it was November and the ground was frozen. Bertha's body would be placed in the crypt at Factory Point Cemetery. For a long time he looked hard at the Reverend and Mrs. Banford, thinking this would make him believe. It was like being drunk, he guessed, because he moved, he talked to people, he understood what they were saying and even answered them, but nothing touched him, nothing had any connection with him, with Bertha.

The night after the service he walked out to the cemetery. It was a cold night with a sharp wind down from the mountain. As he was pushing open the little squeaking gate at the entrance, he remembered that at the end of the play Romeo had gone to Juliet's crypt. Only—he moved on, closing the gate behind him—only Juliet hadn't been really dead; it was just a part of the plot.

Around the crypt, which was at the far end beyond all the rows of stones, there was a low granite shelf and for a time he sat on this, his long legs stretched out before him. Beneath his feet the earth felt hard, covered with a matting of dry strawlike weeds, and as he leaned and plucked the stalk of a weed he tried to recall the ending of the play. Romeo, thinking Juliet was dead, had killed himself, but then Juliet awakened and . . . His mind went blank; he couldn't remember. He ran the stem of the weed through his fingers, studying its feathery top. Bertha would know. Bertha remembered every plot. She would tell him.

He leaned his head back and peered up at the sky, searching for some familiar star, but the clouds were too thick, too low to see through. Bertha would not tell him. Not now. Not ever. And he carefully, deliberately broke the stem of the weed and let it drop from his hand. Then, as if in a daze, he very gently ran his heavy boots across the growth of weeds. In time Bertha's body would become a part of the earth. Her soft dark hair, the young flesh that curved softly over her bones, would feed the soil, but she would not speak, her voice would never speak again. The weeds would go on; in the spring they would bud again, come to blossom and in time go to seed. He sat for what must have been hours. Weeds would go on, but he would never hear her whisper again.

When finally he rose to leave, the wind had shifted, the low-hanging clouds had moved on, and he let his eyes go up to the sky, to the topmost branches of the leafless trees, which were dipping, swaying now against the wind. Stars were out; there weren't many but they were definite, brilliant and white, and to the west over the town he could see Venus hanging low in the sky. Somewhere a dog barked and on a distant hill another dog answered. The worst, the very worst of it, was that the extinction of a young girl's life did not matter. It did not make the slightest difference or in any way affect the movement of the world.

He hesitated by the gate as this thought took shape in his mind, then almost automatically his arms began to stretch up and out, his fingers spread as if trying to grasp some wisp of air, some fragment he might hold. But he knew now, and he let his arms drop to his sides. His need, his loving, didn't matter a good goddamn. His wanting, his hunger and desire, meant nothing to the terrible ongoing forces of creation.

And he would never forget this truth which he saw and accepted that night.

He continued to attend his classes and for a while he tried to go on with his other activities, the glee club, the orchestra, but he found himself going back to Factory Point again and again. He'd walk out at night and sit alone in the empty cemetery. That winter he took the midyear exams, but he failed in almost every subject. By spring it had become clear that he could not graduate; he was president of his class and couldn't graduate. His mother was sent for, and a series of angry meetings followed, some of them in Mr. Brooks's office. Bill simply could not promise that he'd change or improve; he wanted to, but he just wasn't able to concentrate, and finally it was decided that he'd probably do better if he moved to Boston and lived with his mother.

His young years were over.

BOOK TWO

1

In the fall of 1914, Bill entered Norwich University, just before his nineteenth birthday. This was a fine age to be, everyone said; it was the acme of youth, when all life stretched ahead. And certainly it was a glorious time to be an American.

In Europe dark clouds had gathered. Germany had declared war on Russia and then on France and in the same week England had retaliated and was now at war with Germany. But all this was four thousand miles away, and the prevailing view, especially among the students and young doctors who gathered in Emily's apartment, was that Europe's troubles were tragic, of course, but were none of our concern. America had too much to do. We were moving at last, following our own special destiny, and every evening someone would remind the others, half jokingly perhaps but sometimes reverently, that we must remember to thank God for Christopher Columbus.

From listening to such talk as well as from books he was reading in an effort to make up the courses he'd failed, Bill often got the feeling that he'd been born on some blessed promontory that stood high above all other periods of history and toward which all other times had been aiming. He knew that he should be grateful for this, but he could find no way to hitch in with the bright optimism around him. And it had been this way ever since he'd first come to live with his mother and Dorothy.

A door had closed behind him. He had sensed it happening that night in the cemetery, but he had not known it then. It was one of the things he was to learn only by degrees as he walked alone through the little suburbs of Boston or made his way down bustling city streets. For now there was only one thing he knew, and this was that he too would die; just when or under what circumstances he did not know, but the fact of death was with him always.

People said that time heals wounds. He saw no reason to believe them. They said one learns to draw a curtain over certain memories and that in time one is no longer able to see behind the curtain. Then there were those who told him he would find that everything worked for the best, he must have faith. . . .

He wanted to understand and he wanted to follow their advice, but his entire being was haunted by pictures of what might have been and now would never be. He was trying to cling to the one point in his life that had had meaning; he was not yet willing to be torn away.

Just how much the family understood there's no way of telling. In the summer of '13—and perhaps this was an effort to distract him—his grandfather took him down into Pennsylvania. It was the fiftieth anniversary of Gettysburg, and men from every part of the country, rebels as well as Yanks, were gathering to sleep in tents, listen to politicians, talk and remember.

In a way they were a remarkable group, already part of a legend. They were bent now, many used canes and some kept shawls across their shoulders even in the July heat. As they walked out to view the famous battle sites, Bill and Fayette with them, they moved arm in arm, occasionally pausing to look up at replicas of their younger selves, great monumental men in bronze or granite springing from the earth, and they nodded balding heads but said little as they read off the names on gravestones.

But it was the late-night talk that Bill remembered. When the last speeches had been delivered and the formalities of the day ended with the sound of taps across the camp, these old men did not want to sleep. They would begin to congregate in little random groups; flasks and jugs would be produced and passed around and somewhere at the edge of a group Bill would settle down, stretch out and get set to listen.

There seemed something familiar about these men, coming as they did from all walks of life, something about the jugs passing around, about their camaraderie, their warmth. Then he remembered his feeling the first time he'd stepped into a tavern with Mark. In a way it was the same now. But it was more. For these men had been brought here by something important that had happened to them. Once long ago each of them had belonged. Each had moved with and had been moved by a tremendous event that had changed the course of a nation.

And as he listened, as the jugs passed from hand to hand and the summer night fell across the tents like a soft, warm blanket, they talked on and on, telling the most horrendous things, then laughing unsparingly at themselves. And Bill laughed with them. It was their knowing, he figured, that made this possible, all of them knowing in their bowels that what they had in common was stronger and more viable than anything that separated them.

It was as though they could say the things they had to say only to other men who'd been through what they'd been through. And soon he began to notice that this special feeling was not only in the little groups he happened to be with at night. This same communion, this bond, existed among all the men who'd been part of the battle. It wasn't that they dwelt on the fighting, but they *knew*. They shared a secret.

During those days and nights in Gettysburg Bill was lifted beyond himself by something he only partially understood. But that did not matter, for here, for this brief period of time, the whole American idea seemed alive and true and possible.

69

On the fifth day, which was a Saturday, after President Wilson had delivered his address in the great canvas tent and as Bill watched the camp beginning to disband, he felt strangely oppressed, not by the breaking up—this he had expected—and not by seeing friends who had been close suddenly preoccupied with thoughts of others; he understood they had to prepare themselves for what they'd find at home. What bothered him was something he did not want to think about, because he was sure it was once again connected with dying.

Each of these men had been through a battle, each had seen someone die, someone close, yet they had gone on, they had accepted what he could not accept. And now he wondered if this had given them their strength, a faith he did not have.

As he and his grandfather said their good-bys, boarded the train and headed north, his depression grew. The men who filled their train were all veterans and he saw as if for the first time that all of them were men well into their seventies. They had come together to celebrate an event that had occurred fifty years before. Everything that he had responded to—that touch of glory—was all part of the past and it had no connection with him. His eyes traveled across the rows of faces and suddenly he felt himself an intruder, an outsider. All those great emotions he'd been feeling were a part of yesterday. They belonged to these old men, not to him. He'd just come along for the ride.

And in the same way, what was happening to him now, what he was feeling, had nothing to do with them; it had to do only with him, with his own inadequacies.

As the train continued north and the sun sank out of sight, leaving only blackness beyond the windows, he tried to think about what lay ahead—Boston, his mother waiting, possibly summer school to make up the German course he'd flunked—and as he thought of these things he could feel an old fear, a kind of weakness, rising through his body. He could see quite clearly, as if pictures were forming on the window glass, his mother standing by the lake telling him Gilly had gone and would not be back. Then he saw a group of boys in a circle, laughing down at him, Burr and Burton boys, and he knew now that behind everything he had tried to do he had heard that laughter. And he knew there had always been places and groups of men where he didn't belong, where he was just passing through.

These dark moods—this was what his mother called them—these feelings of just passing through were like a disease growing inside him. Emily said they were little depressions and a perfectly natural part of growing up; one learned to override them and she kept harping on the point.

Life had not treated Emily Wilson gently (she did not have to point this out in words; Bill was acutely aware of it every day he was with her), but Emily had gone on, and she took pride in this. She had prevailed and she was determined to pass some of her fortitude on to her son. One must have the proper mental attitude, she insisted, and whenever they happened to be separated during this period, she wrote Bill long letters with the word "succeed" in every paragraph.

On the flyleaf of the little appointment book she kept in her office was a poem of Goethe's. She made a copy of it and gave it to Bill.

> Are you in earnest? Seize this very minute.
> What you can or dream you can, begin it!
> Boldness has genius, power and magic in it,
> Only engage and then the mind grows heated.
> *Begin* and then the work will be completed.

He wanted to begin. Above everything he wanted to be engaged in some high purpose, but he was held in a terrible paralysis and he knew he was powerless to shake it off. He, more than anyone, understood Goethe's words, but he understood them only with his mind; he could only feel like a young boy who had lost the one thing he wanted.

He did everything he could think of to exorcise all thoughts of

Bertha and concentrate on the job at hand. But he had no energy. This was, Emily pointed out, because he had no interests, but Emily, who at the time was giving nightly lectures in Boston on nervous diseases, began to fear it was only a matter of time before Bill's physical health would be affected.

Still he tried. In the late summer he returned to Burr and Burton, took the senior examinations and somehow managed to pass enough of them to graduate. In the fall and winter of '13–'14 he attended special courses at Arlington High which were meant to prepare him for the Massachusetts Institute of Technology—Emily having decided that because of his boyhood interest in science he was cut out to be an engineer. He even took the M.I.T. entrance exam, but he failed almost every subject. After that a search began for a less demanding college, and finally they hit upon Norwich, the Vermont military academy, which was accepting young men on the basis of a high school diploma, so there was no need of further testing.

In the summer of 1914 one important event promised to relieve the monotony, the uncontrollable discouragement. After a series of jobs—carpentry work at the Equinox Hotel in Manchester, working beside Mark as a lineman for the phone company—and with some financial help from his grandfather, Bill, at last, made a trip west to visit Gilly in British Columbia.

Gilly was the same tall, gaunt figure he remembered, the same outgoing contented man. He took Billy everywhere, introduced him to all his friends, and apparently he was the same great storyteller too. "He must know a million stories," Bill wrote Dorothy. "The men all love Dad, and you know, I never heard him tell the same story twice." Yet somehow Gilly was not the same—and Bill knew this as soon as he arrived. He was a little older, a little slower in his movements, but above all Gilly was a man in charge now, in charge of his men, his place in the world, and in charge of himself. And possibly it was this that Bill had not expected.

Bill had a need, and at times a compelling desire to share this need with someone. On the way west he'd been convinced that his father would understand and they would be able to talk; he had actually rehearsed a few conversations. But in his presence there seemed no way to broach certain subjects. It would have been uncalled for and wrong to mention problems when Gilly seemed so pleased with everything.

It was as though all his father wanted was for his son to be a generous, decent, untroubled young fellow. So—it was easier—he was that fellow, or at least during his whole stay in the West he tried to play that role. Then, too, he began to sense that Gilly had another interest, and after being with him less than a week he discovered what this interest was. It was Christine Bock, an attractive, round-faced woman just Gilly's age, who had been a schoolteacher. On the last night of his visit Gilly told him they planned to marry.

Traveling east again, Bill tried to sort out his feelings. His father loved him, or loved what he saw him as, and his father was a good, a genuinely happy man, the sort everyone should want to be. So once more what had gone wrong had to be his own fault. He had been expecting answers from his father that would put his life in focus again but, afraid to interrupt his father's happiness, he had not dared even to ask his questions.

The trip home was one of the most forlorn times of his life. From the train window he watched a continent unfolding, the majestic hackles of the Rockies, the plains and prairies that so recently had been frontiers, endless miles of wheat swaying in the sun and at night lonely little stations with their dim lights moving past. Then, for an hour or so, he would be alive, completely aware of everything. And what he was seeing was both sad and glorious to him. He was a part of it and it was a part of him. But only for an hour or so. Gradually the feeling would fade and he was left with the hollow shell of his aloneness, staring at nothing, listening to the sounds of a train—wheels pounding, the bell, the high, shrill whistle wailing through the night. He remembered what these sounds had meant when as a boy he had heard them from his little attic room, those golden, secret promises they always woke, wild and dangerous plans to join Gilly in the great Northwest. Now still another door was closing and he was going back to what everyone called his home.

Listening, staring straight ahead, he wondered if he was ever to know a home. Or was he destined to roam and become a part of that great American phenomenon, the rootless hobo traveling on his thumb, belonging nowhere, searching everywhere for the place where he'd fit in? Deep inside his clumsy, gangling body he was sure there was a man—the man he had expected to be—who was imprisoned, struggling to be free. But free to go where, to do what . . . ?

So for these, as well as for other reasons, Norwich represented a challenge, his chance to get hold and find out who he was. He understood this and he wanted passionately to heed the advice in Emily's letters. "Sometimes one can have too many opportunities," she wrote in September, "and one does not appreciate them until they are gone. I pray you will not let this be your fate. There is too much at stake to throw it all away."

When he read her words he was sure he wanted success as much as she wanted it for him. But he'd been at Norwich only a matter of weeks when he began to sense that the setting might be new, but he was just the same, plagued by the same fears, the same doubts and anxieties.

With Bertha he had believed himself a winner—and he *had* been one. Without her he had to face the fact that he was second-rate. Not that his classmates were socially superior; that would not have mattered in the military regime of the college. They were simply better at everything they did.

He tried out for baseball but wasn't good enough for the team. Another freshman was clearly more talented on the violin, so there was no place for him in the orchestra; and it was the same in the classroom. It took all the concentration he could muster to maintain a passing grade and when the rush for fraternities was on in the late fall he didn't receive a single bid. Curiously, it was at just this time that he developed an overwhelming need for sleep. When reveille would sound at 6 A.M., it seemed more than he could do to get himself up.

One morning when the ground was covered with ice and he was rushing to make a class, he slipped, fell and knocked his elbow out of joint. X-rays showed it to be a fairly simple fracture but since it was his right arm, the one already somewhat crooked from his excessive pitching practice, he would allow no one to touch him and insisted upon being taken to his mother in Boston.

Dr. Emily had the fracture reduced and while she was at it, in a most professional way, she had some adenoids raked out. Then after he'd had a suitable rest, she prepared to send Bill back to college. But now the thought of the discipline, the drills and above all the constant reminder of being second-rate, were suddenly too much.

Waiting at the Boston station, he became aware of a strange sensation in the solar plexus; his heart began to pound and skip beats; his body was swept by a wave of panic, and alone on the platform he was convinced he was about to die. On the train the sensation increased, but now there was added a terrible shortness of breath, his fingers went rigid and a paralytic spasm seemed to immobilize his legs. But far worse was the feeling that he could not get enough air. In a panic he stumbled from the coach and threw himself down in the vestibule between cars, his nose close to a crack in the flooring, frantically fighting for air.

Back at Norwich there were more attacks. He would be asked to do a few simple exercises, and palpitations would set in, his knees would begin to wobble uncontrollably and he'd be forced to cling to a railing or the side of a building to halt the tremors. He would be taken to the infirmary and examined, and he was always told there was nothing wrong. It was mental, they said, and nothing to worry about, though the doctor was willing to admit the palpitations were actual and often very heavy. One afternoon, while waiting for a medical report, he overheard a snatch of conversation in which the word "heart" was mentioned. Since no one had bothered to explain that if he were indeed suffering from a heart condition, it was simply a functional disorder that would be cured by time and rest, he immediately dropped into a pit of hypochondriacal terror.

By February it had become clear that he could not continue in college and after still another humiliating family conference it was decided that he should drop out, go down to stay with his grandparents and, if possible, come back for his second term the following winter.

At East Dorset things were no better. He would be seized by a fit of palpitations and the doctor would have to be called, often in the middle of the night. He'd be given a bromide, reassured and told to buck up and get hold. And he knew that the following morning he would have to face the unspoken questions in old Fayette's eyes.

Later Bill was to write that it required no profound knowledge of psychiatry to understand what had been going on. He saw no reason to live; a part of him wanted to die; but another part was terrified by the thought of death.

There were times, especially after a visit from his mother or after his grandfather had tried to reestablish their old relationship and have a talk with him, when even this terror was trivial compared to his feeling of inadequacy. Manhood and character, these were the things he must have. And it wasn't only the family that reminded him of this. Everyone seemed to be waiting, to be expecting too much.

Some part of him, he was sure, still wanted to be like others, to love and be loved and find some way to live without excuses, apologies, evasions. Yet as the winter wore on he was convinced that the ability to do these things had been taken from him.

But even in Vermont winter cannot last forever. The coming of spring has its special quality everywhere, but in the valley between the Taconic and the Green there is a rare and heady quality about it. The first hint of change is in the feel of the winds coming off the mountains. The wind is no longer an enemy. Old men feel this in their joints. Then there is the first tinge of green across the hills, tinting trees that have been dead, gray and leafless; then it's there across the meadows. Knobs of crocuses and hyacinths push their way up through the hard earth and there's a promise of lilacs along backyard fences. But above all it's the feel in the wind that carries with it a sense of expectancy, of new beginnings.

When this happens—old Frank Jacobs had once explained this to Bill—another curious thing occurs: the mental and spiritual life of the valley moves hand in hand with the physical. Men smile without knowing why. They arrive home from the quarries surprised to find it still light and they tease and joke with their women. And in this spring of 1915 the weather held, warm and dry and sunny, and Bill had these handsome days to do with as he chose, to wander with his gun along winding paths up to a clear mountain pool or sit all day if he liked, his back against a tree, studying a stray cloud sliding across a greening hill. Sometimes he would hitch a ride or hike it down to Manchester to watch the town beginning to stir and stretch itself back to life in preparation for the summer people. Houses that had been deserted all winter were being painted, opened and aired; gardens were being tended. There was a bustle of anticipation in the notion of so many people arriving and another season starting, and gradually Bill found himself wondering who would be back this year, found himself looking forward to seeing some of them again.

The Thacher house was always one of the first to open. Bill had known the Thacher sons at Burr and Burton, five heavy-drinking fellows from Albany, all fine company. Their family had made a fortune in iron stoves, so the story went. The Burnham house was being rented, he'd heard, the family staying out at their place on Emerald Lake. Rogers Burnham was just Bill's age, and his great passion in life the last time Bill had seen him had been automobiles. He knew everything there was to know about motorcars, and Bill had the feeling Rogers expected his whole life to be one fast sweet ride. It would be good to see him again. Then, too, Rogers had sisters and in particular one older sister, Lois. Bill wondered when the Burnhams would be coming up.

Lois wasn't like any girl Bill knew. She was a "good looker," all right, but it wasn't that which made her different. There was a kind of force about Lois. It wasn't necessarily a force he wanted to tangle with now or believed he could ever handle, but it was a very definite force, and for some reason (maybe it had to do with spring) his mind kept returning to her and he wasn't at all sure how he felt about seeing her again.

2

Lois's father, Dr. Clark Burnham, was to have a tremendous if somewhat indirect influence on Bill's life. Mark Whalon had first pointed to Dr. Burnham as one of the rare individuals who was able to move in any direction, either up or down in Manchester society. Perhaps if Mark had traveled more, or if he'd had a deeper understanding of the moment, he would have seen that this particular man would have been accepted and would have felt himself perfectly at home anywhere in America.

In a way Clark Burnham and his family were products of their time. The doctor was little, standing at least eight inches shorter than Bill Wilson, but because of his chiseled good looks, his buoyancy and his radiant, almost contagious good health, no one considered whether he was short or tall. People instinctively responded to his enthusiasms, his confidence and most of all to his supreme fearlessness in what he knew to be this best of all possible worlds.

One of ten children, Clark Burnham had arrived in Brooklyn with a diploma from a Pennsylvania medical school in his pocket and had immediately checked into a boardinghouse on Clinton Street. His first calls were made on horseback, but it seems that from the beginning many of Dr. Burnham's patients came from the wealthier families along the Heights. By 1888 he had rented the entire house where he boarded and had married one Matilda Spelman, a handsome woman somewhat younger than he who was blessed with a supple intelligence and what appears to have been an incredible sweetness of disposition. By the turn of the century the family, which had been growing at suitable intervals, was spending half its time in Vermont, half in Brooklyn, and by then house calls were being made in a three-horse buckboard. (By the time Bill came into their lives the buckboard had given way to a series of touring cars—Peerlesses, Pierce-Arrows.)

The six months in New England fitted in perfectly with the doctor's social as well as medical views, for he believed that most human infirmities could be overcome by maintaining a good diet, a spartan discipline and a strenuous outdoor life. And what place on earth was so well suited to such a regime as the hills of Vermont? By 1910 he owned a home in Manchester and two smaller houses, "the camp," on the edge of Emerald Lake. There every evening without fail, just as the New York train hove into sight, he would gather his brood about him, take up his rifle and, like the fulfilled, happy man he was, he'd fire a shot into the air. The firemen always answered with a long, loud whistle that came echoing back across the hills.

Indeed, Clark Burnham had reason to be satisfied with himself, his life and the fortunate background against which his story was unfolding. In those first years of the century the United States of America seemed God's own country, a land of plenty, always expanding. In the West, fresh territories were opening up with grain and cattle. We had the machinery and the know-how to build great new cities. Enough for everyone. Just come and get it. And we were powerful too; we'd proved it. Surely we were capable of whipping any force brash enough to challenge Uncle Sam.

At such a time, in such a place, it was easy to ignore, indeed in many cases to be downright ignorant of, the subterranean rumblings in Europe which newspapers kept reporting. We had our hands full, as people said, tending to our own problems, because of course everything wasn't yet perfect or, in some instances, even just. There was much that needed fixing, but with hard work and Yankee perseverance, by God, we'd fix it. We were working out our unique system, which, everyone understood, was capable of improvement. Meanwhile jobs were plentiful, wages on the rise.

At such a time and for such a man as Clark Burnham it is not surprising that there appeared to be one outstanding figure, one hero who came roaring across the scene, as if Heaven-sent, and whose expansive personality epitomized all our rugged aspirations: Theodore Roosevelt. The thought that there might have been something fabricated about this extraordinary character—born an aristocrat, timid, weak and asthmatic, who, with super-human energy, had created himself the opposite—never occurred to Clark Burnham. And if, by the same token, there was something of the performer in Dr. Burnham's nature, certainly his audience was too impressed, too in awe of his vitality, ever to ask questions. It was as though his patients, many of whom followed him to Vermont for the summer, felt a need to be close to this extra charge of life, as though his family felt that by trying to keep up with him, some of his zest for living might rub off on them and they themselves would become stronger, more alive.

The doctor's family also represented a central ingredient in his story and they were certainly a remarkable clan. All the children—two sons and three daughters—were robust and very fair. Among the summer colony these were the golden children; their hair was blonder, shinier, their cheeks rosier, their teeth whiter than the average child's. Both Clark and Matilda were aware of this and felt a certain pride in the fact, though their pride was always conveyed in a tacit way. All the young ones talked constantly and laughed a great deal, but their voices were soft and musical, and they were never let off any breach of manners. Just where their special style came from has always been a question— was it something the doctor acquired on his upward climb or was it a natural part of Matilda's endowment? Wherever they found it, a distinctive style in dress and manner was a mark of all the Burnhams. They were at home in their bodies and their bodies were at home in the world.

Lois, the eldest of the children, was unmistakably the doctor's daughter. She had his good looks, his slim, athletic body, and she had his smile: a smile that appeared first in her eyes, which suddenly grew wider, brighter; then her brows would shoot up as if surprised, as if waiting, wanting to be sure that others found the situation as amusing as she did. But this was only for a second; her lips would part and her entire face would become involved. And the smile had a way of lingering at the edges of her eyes even after the conversation had gone on and the rest of her had finished smiling.

In the summer of 1915 she looked a little older than she had as a girl of sixteen and a little younger than she would at thirty-five. She was radiant and utterly alive, for she'd also inherited her father's sense of adventure, his passion to taste not only the beauty of life, but the excitement, and above all she had his assurance. Yet even her vivacity could not quite hide the seriousness of her nature, and it may have been this that gave her what Bill called "Lois's famous social sense," her belief that no matter what situation might come up, somehow she would be able to cope and rise above it. And the situation she found herself facing now surely demanded something. For early in the summer Lois Burnham, in her middle twenties, had discovered that she was deeply smitten by young Bill Wilson.

Wise men since the beginning of time have warned that we had best be careful about what we want in our youth because we may find in our later years that life has given us just that. But it must be added that had Lois known, had she been endowed with the gift of prescience and been able to see all the terrors the next twenty years would hold, there cannot be the slightest question but that she would have gone ahead and done exactly what she did. She had seen Bill, and like Emily Griffith with Gilly, she had made up her mind she would have him.

Bill had first become aware of Lois the summer before. Foolhardily, he had challenged her to a race on Emerald Lake. That afternoon she was sailing a tight little skiff which had been bought in New York. He had a rough improvised job he'd put together himself from an old rowboat and some tattered sails. Lois won by many lengths. But it was not the winning that mattered, she said, it was the fun of racing. She was full of such sayings, but the point was they weren't just sayings with Lois. She had a way of putting things that always seemed to imply more than the words really said, yet curiously they never sounded pompous or cliché. They were just what she honestly felt, and this may have been one of the reasons Bill remembered her.

He had been a little shy about seeing her at first, but after a time he found he was completely at ease with her and he knew that he could trust her. She and Mark Whalon were the only two people, he realized, who never seemed to treat him as someone other than he was. Lois did not, for example—as did his sister Dorothy's friends, as did all the other girls in the summer colony—look upon him as "one of the natives," a boy who happened to be out of school now but who would one day soon solve his problems. Lois saw him as himself, as if he were a person now.

When the Burnhams came back in the early spring of '15 everything was the same, only a little more so. Lois was prettier than he had remembered and she seemed brighter too, but he was still able to relax with her. The way she looked him in the eye and took hold of his arm as they walked along was meant only to convey her warm and uncomplicated good feeling, and he felt again that here was a girl he could be friends with without any fear of misunderstanding.

Soon after the Burnhams returned, Bill began turning up at the camp every few days without really thinking about it. Then

he got into the habit of staying on later and later until Mrs. Burnham was obliged to invite him for supper. Meals with the Burnhams were unlike anything he had experienced. There was
usually an uproar at the table because they were all tireless
talkers and their conversation was laced with family jokes and
little family expressions which at first were unintelligible to an
outsider, but in no time—everything was so kindly and comfortable—he was no longer an outsider.

After supper—there was no real reason to go back to East
Dorset—sometimes Rogers would borrow the car and they would
ride up the side of Mount Equinox; then they'd park and hike
all the way to the top. Sometimes there were moonlight sails and
freezing midnight dips. As they'd drive or sail along they would
sing together under the stars, they'd laugh, and sometimes the
whole family would break into applause at one of Bill's stories,
and it was amazing the number of old yarns he could dredge up.
Bill discovered that when he tried he was a damn fine enter-
tainer. And beyond the hikes and the rides, there were so many
new friends to talk to now and oh, God, it was fun to be liked
again.

Of course, if Lois had known Bill from the day of his birth, if
she had followed every step of his story and had devised a plan
to attract him, nothing could have succeeded so well as this care-
free time she gave him. For what was happening was very simple. When Lois stepped into Bill's life she brought with her a
built-in family, complete with a father, a mother, two sisters
(Barbara, seventeen, and Kitty, fourteen), two brothers (Rogers,
nineteen, and the baby, Lyman, eight). They welcomed him,
moved over and made him another member of their circle and—
as with the doctor and Teddy Roosevelt—if all was not what it
appeared to be on the surface, Bill was too bedazzled, too hungry
for affection, to question anything. It was as though he'd been
handed a long, leisurely family novel; it could go on and on and
he'd be reading it, absorbed by it, for the rest of his life.

When he and Lois were alone—and they were alone more and

more as July moved into August—there was a wonderful sense of freedom. They discovered they felt the same way about all manner of things, and sometimes these were important subjects, the ones Bill knew people were supposed to feel deeply about but didn't often mention: patriotism and honor, a man's ideals and the real meaning of loyalty. Lois would use such words with no embarrassment at all, no more than her father might feel when mentioning certain anatomical matters to a patient. Bill learned that the Burnhams were all Swedenborgians, and the mystical aspects of this faith so fascinated them both they vowed to explore it more deeply one day. He also learned that Lois had graduated from Packer Institute in Brooklyn, had had two years of art school and was now very involved in something called the Young People's League and the fine work they were doing. Although she kept filling him in with details about herself and all she hoped to accomplish, Bill never felt pressed. She never asked about his plans. (There was no reason to. Lois knew she admired his character and that was enough for her; such was the supremacy of her confidence that it never occurred to her that someone she admired might not be totally worthy of admiration.)

If as the summer went on Bill was ever aware that he and Lois were growing close or that there was a quality of unreality about the relationship, he quite honestly did not care. He was nineteen, a man returning to the world. He was so startled to feel himself alive again, so flattered by the attention being paid him, he asked no more of life than to be allowed to go on one day at a time.

Then suddenly, in the second week in September, everything changed. The unreality was resolved.

Norman Schneider, a friend of Lois's from the Young People's League, had been visiting the Burnhams. On the eleventh Norman was to return to Kitchener, Canada, and Bill and Lois walked with him to the station to see him off. When the train had pulled out Bill said, quite naturally, "You'll miss him, won't you?"

85

Lois nodded, then she went on about the fine work Norman was doing in Kitchener and his wanting her to join him in it. Whether by this Lois meant to imply that Norman Schneider was asking her to marry him or just to work with him in Canada was not important. Bill's reaction was. It was instant and it was terrifying. For a long moment he didn't know if he could speak, but somehow he managed to ask if this meant she was in love with Norman.

Lois hesitated and—this can happen—time seemed to stop and all sound, all movement, stopped on the station platform, on the road, everywhere. Bill waited, his eyes riveted on Lois. Then she shook her head. She wasn't in love with Norman, she said; she admired him and she knew she always would, but . . .

Bill wasn't hearing. Suddenly an old terror, a weakness in the arms and legs, was sweeping over him as his mind filled with the knowledge that the whole secure world he'd been a part of could evaporate in an instant and he would be alone again with all his doubts and fears.

Only gradually, as they walked from the station and headed south, did he begin to hear and focus his mind on what she was saying.

Then, if she didn't love Norman, he asked, did this mean she was in love with someone else?

It was impossible later for either of them to reconstruct what was said that night, or even to recall the steps of the conversation. But Bill remembered the feeling. It was as if all summer he had been standing in brilliant sunlight and now a great pit was opening and he was going to be pulled back into it, he'd be powerless again, a nothing, a nobody.

As they moved on, and he became less and less certain, Lois's confidence increased. (Maybe their trouble was that they were too analytical, she said, there was a difference between loving a man and being in love, but it was the way a woman felt about a man that mattered.) And now there was that excitement about her, about everything she said, that seemed to reflect all the excitement in the world, and by ten o'clock he could not help it, he reached out and she was in his arms.

It was a long time before they talked again. Their arms were still entwined and they were still a long distance from the camp. She had never been so beautiful. Or so happy. And she wanted him to know just how she felt, how she felt about this moment now, about the future—and Lois had many ideas about the future. She believed in him so, and she knew everything was going to be perfection just as soon as he found out what he was going to do. For one fleeting moment the thought did shoot through Bill's mind that there were some things a man would have to find out on his own, but he never mentioned this. Any such thoughts were pushed away by the look of her and by the knowledge of his miraculous escape. He had been, not an hour before, on the verge of losing everything. Now he was safe. And oh, she kept saying over and over, she believed in him so.

He had been able to stand back from her flattery, even from her beauty, her tremendous physical attraction, but now he was helpless before her unabashed declaration of faith. By eleven o'clock they were engaged.

3

Lois left for Brooklyn the following morning. Before saying good-by Bill promised he would write every day and for the next months he did manage to get off three or four letters a week.

All his life autumn had been a special and somehow an extremely personal time for Bill. When the summer folks depart and the children are back in school a strange stillness settles over Vermont. Days begin to close in, and the trees across the mountains are draped in heathen crimsons, golds and oranges. Life is supremely good at such a time and it is easy for a man to believe it may just go on this way, this might be a year without winter. But that fall there was a difference. The whole valley seemed to be waiting, resting in a state of abeyance.

Bill's daily life was much as it had been in the spring. His position at home, it's true, was less anomalous now that he was definitely going back to college, and he was able to recover his old closeness to Fayette and talk with him about all manner of things, but everywhere everyone seemed to think of this fall as a last long vacation.

He managed to get a bit of this into his letters. Sometimes these would be brief because halfway through an opening paragraph Lois's face would be back before him, so clear and so beautiful he could not see around it; then, when there was barely time to catch the last mail train he'd scribble a request for her to write him "some more mush," promise to do the same himself and sign his name, always, "I.L.Y. I.L.Y.—Billy." His feelings when he thought of her now were a mixture of joy and complete incredulity that he could feel this way again.

Sometimes he did write at length, but despite their resolve always to be honest with one another, some of his letters may have been a little less than truthful—not that he lied in fact, it was more in emphasis, in coloring—and they both, without meaning to, created images in one another's minds.

Bill wrote about Mark Whalon, telling her Mark was the only one in town he'd been able to confide in. "She loves you because you are Bill Wilson," Mark had said. "So never try to be anything but just your plain ordinary self; you are enough." After that he told her about his concern for Mark, who was drinking heavily now, and Bill thought he saw signs of what alcohol was doing to that "noble mind."

In other letters he tried to describe his father, and in doing so he poured out his ambivalent feelings toward Gilly. Early in the fall he wrote of meeting an old woman who recognized him as Gilly's son and wouldn't let him go. She just wanted to talk on and on. It was the same everywhere, he wrote: in Vermont and out West people worshiped Gilly. But only a week later, when his stepmother sent word that he had a new half-sister, he wrote Lois that his father "really wasn't much of a fellow" and that he was afraid he might have inherited some of his tendencies and would always have to struggle to overcome them.

But in the flood of letters that made their way from East Dorset to Clinton Street there were two overriding themes: Bill's desperate need to make enough money to get down and be with Lois and his need to know that now that they had found each other she would help him, teach him, guide him.

Through an arrangement with his grandfather he began chopping wood, for which he was paid four dollars a cord. Also there were jobs now on weekends playing fiddle with a small band, the

Aeolians, who were developing something of a reputation barnstorming the county, playing at high school dances and other special events. If Bill was on vacation, it was one in which a lot of work was done, and it was one he always knew would have an ending.

Nothing had prepared Bill for Clinton Street. Originally he'd planned to be there for Christmas, but several big engagements with the Aeolians compelled him to postpone the trip until January.

He had never stayed in such a handsome house and at first this confused him. Always before life with the Burnhams had been easy and natural; in a way they had been like the camp beside the lake, where the rustic little buildings fit in so comfortably with the trees and shrubbery they seemed a part of the terrain, a part of nature itself. A fellow could be himself out there, wear what he liked and think nothing of it. Brooklyn was another matter.

Before Brooklyn Bill had thought, if indeed he had thought of it at all, that the purpose of a house or a room was to be functional; that it might also be beautiful had not occurred to him. Yet here at 182 Clinton he saw that the colors of the walls, the covers of the chairs and sofas had been chosen with considerable care. The walls of the living room above the doctor's bookcases were lined with engravings and paintings, not forbidding, foreign paintings but pleasant views of mountains and lakes; even across the floors were scattered little rugs of bright yet wonderfully harmonious colors. But he was more struck by the realization that this was where Lois belonged than by the beauty of the rooms. All this was as much a part of her as his grandfather's house was of him. Then, too, along with the constant family chatter there was a sense of excitement about Clinton Street, which he couldn't quite pin down, a suggestion of great events taking place, of people arriving and departing, of young men driving up in expensive automobiles, calling for the Burnham girls.

On the first night, especially when he found himself alone with Dr. Burnham just before dinner, he was not comfortable, for now he couldn't escape the thought that he was being judged as a potential son-in-law. The doctor made no reference to this, but Bill knew it was no time to relax, and he made a conscious effort to keep the conversation rolling. It wasn't the famous vitality that put him off; he was used to that. It was the doctor's authority, as if he were always speaking from some great height of security which Bill doubted he himself could ever reach. In a way it was the same feeling, the same desire to please, the same necessity to be on guard he had with headmasters, with his mother, with anyone who held power over him. It would have been different, he knew, if he had a job, or if Lois didn't have one, or if he had money. . . . It wasn't the only time that weekend he remembered Mark's words about the rungs on a ladder.

When they moved in to dinner there was another awkwardness. Beside his place there were not just a knife and a fork, there were several forks and several spoons, and which one he was supposed to use presented an insoluble problem. But as they sat down he felt Lois nudge him. Whether this was accidental or not he wasn't sure—he was sure of nothing now—but then he saw Lois smile, reach down and pick up the outside spoon. He followed suit and immediately felt himself relaxing. Any girl who could understand and do a thing like that without making a man feel a fool was no ordinary girl. From then on everything was right. The family behaved as if it were the most natural thing in the world for Bill Wilson to be here for a visit, and before long he was telling his stories, everyone was laughing and he was as much at home as he would have been on the dock at Emerald Lake.

In fact, that smile and that showing him which spoon to use marked the beginning of what was to be the perfect holiday, the one that would always come to mind whenever anyone mentioned holidays. There was the Metropolitan Opera one night, and a concert by the Philharmonic another. They went to a Broadway play with the Shaws, who were newlyweds. Elise had been in school with Lois and Frank had important connections with a Wall Street firm, but they weren't at all what Bill had imagined sophisticated New Yorkers to be. He liked the Shaws. Then there was a party to meet more of the Burnhams' friends. But through everything he knew that Lois was beside him and Lois was taking care.

That smile may also have been the start of what Bill called his social education. And the point to remember is that Bill asked for this. He wanted to be taught. And Lois Burnham was a born teacher. Not that there was anything wrong with Bill's manners. He was certainly not, as he sometimes enjoyed painting himself, a backwoods clown who'd come to the city. He was young; he'd been alone a great deal, and some of his expressions may have seemed a little quaint, some of his gestures rough-hewn. In a way it was like the difference between the furnishings of his grandfather's home, which were made from plain, sturdy cherry wood, and the more urbane mahoganies of Clinton Street.

Saturday they set out for Manhattan to buy a ring. Lois led him first to a few of the less expensive jewelers along Maiden Lane, but Bill would have none of these. He'd set his heart on a Tiffany ring. He was adamant about that, and after crossing and recrossing dark, narrow streets Lois had no choice; she headed him uptown. As they dodged in and out of crowds they were developing a sort of shorthand speech. Bill would be halfway through a sentence and he'd stop. Lois knew what he was going to say.

It was extraordinary, too, the number of things they agreed about. For instance, they decided New York was a city for lovers —you could be more alone in a crowd than you ever could be in a little town. Even so, they were never going to allow it to be all of their world; there must always be a place for the outdoor life. And there must be music too, some music every day. They had a good start here, but they would work and know more.

Tiffany's was just closing when they arrived and to Lois's amazement, if not to Bill's, there was a ring at precisely their price, a small amethyst for twenty-five dollars.

And Bill would remember the two of them late at night. After Lyman and Rogers had gone to bed and Barbara and Kitty were back from their parties, the house was silent. They would turn the lights low in the parlor and when he pulled her to him and kissed her she made herself small in his arms and tilted her face up to be kissed again. A new, clean confidence filled him then and he knew that he was loved.

On his way back to Vermont Bill stopped off in Albany to visit the Thachers, those jovial brothers from Manchester summers and his Burr and Burton days, and once more he found himself moving in a beautiful world, miles away from any he had known, where any problems that might arise would never be about money or finding the right sort of job so you could marry a girl.

While Bill was there, Ebby and his brothers took him to his first nightclub. There was a lot of heavy drinking and talk of joining some available girls. Bill at this point was honestly and unashamedly afraid of drinking and after his nights in the parlor at Clinton Street he wasn't interested in another girl. Still he felt comfortable. The Thachers wanted to hear about Vermont and he told them stories about Mark, Barefoot Rose and old Charlie Ritchie, even about the little hick band he'd been playing with. They all laughed, and for a time it seemed wonderful that they weren't putting him in the same category as the natives but were accepting him as one of themselves on their more elevated plane. Then suddenly it troubled him that he was thinking this. These were the Thachers, for God's sake, they were half-Vermonters themselves, and the notion that he could have felt that way bothered him so that from then on he didn't tell any more stories.

Back in East Dorset there was much to digest. The company of the Burnhams and the Thachers had left him elated. He'd

been victorious in every detail, yet there was something unre-
solved, unclear. The constant movement of the city had impressed him; it had seemed young and confident, filled with an
energy that was so different from the quiet streets of home. He
knew New York was a challenge he couldn't resist, yet at the
same time he wondered how much a man would be giving up if
he exchanged the stars over their mountains for the lights of a
city? Common sense told him he should go slow here and think
this through, but some other impulse said no, he was on his way
now, he must keep moving.

And this wasn't difficult. There were many things to be done,
many people to see before leaving for Norwich, and with it all
there was a new, inexplicable sense of light-headedness, almost
as if he were playing a role. If earlier he'd thought of the Burnhams as a family novel he was reading, now he was entering the
story.

Years later Bill said that he had been slow in maturing. Looking back at this period, he wrote that when Lois came along,
"she picked me up with all of the loving care a mother might have
shown for a child and this was doubtless a tremendous compo-
nent in her love."

Perhaps the only harm, he pointed out, in being fast or slow, or
in trying to by-pass one of the so-called normal stages of development, is that we are destined then in the secret nature of things
to live over those stages at some later and less appropriate time.

But there is one other element in Bill's story—one which a man
may never fully realize about himself—and that is the important
and mysterious matter of timing. Bill and Lois met and fell in
love at the beginning of World War I, and the war was to affect
every segment of his being—his view of society, society's view
of him and, to a great degree, his view of himself.

4

Although the First World War shook the foundations of the world in which Bill had grown up, for him, and for Lois, it served to place a platform beneath their feet, to create a stage on which they could perform, a background against which their actions would be accepted. For who would object to a pretty girl going anywhere with a handsome young man who might be sent off to fight and possibly die for his country?

In many ways the advent of war may have had as much to do with the forming of Bill's character as did his life with Lois. But the changes did not happen overnight.

When he returned to Norwich in February 1916, Bill was still technically a freshman, enrolled to finish out his second semester. This was not an easy time for him. In the last few years he had developed no habits of study. Some subjects interested him and he did brilliantly; others bored him and he failed miserably. He made innumerable fresh starts, flunked and started again, and each new start, each failure, he reported to Lois. Then in the spring the hazing incident occurred.

One night Bill's roommate, who was a sophomore, told him they were off to get the freshmen, and since Bill had been there the year before and most of his friends were sophomores, he was invited along to watch. In the beginning everything seemed innocent; freshmen were paddled with straps and staves; but before long the whole freshman class turned up and the freshmen were carrying clubs and bayonets. It took time to disarm them; heads were smashed, some bones broken, and quite a number ended up in the infirmary. The next morning there was a trial, and the commandant decided to expel eight sophomores whom he considered the ringleaders. But the other sophomores insisted that if eight must go, they all would go, and they all, including Bill, signed a paper to that effect. The following night it was announced that the entire sophomore class was suspended indefinitely. Some of Bill's friends argued, and persuasively, that since Bill was not really a sophomore, since he had been involved only as an onlooker, there was no reason for him to accept the punishment. But he had signed his name to the paper, he said, he'd given his word, and he walked out with the others.

There is no telling what might have happened if the hazing incident had not been followed almost immediately by the Mexican incident.

All spring the newspapers had been filled with accounts of revolutionary activities south of the border. Congressional pressure had been mounting for some form of military intervention against Pancho Villa. Finally forced to abandon his policy of "watchful waiting," President Wilson ordered General Pershing to head a punitive expedition and pursue Villa back into Mexico. At the same time he called up various state militias to be stationed along the border.

For generations the Norwich cadets had been a proud part of the Vermont National Guard, but there was a slight problem now; one-quarter of the school had been suspended. The problem was quickly resolved, however. Early in June they were all back in school and on the twenty-second they were sent off for mobilization at Fort Ethan Allen.

Bill found himself a corporal in charge of drilling raw recruits. His letters to Lois were mere scraps now: "Have found I'm first in line for promotion to sergeant. . . . Tried to get away to telephone you, but couldn't get permission. Hope you will decide to come up. . . ." ". . . Morning: it was wonderful of you to think of marrying me before I go. We'll talk it over when I see you. . . ."

On June 30 the First Squadron, with a strength of sixteen officers and one hundred and fifty-five enlisted men (upper-classmen), was ready to depart and was finally put aboard a train. The rest of the camp, including Bill, gathered along a siding to see them off. There was a feeling of high adventure here, for these men were no longer playing at being soldiers, they were actually leaving, off to face the great unknown.

Unfortunately, when the First Squadron arrived in Brattle-boro, there seemed to be a foul-up and they were told they were no longer needed and ordered to return to Ethan Allen. Within a week another order had come through and the cadets were demo-bilized and sent back to their home station, Norwich University. For all practical purposes the Mexican adventure was over.

But for Bill it had been a beginning. He had worked hard and well and his work had been respected. What was more, he knew that he'd done it on his own, that he'd been moving in an area where he needed no one's guidance. Indeed, he had been the one the new recruits had turned to for guidance and advice. And this represented something of immense importance to him, as if some crucial element of his nature suddenly had been restored.

Those weeks at camp had given him a sense of himself, yet at the same time he had the feeling of being part of something bigger, a part of what his country was doing. He knew the Mexi-can episode was only a minor incident, and he tried not to exaggerate it; still he had been involved. A connection had been established and he felt a sense of responsibility beyond his per-sonal feelings, and he knew it would be a betrayal of something he believed in if he ever let his own concerns obscure this. He was warmed and stimulated by his acceptance. And along with this he had gained a new awareness, a widening out of interest. If he had been part of the national scene, then he wanted to know about that scene.

In '14 the mood of the country had been fiercely noninterventionist, but as the situation in Europe worsened and our relations with Germany grew more tense, many prominent citizens began lending their support to a Preparedness Movement. Among them was Teddy Roosevelt. He had been off the stage for several years, but now T.R., instinctively responding to the cause, rushed to the head of the movement. By the end of 1915 his criticisms of the administration were being quoted from coast to coast; little training camps where businessmen might spend a few weeks presumably learning something about firearms and drill were cropping up everywhere.

By mid-1916, at the time the Norwich cadets were discharged from Ethan Allen, the number of important people who were demanding action against Germany was growing daily, until even Washington felt the pressure and Congress finally passed a defense bill, which called for an army of 175,000 and authorized the establishment of an Officers Training Corps.

In any serious reckoning it cannot be said that the Preparedness Movement added a great deal to an army that, when war came, would call up more than four million men, but it did lend zest to arguments and it helped change the mood and attitudes of the country. And it lent young Bill Wilson a curious local prestige. Everyone in East Dorset knew he'd done a stretch with the Guard and that he was continuing to prepare himself in a military college. What he was doing mattered now. It was as important as what any other young fellow might be up to with a fine job and an impressive salary. The next time he met with Dr. Burnham the change was remarkable. There was none of his former diffidence, none of his subservient desire to please. They were two men who knew what they were about, and they immediately began swapping jokes about old T.R.'s latest blast at "the cowardly crew in Washington."

All through the summer of '16 and into the fall Bill was aware of subtle changes and shifting attitudes. Although the President was reelected in November on the slogan "He kept us out of war," there was still a feeling of impending drama. All the cadets, Bill among them, seemed imbued with a sense of purpose that gave a reason for accepting the tough strictures of military discipline.

In January, when the President called for a negotiated settlement, "peace without victory," the cadets were at a loss, not knowing what to think. But the German government not only spared the Allies the necessity of a reply by an immediate resumption of submarine warfare—allowing only one American ship to sail each week into one British port—but also helped the students make up their minds. It was the notion of being *permitted* one ship and that one having to be marked like a barber pole that was too much for their pride, and as a body they wanted to know what the hell the President was waiting for.

It was actually only a matter of days before Wilson formally broke relations with the German Empire. Now surely, they believed, he had seen the light, now he would stop equivocating.

And again they did not have long to wait. The Zimmermann note was intercepted and published on the first of March and when the public learned of the deal that was being offered Mexico—if she would join forces with Germany, at the end of the war she would be given all her lost territories in Texas, Arizona and New Mexico—the reaction was instant. A wave of shock and fury swept the country, and even before college recessed for Easter three more American ships had been sunk and before Bill left to pick up Lois in Short Hills, New Jersey, where she was teaching in her aunt Marion's school, there were rumors of Congress being summoned for a special message from the President.

Bill and Lois were together when they heard newsboys shouting "Extra!" They bought a paper and read the President's address:

. . . it is a fearful thing to lead this great, peaceful people into the most terrible and disastrous of all wars, civilization itself seeming to be in the balance. But the right is more precious than peace and we shall fight for the things which we have always carried nearest our hearts. . . .

They read, then slowly looked at each other and their eyes were misty. The thing they had dreaded and dreamed of was now a fact.

5

Thinking back about his war years, Bill remembered them as having little connection with what had gone before or with what was to follow. In memory they always held a sense of exhilaration, of days racing by, filled with events that seemed to leave no more of a mark than a passing image leaves on a looking glass.

Yet, curiously, there were moments, a series of five or six specific, isolated incidents, that for some reason worked their way inward to become a part of him.

The first of these, which he was to relive over and over, occurred shortly after he arrived for training at Plattsburgh, New York. Reporting back to Norwich in April of '17, he had found all his academic classes canceled so that the cadets might concentrate on military studies. Within a matter of weeks he had volunteered—and this he did on his own, asking no one's advice —for enlistment in an R.O.T.C. unit; he'd been accepted and immediately shipped out with a contingent of his classmates for the training camp at Plattsburgh. There the discipline, the easy familiarity with the rituals of drill of the Norwich cadets quickly set them apart as an outstanding group, which of course was extremely good for their egos, especially Bill's.

The moment that so impressed itself upon Bill might have had no significance to another cadet. He was suddenly handed a piece of paper and told to sign his name beside the branch of service he wished to enter. There were four choices: aviation, which sounded daring, flying creaking crates in combat; infantry, which he knew meant danger and the probability of wounds, even death; field artillery and coast artillery. He'd heard the coast artillery was training in the South with large guns that were to become part of the mobile artillery, and they would surely be sent abroad. However, they said the training took a long time and the eight-inch howitzers usually operated some distance behind the lines. The coast artillery, he knew, represented safety.

But that afternoon, in an empty barracks room, as his eyes moved down the sheet of paper, two sides of his nature met, confronted one another and in the course of a very few minutes waged their own brutal war. He wanted to live. He knew that. He wanted to protect himself and hold on to what he had finally built up, his opinion of himself. And as he argued this side of the case it was as though he could see Lois, as clearly as if she had been beside him, could see her smile, the funny tilt of her head. He did not want to be wounded, maimed, not now before he had lived out his life with her, before he had lived with her at all. But just as he was about to sign his name, another thought flashed through his mind, and he remembered old Bill Landon, remembered the drooping eye, scarred by a Minié ball, and he remembered his stories of Sheridan and the battered infantry rising as one man. "Back. We will go back and retake our camps!" The glory and the wonder of those words, that beautiful gut courage, had been a part of him once. As much a part as Lois was now. And yet . . .

To go along with it he would have to sign up for infantry.

Slowly he let his eyes move up the list and at the sight of the word "infantry" a half-forgotten terror swept over his body, he could feel the weakness rising from his legs, feel his heart pounding in his chest. Then he saw that his right hand, holding the pen, had begun to shake uncontrollably. In a panic, he tightened his grip on the pen and signed his name opposite "coast artillery."

That should have been the end of it—he had friends in the artillery, they welcomed him aboard and there were plans and orders about their transfer—and it would have been the end if, two weeks later, the night they were to depart for Fort Monroe in Virginia, a group of fellow cadets had not come down to see them off. At the time they seemed to represent half the camp, men who'd signed up for aviation and infantry, and they stood along the tracks yelling and cheering. Everything was friendly and it was exciting too. But then, just as the train pulled away, one little group of four or five men began to jeer directly outside Bill's window. "The artillery. Yeah, yeah . . . playing it safe, aren't you? Playing it safe . . ."

All that night as the train headed south he couldn't sleep. He kept hearing those men and he kept remembering, first, his grandfather, then the old boys at Gettysburg and then Bill Landon. And he remembered a skinny ten-year-old kid charging up a hill, his Remington at the ready. "Back. We will go back . . ."

But there was no time to think or analyze his feelings, no time to regret a decision. Once at Monroe he was surrounded by engineers and technical experts, and the student officers were worked sixteen hours a day. If Emily had believed Bill cut out for M.I.T. and a career in engineering, that belief was being put to a grueling test.

Life around a base in Virginia with its hell-hot days and soft, dark nights cooled by breezes from the sea was unlike anything he had experienced, but he knew he wasn't the only one whose life was changed. The war had become a whirlpool drawing everything into its center. Wherever he looked he saw it happening: on trains and station platforms—where young couples saying good-by might be saying it for the last time—with soldiers he passed on the street, there was the sense of sharing an experience.

If occasionally there was still the feeling of playing a role, if he wanted time to find out what he really thought, well, that was all right too. He was sure others were feeling the same. The

President had said, "It is not only an army we must shape and train for war, it is the nation."

Whenever there was hope of a few free hours, a Saturday or a Sunday off, Lois would manage to get down and check in at a nearby inn—and in this summer of '17, the sight of a beautiful woman on the arm of a tall young soldier was about the most touching America could offer. And Lois, more than anyone he knew, understood and responded to drama. She saw all the wonderful qualities a war can bring out in people—the self-sacrifice, the unselfishness—and most of the time she could find the right words for her feelings; at other times her laughing eyes would fill up with tears just at the thought of what Bill was doing.

In this mood, then, and to this accelerated, hypnotic rhythm, believing the nation stood behind him, Bill marched off to war.

At the end of eight weeks at Fort Monroe he graduated and became Second Lieutenant William Wilson.

The next incident just happened. There was no premonition to warn him. On a beautiful summer night it simply happened.

After Monroe, with his new commission and a set of brand-new uniforms, Bill was stationed at Fort Rodman, Rhode Island. One evening, he was invited along with some other young officers, to a party at the Grinnells' in New Bedford. Although he had stayed with the Burnhams and with the Thachers in Albany, he had never even imagined a home like the Grinnell mansion or the kind of lavish entertaining the Grinnell daughters extended every weekend to "our brave boys in uniform."

The party was already under way when he arrived in the great main hall, and he could see that it not only filled the hall and two vast drawing rooms on his right but was overflowing onto a terrace. At the end of one room a small orchestra was playing a medley of sad sweet songs and a few couples were dancing. He edged his way around the dance floor and out onto the terrace and saw the gardens below filled with little tables and Japanese lanterns. At each table there were even more guests, laughing and talking.

For a time he stood by the garden steps, not knowing where he belonged and, trying to appear nonchalant, peered up at the night. Then he turned and concentrated on the dancers, then just wandered around, in and out among couples and groups of people he didn't know. Here and there he did spot someone from camp, but it was always an officer who outranked him, and he wasn't sure yet about protocol: did he nod first, or sketch a mock half-salute? It was like the first afternoon at Clinton Street—he felt ill at ease, awkward, and he didn't know what to do with his hands—and the worst of it was he knew there'd be no Lois to nudge him now.

As far as he could see, people were herding into little groups— he was the only one adrift—and the groups seemed to be constantly changing, swelling with new arrivals, then dissolving to form other groups. At first he'd thought someone would smile and ask him to join a group. But this wasn't the way it worked, and after a time he was sure that even if the most attractive girl there started talking to him, he would be too uncomfortable, too out of it, to think of a thing to say.

On his way in he had noticed a long bar set up beneath the stairway, and although it was surrounded by confusion, with waiters coming and going and a great many civilians trying to attract the bartenders' attention, still it seemed to represent a haven, a place where a man might stand alone without being conspicuous. Also he had spotted a small door across from the bar, which he was sure led to a side entrance. He was just considering if it might not be possible to step through this door and make an exit completely unobserved when someone spoke to him. She was tall, not young, with a bony face and a hearty but at the same time haughty manner, what in East Dorset would have been called a "socialite."

Her hand rested on his arm and she immediately began asking

a series of foolish questions—wasn't he enjoying himself, didn't he think the orchestra divine?—but what he had feared came true: he could not think of a thing to answer.

He nodded, tried to smile. When a waiter carrying an immense tray that must have held at least a dozen glasses paused before them, the socialite beamed, reached out and took two glasses from the tray. This was something new, she said as she handed Bill a glass; it was a New York drink, a Bronx cocktail. She knew that he would love it, and she held up her glass in a silent toast. Bill had never been more miserable. There was nothing else he could do, so he held up his glass. Then they drank.

In a matter of minutes, no more, the same waiter was back. Bill's new friend took his glass, placed it on the tray and handed him a fresh one. For a long, long moment he looked at the beautiful glow shimmering in his glass, then he lifted it and drank again, emptying it in one swallow.

Perhaps it took a little time, but it seemed to happen instantly. He could feel his body relaxing, a stiffness going out of his shoulders as he sensed the warm glow seeping through him into all the distant, forgotten corners of his being. Then, unaccountably, the room was tilting, and he was sure he would slide down to the floor, but gradually everything evened off. And he found he was beginning to talk—not just answering now but bringing up subjects on his own—and apparently he was being amusing. His socialite friend was smiling, then she was laughing, and he'd been wrong: she wasn't haughty at all and when she laughed she was far from homely.

There were people she wanted him to meet, she said, and locking her arm in his, she ushered him about, introducing him to some of the prettiest girls he'd ever seen. Soon he had the feeling that he wasn't the one being introduced but that people were being introduced to him; he wasn't joining groups, groups were forming around him. It was unbelievable. And at the sudden realization of how quickly the world can change, he had to laugh and he couldn't stop laughing.

It was wonderful to be so free and so witty; and he must have been witty because his remarks were being repeated all around the room—"Did you hear what old Bill said?"—and before long strangers were asking if he could come to a party next weekend and what about the one after that. . . .

At one point—and this may have been after his third drink, possibly his fourth (he'd lost count because every time he put down his glass the same waiter with the same tray was beside him)—as he was taking a fresh one, he hesitated for no reason, the glass halfway to his lips.

A dim cloud passed over the room, faces around him became hazy, and for a moment his mind seemed to be slowing. He stared at the drink in his hand and as he did he felt a numbness in his arms and legs, a sudden pounding in his chest, all the old signs of terror grabbing him. But by some great, inexplicable miracle, it lasted only a moment. Then another, older, wiser, infinitely stronger Bill seemed to be there and to be taking possession of him.

He slowly straightened up and, standing considerably taller than those around him, thanked a girl for an invitation to supper, smiled, and went on with the conversation he'd been having with a captain and a major he'd just met. It was a miracle. There was no other word. A miracle that was affecting him mentally, physically and, as he would learn, spiritually too.

Still smiling, he looked at the people around him. These were not superior beings. They were friends. They liked him and he liked them.

A little awed now by the speed of his recovery, enchanted by the way he was handling himself, for a time he continued to sip his drink, continued to talk and to listen. Then, with great authority, he held up his hand, signaled the waiter and, when he had another full glass, stepped back, bowed politely and excused himself.

With a thrill of pride at the way his mind was working, at the magnificent clarity with which he was now understanding everything, he walked quietly across the hall and through the little side door, and yes, once again he was right, it did lead onto a driveway.

Surprised and delighted to discover he had brought his drink along, he held it before him and twirled the glass slowly, gently in his hand.

His fear, that sudden momentary attack, had come from what he'd been taught, from all the stories his mother and grandfather had drummed into him about alcohol, what it could do, and what it had done to his father. But the one thing they had not told him—he stopped now and, standing in the middle of the gravel driveway, leaned his head back and looked up at the star-spangled sky—the one thing they hadn't known was that he was not just Dr. Emily's son, not just Fayette's grandson; he was also Gilly's son. And more than that—he smiled at the night and held his glass before him—oh, much more than that, he was himself.

At his back he could hear the whine of a saxophone, little waves of voices rising, falling, but now they in no way ran against the overwhelming joy he was feeling. His world was all around him, young and fresh and loving, and as he made his way down the drive he moved easily, gracefully, as though—he knew exactly how he felt—all his life he had been living in chains. Now he was free.

6

It was always an amazement to Bill that anything which in the end could drag a man so low could in the beginning lift him so high. For there was never any doubt that his evening with the Grinnells was the beginning of the highest, happiest time of his life. From that point on he drank whenever and wherever there was a drink available.

When he had left the house, heading back to camp, he had left the sounds of the party, the music, the bright chatter of the guests behind, but he knew he was leaving more than that. It was as though back there in the Grinnells' drawing room he had turned a corner and in doing so had rid himself of his timidity and all the muddled unsureness of youth. Now he was moving into new worlds. A barrier which had always existed between him and others had been dissolved. Now he was part of life. And oh, God, with a few drinks under his belt, what a wonderful world it was.

And what a wonderful position he was in. There were a few minor problems, of course. From the beginning he seemed to lack any inner censor such as other men had to warn them when they'd had enough, and often after the third or fourth drink he would become physically ill and have to go out behind a tree or hurriedly find a men's room. The next morning he would be hazy, his mind blank about certain events everyone else remembered. But this was all part of it, he guessed. He'd just passed out, the older officers said. Sometimes they said he'd blacked out, but they were saying it as a joke, and since everyone he knew, or everyone he chose to know and drink with, was a heavy drinker and they all admitted to having had similar experiences, there was no reason to be concerned.

Curiously, his drinking in no way affected his work during his long stay at Rodman. He was up at the first sound of reveille, the first one on the drill field, and his performance there was watched with something like awe by his fellow officers, for he was not only popular with his men but continued to be one of the most efficient officers on the post.

The only explanation was that at twenty-two Bill Wilson had the constitution of a horse. And frankly, when he was honest with himself, he had to admit he felt a little secret pride in his resilience.

There was one problem, however, that did concern him and it had to do with Lois. Not that the Burnhams were teetotalers. He was sure Rogers would be a fine drinking companion, and he knew the doctor's cellar in Brooklyn was beautifully stocked with wine, but he couldn't be certain what their attitude would be. The first time Lois came to Rodman for a visit and they went out in the evening with a few of his new buddies, he noticed that she had a way of sipping a drink, sometimes putting it down and then forgetting about it. It obviously meant nothing to her. And he could see she was disturbed when he'd had too many. Although she didn't say anything. The next night he made an effort to nurse his drinks by adding water to each one. But this made him feel nervous, not himself, and their conversation became awkward. He soon gave this up.

On that first visit he also saw how quickly and how easily Lois could find her own explanations. The tensions they were living with and the terrible uncertainties about what was to happen next were, she knew, enough to make any man take too much.

He tried to make her see that there might be something else involved, something important and personal, but he could find no way of explaining what he meant.

There were tensions all right. The post was a hotbed of rumors about which units were to be shipped out and when they would sail, and it was these very rumors that finally made Bill and Lois decide—and the Burnhams went along with the decision—to move their wedding date ahead. Originally they'd planned to be married the first of February. Invitations had been ordered, but when, after Christmas, it seemed likely that Bill would be off to France at any moment, the invitations were changed to announcements and they were married in the Swedenborgian Church in Brooklyn on January 24, 1918.

Rogers Burnham stood as Bill's best man, Lois's sister Kitty and four girls from Packer were bridesmaids, Elise Shaw was matron of honor and her sister Barbara maid of honor. Dr. Emily, due to a sudden attack of flu, was unable to come down and Dorothy stayed behind to nurse her mother. Also, perhaps because of the rush, Fayette and Ella were not there, but nothing, not even a lack of family on the groom's side, could dim the quiet glow of the occasion, a young lanky soldier standing beside his bride—and no one who was at the church or at the reception on Clinton Street was apt to forget them.

They took the night train for Boston and next day, after paying their respects to Bill's mother and Dorothy, they hurried on to the apartment at 33 Seventh Avenue, New Bedford, complete with piano and woodburning fireplace, that Bill had rented for thirty dollars a month.

Now that they were lovers in every meaning of the word, Bill felt he'd taken a giant step toward becoming the man he had waited all his life to be. Here in the little upstairs apartment they were at that early stage of loving where they could not stay apart and where they had no need of any other person. And at that same time, his feeling for Lois seemed to be enlarging his feelings for all sorts of other things, other people. He

111

wrote long letters to his grandparents and to his father. He wrote Mark Whalon, asking him to come for a visit.

They entertained often and well. Bachelor officers and other stray sheep from the post were always welcome for a meal. Lois was learning to cook, failing, then valiantly trying again, and there was always plenty of booze.

At some point during these months it must have rained, but they were two healthy young people who wanted each other and in memory these were golden days. They were happy and they were secure. And this seemed even truer when in April the Sixty-sixth C.A.C. was transferred to Newport and Bill found himself stationed at Fort Adams. Here, since Adams was a last stop before embarkation, he had to sleep on the post. Lois stayed in a boardinghouse, and they had only their weekends. Still a spring weekend in wartime Newport, when the most famous hostesses in America were opening their villas to servicemen, was an experience not every young couple could enjoy.

Sometimes at a great gala, when Bill would wander off for an extra snort with the boys, he would glance back and see Lois sitting at the edge of a group, a little out of it perhaps, but she was never uncomfortable, never apologetic. She might not yet be sure what she thought—having been led from one world into another, she was getting the lay of the land—but she was still Lois, still confident.

If, as did happen, Bill might have a few too many and an older officer had to take him home, leaving a young shavetail to see to Lois, and she would arrive back at the boardinghouse to find him stretched out across the bed, a pail below his head, still she said nothing. And what, after all, was there to say? In the morning he would be sorry; everyone would laugh and he certainly was doing no one any harm. In the time they had been together it was almost as though she had actually seen him growing. He seemed taller somehow, stronger. She knew he'd put on a little weight, but he also was putting on a kind of authority.

112

He never raised his voice in argument or to give an order, yet the enlisted men never questioned Bill.

On special afternoons, when the public was allowed on the base to watch a parade or a practice maneuver, Lois always got there early to find a place at the front of the grandstand. When the band struck up, there'd be a strange tingling through her body, and when she saw Lieutenant Wilson lead his men across the field tears would blur her vision. Even with all that was to happen in the future, this was the proudest time of her life. For these afternoons made one thing crystal clear. Clark Burnham's daughter had married a leader.

Their last night together was in July. The Sixty-sixth C.A.C. was to sail from Boston on the eighteenth, and on the night of the seventeenth they went out to the shore for a lobster supper along with another young army couple. And there high on a cliff overlooking the sea, one of those things happened that for many years made Bill think he was unlike other men.

There were drinks at supper, but for some reason they did little to lift the dark mood that had fallen over the evening. Finally, unable to break through the gloom, Bill and Lois walked off along the shore, up over dunes, and came to the cliff.

At their backs a copper sun was sinking into the hills, but before them the east was still ablaze with thin, narrow clouds, rose-colored streamers flecked with gold, and for a time they stood quietly, hand in hand, gazing across the sea toward France. Then still without speaking, they sat and looked down at the harbor.

Two battleships were anchored side by side, already beginning to light up for the night. Yachts and pleasure boats were moored closer in and tiny white launches darted about, bringing men ashore. They sat, his arm across her shoulder, and as the sky darkened their bodies relaxed and their nerves calmed. The first hint of a star appeared and a breeze came up from the sea. For

113

a time then it seemed all nature was contriving to create a memory they could keep and carry with them.

Occasionally he brushed his lips over her hair, his fingers barely touched her fingers, yet in all their nights of loving they had never been so close, they had never read one another's thoughts so clearly. There was a great possibility that Lois already was pregnant and somehow the realization of this was not only part of their thinking now but seemed part of all they were seeing, all they were feeling. In the morning he would sail, he would do what he must, then he would return—he looked into her eyes and she was so convinced of this, he could not doubt her—he would return and she would have borne his child. Above all, he wanted to cling to this one thought because the idea of a child filled him with a kind of joy he had never known, joy and a sense of growing wonder; thinking of it seemed to open his mind, to draw him on toward some other distant reality.

He did not speak and he prayed that she would not speak because he knew words could destroy the feeling he had of hovering near some deeper, further meaning just beyond his reach. Was this what old Fayette had meant when he spoke of his son, his link with the future? What Gilly had been saying when they stood under the stars? Was it part of an answer to his fear of dying, to all those agonizing questions he'd battled with when they had buried his girl? If a man lived on through a son, was this then a kind of immortality?

Still without speaking, he got to his feet and took a long deep breath, then pulled Lois up beside him. He had no answer—and he knew the answer might never be found in thinking—but some deep intuition told him there was a path now, a way toward something that was larger, finer and at the same time more remote and undefined than anything he so far had known. And just knowing it was there filled him with a particular kind of pride.

They ran then, two children out of school, all the way down the cliff. And in the morning some part of the feeling was still

114

with him, and when they stood by the train and finally had to part it was nothing like what he had imagined. Their eyes met, their eyebrows lifted slightly, and in the look that passed between them there was an awareness that set them apart from everyone else on the platform. They knew they were together and they were indestructible.

There were two other moments or incidents—Bill never knew what to call them—and they both occurred before he reached France.

When the old British liner *Lancashire* sailed from Boston, cut down to New York to pick up more troops and then headed toward England, there was a tremendous sense of adventure about everything. On his second night at sea Bill struck up a friendship with several of the ship's officers and with them he had his first drink of brandy (this introduction to real French brandy and what it could do for a man's spirits was by way of being a memorable moment in itself). Ten days out, however, when they were moving into the Irish Sea, which they knew was filled with subs, the mood changed suddenly and dramatically. Apprehensions and little anxieties which until now had been successfully hidden all came to the surface. Blackout regulations were enforced—portholes covered, no lights on deck, not even lighted cigarettes—and all junior officers were issued revolvers and put on a rigid schedule of watches. On each deck an officer manned the small open landing beside the stairs leading down from the hatch openings so that there would be someone to take charge and control any panic in case of a hit.

On their last night out Bill drew the death watch, midnight till 4 A.M. He was stationed on the lowest deck, practically along the ship's keel, but somehow even that was exciting. He could look up and see through the open hatch a bit of sky. He liked the atmosphere of tension and silence and he liked the new authority that had been thrust upon him. His only question—and for most of the night he managed to push it down and not

115

think about it—was the old one of how he would perform in an emergency. At times he was aware of his fingers caressing the edge of his leather holster and he wondered if he would have the nerve to take the pistol out and actually use it. But as the hours slipped by he relaxed and gave himself over to the unreality of the scene, of Bill Wilson being at sea surrounded by strangers.

Behind him Lois was waiting, ahead there were only uncertainty and darkness, but for this moment, cut off from land, from his past and his future, time stood still, and there was a mysterious headiness in the thought.

All around him the vessel was packed with men sleeping, lying flat out, some snoring, some with their mouths open to the night, not worrying in the privacy of sleep, not trying or having to be brave, just being. High above there were officers on the bridge, but as far as his eye could see, his little landing by the stairs was the only spot of consciousness. In a way he felt he was joined to these men and they to him, for in their sleep they were all dependent on him.

He was just examining this thought when there was a crash so overwhelming that it toppled a small table and sent its contents flying to the floor. For a moment Bill stood staring stupidly at the table; he felt a wave of nausea sweep over him. In another second every man was awake, out of his bunk, racing for the stairs. But Bill's pistol was drawn, and he was barking orders. And there was no doubt in any of their minds that he meant them. If they moved, if they dared take one more step, his pistol would be used. They waited, all eyes staring up at him, but there was no second crash, only the sound of the motors as the *Lancashire* moved steadily ahead. Later, they found out that a destroyer sailing very close at their side had spotted a sub and dropped an "ashcan" off her stern, and the crash of the impact so close to the *Lancashire*'s hull had given every indication of a direct hit.

When finally Bill was relieved of his watch and had crawled up the hatchway and out onto deck, the sky was growing brighter in the east. A thin rim of gold had appeared on the horizon and at its center he could see, or thought he could see, a dim shadowy indication of land straight ahead.

The sun came up strong and bright and he had been right, the dot ahead was land. Within minutes he was in the midst of a sparkling world of blue sea and tumbling whitecaps. Then suddenly there was another dot, higher up and moving toward them—a British blimp coming out to meet them. The sight of it drawing nearer and nearer pierced him with a thrill of delight. They had made it. The old tub had held beneath them and the speck of land ahead looked solid and hospitable. But more, much more than this, *he* had come through the night, faced terror and escaped humiliation. There'd been no panic on his deck because he had been there, and as he stood watching the blimp's approach he felt more complete in himself than ever before.

He was in harmony with himself, with everything that was happening. And yet, it was the damnedest thing, at this moment of relief, pride and physical excitement, there was once again that sense of something more, as if he were on a borderline of understanding something just beyond what he was conscious of. He couldn't explain the feeling.

The other "moment" occurred in England. The Sixty-sixth C.A.C. disembarked at Southampton but instead of being transshipped for France immediately, they were stationed outside Winchester, where a minor epidemic in the camp was to delay them even longer. Having managed to wangle a leave, and eager to discover as much as possible about the English, as well as their drinking habits, Bill set off alone one afternoon to visit Winchester and its ancient cathedral.

Possibly he was worried that hot August afternoon, possibly his mind was filled with thoughts of France. News from the front was anything but reassuring. In their spring offensive the Germans had got within fifty miles of Paris; Americans had arrived and they'd been thrown in everywhere—Belleau Wood and

117

Château-Thierry—to block the advance; but now England was buzzing with stories of a second battle of the Marne. Bill had no idea where the coast artillery would be needed or when they'd be sent. But the moment he stepped into the cool hush of the cathedral, all such thoughts, indeed any kind of conscious thinking, seemed to be taken from him. He moved slowly up the great main aisle, then, halfway to the altar, he paused. His head went back and he stood transfixed, legs spread, gazing up at a shaft of pure light streaming in from the uppermost point of a stained-glass window, absorbing the total silence around him, which seemed part of some vast universal silence, and all his being yearned to go on to become a part of that silence. Then, hardly knowing he was doing it, he moved into a pew and sat, his hands resting on his knees.

How long he sat or what happened or even what state of consciousness he was in he did not know, but he was aware for the first time in his life of a tremendous sense of Presence, and he was completely at ease, completely at peace. In this place, in this state of being, he felt again what he had felt on the Newport cliff, what had seemed just beyond him on the ship at dawn—he understood that all was good and that evil existed only in the mind—and he knew that now, for these fleeting moments, he had moved into some area beyond thought.

When finally he rose and started back down the aisle, the chimes in the high tower had begun to play. He vaguely remembered the hymn from childhood, but he could not recall the words.

Out in the graveyard, a little beyond the entrance, he paused again, listening to the bells ring across the valley and looking back at the cathedral. Something had happened, something he had no way of describing, but the important thing was that it had happened and if it had, could happen again. He was sure he had a long life ahead, and one day he might be able to grasp what it had been and pull it further into the light. Until then —he turned and started along the path—until then he knew he had only to wait, even though he couldn't be sure just what he was waiting for.

At the edge of the path he hesitated again, thinking he would cut through town, find a pub and have a few short beers before returning to camp. As he started off, his attention was caught by a name carved on a headstone: *Thomas Thatcher, died age 26 in 1764.* He smiled, remembering Ebby Thacher and his brothers in Albany, then he leaned down and read the full inscription. He read it again:

> Here sleeps in peace a Hampshire Grenadier
> Who caught his death by drinking cold small beer.
> Soldiers be wise from his untimely fall
> And when you're hot drink Strong or not at all.
>
> An honest soldier never is forgot
> Whether he die by musket or by Pot.

Like thousands of others, Bill and Lois had worked out a private code that was designed to get past the censors and tell her where he was, or at least how close he was to the fighting. If he signed his letter "Billy" with the *y* going straight down, she would understand that he was safe in some rear area; if, on the other hand, the *y* had a curve, it meant he was near the front. In all his time abroad he was able to use only a straight *y*.

Shortly after Bill had sailed, Lois discovered that she was not pregnant after all, but even that news did not dishearten him. He wrote back that they had the rest of their lives to try again. At one point it even seemed likely that she would be able to join him in France. She'd been taking courses in occupational therapy while at Walter Reed and she'd found out that the Y.W.C.A. was sending women overseas. But after applying, and pulling what strings she could, she was notified that the Y. did not consider Swedenborgians an acceptable Protestant denomination. Still his letters show no sign of depression.

He believed deeply in what the war was about and there was

never any doubt that he was where he should be. Some said later that Bill had gloried in the war. That may have been true, but if he did, it was not because he loved bloodshed but because of his staunch belief in the rightness of "our cause" and because the army was offering him a new outlet for his energies. Also, aside from missing Lois, there was no doubt that he was where he wanted to be. He loved France and he loved the French—the bright cafés at night with a few familiar tarts, the old men arguing over their wine, and always everywhere the young lovers embracing in public, wandering down country lanes—and he loved their feeling for Americans.

During his time in France he was not to know another such moment as he'd experienced in the cathedral—in fact, he was not to know such another for sixteen years—yet there were nights when it still seemed more real than anything that was happening around him. Often in the evening he'd walk into town, order a bottle of wine, then sit back and try to recall exactly what it was he'd felt in Winchester, try to draw it back into the light, so that he might feel again the power he'd sensed just beyond himself.

Mostly he drank, as he always drank, when a drink was available, and in France there was always someone to offer a soldier a drink. Their attitude toward alcohol was a constant delight. One farmhouse where he was quartered was run by an ancient grand'mère, all the men being off at the front, and this good woman would awaken Bill each morning with coffee and a bottle of rum. He often watched fascinated as she doled out a morning tot to her four-year-old grandson— "*Ça ravigote, vous savez, ça donne un coup de fouet*"—and to his astonishment it never seemed to have any dire effect on the boy.

It was in this congenial world that he began to refine his talent as a storyteller and to experience again the delights of holding an audience. At night with other officers in a café, or with enlisted men gathered before a tent, someone would invariably say, "Bill, give us that one about . . ." and he would lean back, take a swig from a bottle, stretch out his legs and begin, a relaxed and happy man. He was happy at such times partly because his relationship with his men had become important to him. He made no close friends in the army, had no special pal—in many respects he was still a loner—but he was on better than good terms with all the men under him. Corporals and sergeants outdid themselves for him and they came to him in their off hours just as the young recruits had done at Ethan Allen. They brought him their letters from home, confided their intimate worries and fears, told him their troubled secrets. And Bill would listen, encourage them, sympathize and often tell them about his own concerns. Sometimes he would make them laugh, and he would always offer them a drink. If he didn't altogether understand the respect they seemed to have for him, it was because he didn't yet realize that his willingness to share and enter another man's life was not a usual thing.

When the Armistice was signed in November, the C.A.C. did not immediately disband and return to the States. It was not until March that Bill boarded the S.S. *Powhatan* in Bordeaux and sailed for home, and not until May that he was discharged from Camp Devens. But that winter and that spring were extraordinary times to be an American and in Europe.

It was an extraordinary time just to be alive anywhere. Four years of slaughter had ended with nine million dead, twenty-two million wounded and the eyes of an exhausted world focused on the peace conference, where an American President was addressing not just his countrymen, but all mankind. He had become the spokesman for a new world order that was to outlaw war forever and drag the old rudderless hulk of humanity onto a brand-new course. In that winter and spring the President spoke as a deputy for all men who had believed in, dreamed of and fought for democracy. And for a brief time the world listened.

It was a time when the very air seemed filled with a sense of history, such as a man may know only once or twice during a lifetime, and as the *Powhatan* steamed into New York harbor the course ahead—for the world, for the country and for Bill Wilson—was clear and straight and infinitely hopeful.

BOOK THREE

1

When Bill returned from France there was a marked change not only in the amount he drank, but in the reasons for his drinking, in what drinks did for him.

He knew that certain situations always seemed to bring out his sense of responsibility, while others played upon his insecurity. The period immediately following the war did both, because now he was living in a city and now for the first time in his life he found himself face to face with a highly competitive world.

His first weeks back were happy, everything that a returning hero could wish for. New York was filled with uniforms that spring, and whereas all servicemen were respected, those who had actually been overseas were a special group looked on with particular admiration. For these were men—or so civilians believed—who had tasted real life. They had been exposed to danger and many must have known the feeling of killing other human beings; because of this it was assumed they had discovered a secret that stay-at-homes could only guess about. When strangers came up and offered to buy Bill a drink or a bartender would shake his head and refuse to let him pay, he experienced a peculiar sense of pride.

For a little while he was getting all the adulation he craved.

But even more than the flattery was what he felt about himself. He had been part of a great endeavor; he had done something worthwhile. Once before, as a schoolboy, he had known this same sureness, but something had happened then, he had lost it—and he had been lost. Now he was determined at any cost to hang on to what he'd found. Never again would he think of himself as Dr. Emily's little boy or the Burnhams' backwoods son-in-law.

One small incident occurred the first day he was out of uniform. He was going down into a subway on his way back to Brooklyn as a group of some ten or twelve enlisted men was coming up the steps. They were apparently in a great hurry and they brushed past Bill, knocking him back against the wall. For a long moment he stood looking after them, watching them disappear into the street. Not one of them had stopped. Not one of them had stepped back and saluted. It was a small incident and nothing to be upset about. In time he even managed to laugh and create an amusing little anecdote out of his reaction. But he remembered his feeling.

During the next weeks, although no one ever put it into words, he got the impression that he was being watched, studied. The time had come when he must get hold and brace himself for what was called the serious business of living. Everyone said he'd have no problem, he could write his own ticket, but there was a question: a ticket to where?

Most of the veterans he talked with were eager to get going again and take up their interrupted lives. But before the war, before Lois, he had had no life. Each morning he read the help wanted ads. In his letters from France he'd debated the possibility of going west and living the sort of life Gilly lived, but there was no mention of this as he began taking his place in the long lines of ex-servicemen applying for jobs. But there appeared to be definite limits as to what a former lieutenant with no college degree qualified for and after a time he himself began to wonder exactly what he was equipped to do.

For several weeks he worked on the New York Central piers up near West Seventy-second Street in Manhattan. His job was driving spikes into planks after carpenters had sawed them and laid them in place, but there was a lot of talk on the piers that summer about the workers taking over the railroad, and when finally he was threatened with violence because he wouldn't join a union, he decided to move on.

For a time he decoded cablegrams for a concern on Forty-second Street, for which he received twenty dollars a week. He went through the motions, all the little office routines, but he soon grew listless and knew he had no energy because he had not the slightest interest in the work. He wanted a job with meaning, with some purpose, and he realized his future here depended on the whims of an aging office manager, a stranger.

He was confused, angered, and at times filled with a gnawing self-pity, but mostly he was confused, and at the end of the business day he got into the habit of stopping by a local pub. With a few drinks in him—why was it always easier to think straight and regain his old clarity in a bar?—when he'd pull out and start heading back to Brooklyn, he quite often had reached the conclusion that tomorrow, or next week anyhow, he'd look around for the right job. And always as he approached the house on Clinton Street he'd say a little prayer that tonight Dr. Burnham would not ask his question about how things had gone at the office.

Dr. Burnham, whom Bill now referred to as "boss," was still a man of influence in Brooklyn and during the summer he pulled many strings and arranged some important interviews for Bill, but again it was the old story: without a degree his opportunities were limited.

He became aware of a subtle change in the family. Oh, there was still the same warm excitement around the house, the same contagious friendliness. Lois's family loved him, he knew it, and he loved them, but in the year he'd been away the girls had grown into young women. Their talk was all about their work, and the young men who called were serious suitors now. Some-how they seemed more self-reliant than he'd remembered, as though each of them possessed an independence he'd not recog-nized before. At this point Rogers was still overseas and some-times Bill wondered whether he would understand if he were back; would Rogers have the same questions? For it was not only the Burnhams who seemed assured of their world. God knows, Dr. Emily had no doubts about the course she was sailing and his little sister Dorothy was writing from Chicago, where she was studying, that she had met a young med student, Leonard Strong; her letters were full of their plans. Everyone was moving, going toward something or someone new.

In a way, on certain days, he could believe this true even of people he passed on the street. Everyone had been assigned a part and was getting on with the special job he was expected to do, all of them heading toward a fulfilled life. Only he seemed uncertain of what role he was supposed to play.

Of course, the way to cope, as Bill realized, was to appear as confident as everyone else, and also, of course, nothing was so helpful with that as a few little drinks after work or maybe just a couple with lunch.

Some of this he could talk over with Lois. Some he could not, and if at this time she had any suspicion of how concerned he really was, it has to be remembered that she had her over-whelming faith. Everything would be all right. Somehow she would make it right.

At the end of his first summer back, partly because they wanted to be alone, partly because Lois believed it a good idea to get Bill away from the bars, and partly, too, because they wanted to get away and think, they decided to take a walking trip. From Boston they took a boat up to Portland. There, carry-ing packs and army pup tents, they started off across New Hampshire and on down into Vermont, and almost the first day they were out of the city a change began to take place.

All Bill's life part of him remained a country boy. Reared on a farm, he kept a farmer's skills. He could lean down and take up a hunk of earth and he believed he could feel the growing between his fingers. This part of him responded to every aspect of nature—to winds and rains, to the stars at night, the shifting autumn colors. It was as though nature helped him keep his soul his own.

He loved the rhythms of walking and the chance to look at himself away from the details of city life. This, plus his ability to let his mind wander free, produced a kind of intoxication not unlike what he tried to get from booze. While hiking, he said, he saw himself in perspective.

At such times Lois was a constant wonder and a constant delight. With her inexhaustible energy, she was incapable of fatigue, and he knew that he could have looked the world over and never found another girl who so completely enjoyed the same things he enjoyed or had such total confidence in him. This was what amazed him. As they'd stride along, he'd look down at her and wonder what it was that had given her this faith.

At sunset, or sometimes in the early hours just after dawn, they would stand side by side on a mountaintop, having skinny-dipped in a clear mountain stream, and they would look out over endless miles. Then they'd lean back against the wind and it was as though they could feel themselves growing taller toward the sun. All their problems dissolved, all their worries seemed to be sucked up, absorbed in the sun as easily, as simply, as the moisture evaporating from the earth around them. They were in love and they knew in their very beings that all was right with them, and they also knew that if only they could keep this they could do anything. If they, if all people, could have and hold this feeling, there would be no discord anywhere, no fighting, no wars, no pain. Here on a mountaintop the few words they spoke were a hymn, a cheer, and above all an affirmation: they belonged in the world, and for them the world was good.

But how to keep that feeling while penned up in an office on Forty-second Street? As their trip drew to its end and they moved down toward East Dorset, this and other questions about the future began to plague them.

At first East Dorset appeared exactly as Bill remembered it. All the old folks were there—his grandparents, old Bill Landon, Barefoot Rose—but after only a few days he became aware of a subtle change. For example, there wasn't one house he visited where he didn't hear a story about some young person taking off and going to live in the city.

Mark Whalon was also around that summer, as articulate and as eager as ever to explain the world. Of course there was a change, Mark said, but it wasn't only in Vermont; the same thing was happening everywhere. Americans had fought a great war and they'd fought it wholeheartedly, accepting rationing and meatless days; they'd bought Liberty Bonds and worked in defense factories and now that it was over they wanted to return to what the Republicans were calling normalcy. Already politicians were out on campaigns calling for no more entanglements in Europe, no more sacrifices.

But Mark's point was that it was too late. The change had already taken place and Americans always moved forward, not backward. The 1920s were going to be a time such as Vermonters had never imagined, and Mark would whistle "How Ya Gonna Keep 'em Down on the Farm? (After They've Seen Paree)."

The new electricity being installed all over town, and the automobiles, were symbols of the change. He admitted they'd seen a few cars around Manchester before the war, but those, he reminded Bill, belonged only to the Burnhams or rich summer visitors. Now, through mass production, everyone would have his Tin Lizzy and when folks started demanding new all-weather roads, pretty soon they'd see a web of highways clear across the state. It was inevitable, he insisted, and there were bound to be alterations in everything, in the way folks shopped, traveled, did business, in the way the young ones courted. . . .

Although most people were less articulate than Mark or less aware, what they could sense happening had begun to color their conversations and their thinking. The word Bill kept hearing was "progress." Yet curiously, no one seemed to question. Only his grandfather voiced any misgivings.

Fayette was much the same, a little thinner perhaps and his step was slower on the stairs, but there was the same rough-hewn handsomeness, the same inner quiet. Bill knew Fayette might have omitted some things from his life, he might have had more of others, but as Bill studied him now he saw an elderly man of few regrets. Above all, he saw the man who had always taken care of him. As they rode out together in the evening it was easy to fall back into the feelings of the nine-year-old riding beside his grandfather, to recapture a touch of that confidence he'd known after he'd met the challenge of making a boomerang or mastering the violin. For old Fayette, more than any man Bill had ever known, had been able to clear Bill's mind of cobwebs and leave him with a shining, wondrous excitement about what lay ahead.

Fayette saw Bill's conflict about the line of work he wanted to pursue as a reflection of the shifting attitudes across the nation, and to him these represented a more profound and potentially more dangerous change than any Mark had mentioned. He and, to an extent, Bill himself had grown up in what was already being called a horse and buggy world, but it was a world that had been inspired by the ideals of Lincoln, and now much that was taking place appeared to Fayette to be chipping away at those ideals. Perhaps we were growing too fast. No country in the history of the world had grown more rapidly. But he did know that the old ideals had been basically individualistic and now he could see us becoming a nation of organizations and giant corporations.

Above all, he knew that the Lincoln ideal demanded self-

131

government. Yet he could see our great cities being run by businessmen and corrupt political machines. If our experiment in government was to succeed at all—he paused after those words just as he had always paused, and as Bill waited to hear the rest of the thought come rolling out in a clipped Yankee cadence, he could feel the same tingle of anticipation he'd always felt when he was getting close to a truth, to the very kernel of all Fayette believed—if it was to succeed at all, it would be brought about by the people themselves. "For," he said, exactly as he had always said, "there's no other capital fund I know of to draw on."

Finally, Fayette guessed, it all came down to one thing: whether there were still men who cared enough to assert the old beliefs, clarify some new ones and then try to shape society to them.

As to what line of work Bill should follow, well, he said, he'd always been of the opinion that there were only a few careers worthy of an honest man's efforts. One of these he still believed was farming, but the greatest one . . .

He didn't have to finish the sentence. Bill knew before he spoke the word. And he knew, too, why as a boy he'd always wanted to be a lawyer. He knew the training, the hard work it would take, but he knew now, before they left East Dorset, exactly what he would do.

Back in the city there were problems, but these were not problems of goals now, only of procedure. As a young husband and a man who expected very soon to be head of a growing family, he could not be a full-time student; he would have to find a way to carry his own weight financially. Lois, who'd done so well during the war with her work in occupational therapy, was happy to accept a job at Brooklyn Naval Hospital and after a time, through a friend of her sister Barbara's, Bill was taken on as a bookkeeper in the offices of the New York Central. It was a dull job and one for which he was remarkably unskilled.

Still it paid $105 a month and with this added to Lois's salary, it meant they could move from the house on Clinton Street into a small apartment of their own. It also meant he could enroll for a series of night courses at Brooklyn Law School.

These were full days. Bill was carrying a work load that would have felled a less rugged constitution, for the job turned out to be not only tedious, but a constant strain, demanding complete accuracy in every detail. Furthermore, he discovered that the study of law was not all lofty discussions of the philosophy of justice. His first term he wandered lost through a maze of universal codes, statutes of fraud and civil procedure. ("Mr. Wilson, will you recite to the class the facts of *Hart* v. *McGee?*") Over lunch he plowed into tomes on mortgages, torts, liens, and tried to make his peace with the difference between a misfeasance and a malfeasance.

But in one way, he knew, he was blessed: during his first year there were two professors who looked upon the law not only as a profession but as one of the humanities, and in their classes Bill saw that the law actually had two faces. It not only defended the existing power structure; it could also legalize tremendous changes. It could shield the wealthy and at the same time protect the poor, the helpless. Often in these late-night sessions it seemed that the minds of the young men gathered here to learn to use the law were actually being shaped and trained to run the world.

When the classes ended with a loud ringing of a bell at ten-thirty, and they would wander out into the dark streets, it was natural to want to hang on to these feelings, and he and a few classmates would move on to a speakeasy (prohibition was now in effect) just off the campus. There they'd be joined by other students, sometimes by postgraduates or young attorneys who worked for New York firms and had already argued cases. Over great steins of beer the talk would grow heated, and the opinions of famous jurists—Justice Marshall, Holmes, even the new man, Brandeis—would be quoted back and forth. On such

133

nights in tiny back rooms, it was natural to think of one's self as a physical extension of these great minds. In such an atmosphere grades did not matter. ("But just you try getting a job without them, Bill.") He was a link in a glorious chain, part of a noble tradition.

A man didn't want to pull out and take such feelings down into a subway. He didn't want to even when a picture of Lois waiting at home would flash across his mind, for here he knew he was close to the heart of law and justice, to the very meaning of Fayette Griffith's democracy. At such a time a man just had to order another round. Bill would order another and often he was the last man to leave the speak.

The next morning the alarm would go off and there'd be the long trip into Manhattan, the agonies of adding figures and the constant effort to keep a fountain pen from blotting his ledger, and at 5 P.M. once more he'd battle the rush hour crowds back to Brooklyn.

As part of their courses first-year students were urged to attend as many trials as possible and whenever he could wangle a half day or even a few hours off, Bill was in the courthouse down on Chambers Street. He liked everything about a trial—the solemnity, the drama, the shuffle of a crowd rising to its feet as a clerk intoned the ceremonial "Hear ye, hear ye, all who have business with the Southern District of New York draw near, give your attention and you shall be heard."

Perhaps he was romantic, even naïve, but people in a courtroom, witnesses and members of the jury, seemed somehow strangely calmed. Especially when, one hand rested on a Bible, the other raised to take an oath, they seemed to be exposing some serious and admirable side of their nature. He studied everyone, the judges, the attorneys, and he learned that their impact depended on just one thing: their knowledge of the law. And finally it was this, plus his own lack of knowledge and his terrible slowness in acquiring it, that became so painful. For he knew that he had within him the makings of a fine lawyer. He had an alive, inquiring mind, and he had a knack of being able to see all sides of a question.

But to succeed in such a demanding profession required dedication and total concentration, and at this time his days were being wasted, his concentration focused on columns of figures. This, of course, created an inner conflict. If only he had some other way of making a living, he'd be freer, more able to be himself. By the start of his second term at law school, he once again began to study the want ads.

One morning a notice appeared in *The New York Times* asking young men of "all around abilities" who considered themselves capable of close observation to write a letter to an address in New Jersey. Since no particular scholastic requirements were mentioned, Bill answered the ad, and in time received a call from the Edison Laboratories suggesting that he come to East Orange and take a qualifying examination. On a Saturday in May he arrived in East Orange, along with some fifty other young men. There they were greeted by an employment manager, broken up into smaller groups and led into a huge oblong room. There were drains and sinks and some laboratory equipment along the walls, rows of tables on which their examinations had been placed and, off in a far corner of the room, a battered desk. Sitting at the desk, obviously lost in thought, was Thomas Alva Edison. His clothes were stained with chemicals and across his cheek there was the faint scar that Bill knew had come from an experiment with nitric acid.

Ever since he'd been a boy, Edison had been a hero of Bill's. He knew a thousand details of this man's life, and could quote him endlessly. He knew that Edison had had no more than three months of schooling but had read and trained himself; that whenever he had come across any reference to a scientific experiment he'd gone off and tried it and whenever he'd been near an engine, he'd tinkered with it until he understood it; that he always trusted hunches. It was Edison who had said that the secret of success was to hustle while you work. And now here he was, just across the room, the authentic American genius. It took a little time for Bill to turn back and focus his attention on the papers before him.

In all there were some three hundred questions. One asked about the diameter of the moon, another concerned overtones on a stringed instrument, the next dealt with the kind of wood used for oil barrel stays. Many aimed at testing one's sense of observation.

As the afternoon wore on and the others rose and turned in their papers, Bill plowed ahead. He'd answered all those he could immediately and then gone back because he'd found many that required estimates. (Bill said once that his mind was like his grandfather's toolshed, a spot where random objects could be stored that one day might come in handy. That afternoon he seemed to be using everything in the shed.) Finally, when he was the only applicant left in the room, he glanced up. The great man had wandered over from his desk and was standing beside him. He asked if Bill found the exam difficult and Bill said yes, he thought it very difficult. They talked for a time, quietly and easily, and then Bill rose, thanked him and left.

Weeks passed, and not having heard anything from East Orange, he began looking for another job. One with United States Fidelity and Guaranty Company sounded appealing. It promised to take him away from a desk and there was a chance his time might be a little more flexible. When a definite offer came he accepted it.

The work was primarily investigative, mostly looking into defaults of stock exchange firms on Wall Street. This was Bill's first exposure to the Street, and, as he said later, it was a simple case of love at first sight. For here was much of the drama he'd sensed at a trial, plus the excitement of changing times Mark had talked about. In the summer of '21, America was just beginning to be aware of its resources, its incredible potentials. Ambitious men everywhere were going into business for themselves, and Wall Street, not Washington, was becoming the real seat of power. That spring the Street was a place where anything could happen—and often did—and it always happened at a wildly accelerated pace. A man couldn't help catching some of the contagion.

Then late one night, shortly after he'd started with U.S.F. and G., there was a loud ringing of the doorbell and a reporter from *The New York Times* came running up the stairs. The results of the Edison exams were to be announced in the morning papers and William G. Wilson was one of the winners, the prize a chance to work in the laboratories in East Orange.

This was a moment of extravagant happiness for both Bill and Lois. The reporter wanted to hear all about him—he was a news story.

It was also a time of tremendous inner satisfaction. But even before he went to bed that night, he had made his decision. He would follow his hunch. Right or wrong, he would stay around Wall Street.

He already knew a few important men in brokerage houses. Lois's sister Barbara had worked for Baylis & Co., and she had introduced Bill there, and Lois's old friend Elise was married to Frank Shaw, who was quite high up at J. K. Rice & Co. But every day now he was meeting new people and making new friends.

Men, especially businessmen a few years older, seemed to take an immediate liking to Bill. Possibly they knew he represented no threat, not even any competition. For there was something a touch incongruous about the lanky figure, a battered brown hat always on the back of his head, leaning back comfortably in an outer office. It was that bit of the hayseed that never completely left him. It was in his speech, in the bright friendly blue eyes that had a way of squinting up as though they were more used to studying some distant acreage than the jottings on a ticker tape. He was at ease, that was the thing. Men trusted him, felt they could talk freely with him, and in time they began giving him tips on the market. Sometimes this would be done in an office, or even on the floor of the exchange, but more often it happened after the market had closed for the day, and little groups would retire for a couple of quickies to one of the speakeasies down behind Whitehall Street.

Another element that distinguished this period for Bill was the fact that although he and Lois were far from rich, they had enough money. Lois was making $150 a month, and Bill about the same. In '22 they were able to move from their tiny apartment to a somewhat larger one on Amity Street. Radio was the new thing everyone was talking about, and this just naturally fascinated Bill. While Lois busied herself at decorating the new flat, he would tinker for hours with a set, and indeed he managed to build by himself one of the first superheterodyne radios in Brooklyn. In time he built others, which he was able to sell at a considerable profit.

Bill's dreams may have been growing, but his tastes were simple and he and Lois lived simply. They remembered their vows to keep in touch with nature and often took weekends off to hike in the hills or sail for a day on the Hudson. It was always puzzling to Lois that on these treks Bill never seemed to think of a drink. It was as though the fresh air and the strenuous exercise furnished him with some essential ingredient that away from the country he could get only in booze. Back in the city when the weekend ended, it was always another story. Then his days were spent moving through the dim chasms of the financial district, his evenings in classrooms at Brooklyn Law, and both places—with the exciting talk along the Street and his slowness in acquiring any mastery of the law—gave him a good reason, or at least an excuse, for a couple of snorts. And with Bill a couple always led to a couple more.

Only occasionally now, and this was usually when his friends had left and he found himself alone in a bar, did the old nagging doubt start to come back. Then he would remember that all the bright talk he'd been enjoying had been about another man's money, another man's grand plans. Then, it's true, he did sometimes think of himself as the perennial outsider, an amateur still waiting around wondering what role he was to play. But he had learned by now that when these little fits of depression would descend he could signal the bartender, order another and swallow it—not always as a taste he was enjoying, sometimes more as a medicine a part of him needed—then the happy little changes occurred. He became convinced that even these gray feelings would pass and when he finally got going, when he made his pile, everything would fall into place.

In late December Bill received word that Grandmother Griffith was very ill and probably dying. He hurried to Vermont to be with Fayette.

He made the trip alone. Lois was suffering from the first of what was to be a series of miscarriages. On New Year's Day he wrote her that Ella Brock Griffith was dead, and in this letter he described how she had been a mother to him through the years of his growing up. Then he added, "Dear Gran left us quietly and with no suffering. She had done her work well and now she knows what it is all about."

He was back in Brooklyn in time for the beginning of the winter semester, but now there seemed to be another change in the pattern of his drinking. Just as he was spending more time reading reports and analyses of the market than in reading lawbooks, so most of his drinking was being done in the speakeasies of lower Manhattan instead of those just off campus. And more and more he was drinking alone.

During the day he still had the sense of events rushing by, and with it the old ugly awareness of not really being part of the scene. Everyone he knew was involved and "with it"; everyone was building a family, a secure place for himself. His sister Dorothy had married her doctor. Living up in Tarrytown, she already had one child and another on the way. The Shaws, whom he and Lois visited on Long Island, were prospering, with a whole batch of kids growing up.

Occasionally, alone in a bar, after belaboring himself for a time, he would lift his head, a suggestion of a smile would flicker across his face and he would order another drink. Maybe, he would tell himself then, it was all because he had a different focus on life, and maybe it was all right to be different, to be a misfit. Because didn't all forms of growth begin with some variation from the norm? Didn't evolution itself depend on differing groups? Wouldn't it then follow that all other, all social and moral changes would begin with those with differing values?

But then the next question would come up. Just what were his values? Not finding a ready answer he would have to have another drink.

But it must not be implied that during this period Bill experienced only the solemn, introspective sprees. There were wonderful happy highs, too, and some of these he shared with Lois. They would start out with a few short ones at home, and gradually, beautifully, the whole world would open out. They would move on to a restaurant, enjoy an insanely expensive meal with the best of wines, and on such nights Bill was, or so he seemed, the wittiest, the most articulate, the handsomest man in town. On such nights all dreams seemed possible.

But then, as Lois was learning, it was only a question of time. For after Bill's sixth or seventh drink—it was impossible to tell just when it would happen—there'd be the change. He'd be just as full of what he was saying, just as happy, happier even, but he was now interested only in what *he* was saying, what *he* was thinking, feeling. It didn't really matter whom he was with. He was only hearing cues.

It's a lonely business being with a drunk, and when finally Lois had to take him home, she couldn't help it, she felt like a little girl deprived of something that had been, just a few hours before, so real, so promising.

140

Often next day they would have endless talks. What had caused the change? What had set him off? They were determined to get at the real cause. Sometimes they'd walk all day discussing just this, trying to understand, to find a "cure." These would be followed by mornings when there would not be the slightest reference to the night before. His behavior became the one subject they both consciously avoided.

For Lois these mornings were often a time of self-reproach. She seemed unable to shake off the feeling that in some way she was failing as a woman. For Bill they were a time of silent remorse, of occasional stammered apologies. Also they became a time of high resolves. But somehow these never worked out.

By Christmas 1923, there had been so many disappointments, so many bad nights followed by gray, silent mornings, that for her Christmas present Bill wrote on the flyleaf of their family Bible:

Thank you for your love and help this terrible year. For your Christmas I make you this present: No liquor will pass my lips for one year. I'll make the effort to keep my word and make you happy.

Two months later there was another such vow. As time passed, there would be still others.

2

If the death of Ella had been like the loss of a mother, Bill had no words to describe the impact of Fayette's death.

When he arrived in Vermont for the funeral he again felt that immediate identification with his surroundings and it seemed fitting to leave his grandfather in the little hillside cemetery surrounded by his ancestors. But at the close of the services, as he stood by the grave watching old friends and relatives slowly depart, he was filled with a kind of emptiness he had never felt before. For not only was part of his own life ending, but a great and indefinable part of America was ending too.

Fayette had been his anchor and his pole star. Shortly before he died he had sent Bill a letter filled with news of the town, telling him that he had heard William Jennings Bryan speak and not been too impressed, thanking him for the radio—it was working just fine now with very little buzzing—and, as always, there'd been a line about this noble universe and a line of encouragement about his law exams. He had been Bill's link with the past and, in a way, with the future too, because it had been old Fayette who'd made him see that through a son a man might live on beyond his years. But Bill didn't want to think of that now. The spring before, Lois had had her third miscarriage. (His mother, he remembered, had written them most sympathetically at the time and in the same letter she had announced her intention of marrying again.) No, his link with the future would have to be worked out along some other line.

Fayette, he remembered, had never had to sign a contract for the sale of his lumber. A handshake had sealed the deal, and when Bill had asked about this, he'd been told: A man's word is his bond. Now these words came back with a special resonance. They seemed to epitomize all the values of self-respect, decency and communal responsibility that Fayette believed had made life vital and civilized.

Now as Bill moved down from the cemetery and made his way through back roads toward town, Wall Street and the frantic pressures of Brooklyn Law were far away, and not only in miles: a century seemed to separate them from this quiet, orderly world. Down in the financial district he'd been excited by the rush and change, the constant state of alert, but with only the familiar clop of a horse's hoofs on a hard dirt road he saw that it wasn't only the outer physical comforts, not only the highly touted standard of living that was changing there; attitudes were shifting too. With the economy moving so fast, with production galloping ahead, the problem was to create enough new customers. Already the salesman, not the producer, was becoming the big wheel. Advertising and the hard sell were all the rage. But far worse in Fayette's terms, a part of the old ideal was beginning to do duty for the whole. In place of his grandfather's "balanced humanity," everyone on Wall Street, in fact, everyone he knew, was out to make a killing, chasing after his own big payoff.

But for better or worse, he realized that evening as he moved through the silent, empty house, packed his belongings and prepared to leave, for better or worse, this was the world he lived in now.

Or almost lived in. Because as he shook hands and said his good-bys, he couldn't escape the knowledge that he hadn't done much of a job of living in either world. He no longer belonged in East Dorset with its little buyings and sellings, its absorption in the raising of children, in weddings and funerals. And he'd made no real place for himself in the city. The war was six years over, and it was a little embarrassing still being a student at age twenty-eight.

Mark Whalon walked with him to the depot. Although of course nothing was said about it, he knew that he'd not moved up on Mark's famous ladder. Maybe he'd married a rung up— was that it?—because even his fine contacts along the Street, the men at Baylis, Frank Shaw at Rice & Co., he'd met directly or indirectly through the Burnhams.

Mark had been drinking that night. He hated to see Bill leave and he kept reciting a poem by Henry David Thoreau. "Though all the fates should prove unkind, leave not your native land behind. . . ." Then there were a lot of lines about no matter where the ship might sail, or what she carried in her hold, a New England worm would bore her hull and sink her. But Bill knew better than to take the words of a drunk seriously. It was to be another five years before he understood what Mark was trying to tell him. That night as he boarded the train and headed south for Brooklyn, he understood one thing: he'd accomplished nothing. For six years he'd been drifting aimlessly, waiting for the break that would not come, and now there would be no Fayette to turn to.

One might suppose such thoughts would be sobering thoughts, and for many men they might have been, but for Bill they seemed to have had the opposite effect. Back in Brooklyn, his questions about himself increased, and the drinking increased. Somehow he was able to hold down the job at U.S.F. and G., but he saw that was exactly what he was doing, holding it down. There was no hope of the job taking off, opening out and leading him on to higher ground. In the beginning, law school had seemed to hold the answer; he'd been stimulated by

144

acquiring each new bit of information, but he'd never really latched on, and now he knew there were young men in his class far brighter than he. At his final exams he was too drunk to see the questions.

As the hot summer nights settled over the city, he was determined to pause, take a realistic look and find some way to halt the terrible sense of drift.

Always—and he knew this might be part of the problem—ever since he was a boy, he'd been trying to please others. Decisions had been made by others or by his desire to please them: Lois, his mother, his grandfather, Gilly. In some corner of his mind he had always been seeking Gilly's approval. But he could change all that. He had done it before. Once, and not too far back, *he* had been in command.

One night, sitting alone at the end of a bar, he lifted his glass and announced that he had a new ambition for the world: "Each man his own father by Christmas."

The remark may have confused the bartender, but it made tremendous sense to Bill, and he knew he'd remember it.

Buoyed up by this decision to take life into his own hands, during the next few weeks he began what he thought of as a personal inventory and he reached back in his mind for those times when he had been in control, when others and the opinions of others had not mattered.

As he worked with his radios in the evening—conscientiously cutting down on his drinking—and as Lois busied herself around the apartment, he remembered the boy at Burr and Burton. He'd wanted "power" then, and somehow he had found it. He'd seen himself as a loner then, surrounded by adversaries, and he had determined that he would become the number-one man. Although he half smiled at the phrase, he had to admit he felt a certain little thrill of pride remembering that boy ("I'll show them all."). Challenged, he would formulate a plan, pursue that plan, and that decision, that simple pursuit, had guided his every action. And now, as he remembered those obsessions

145

of fifteen years before, gradually another plan began to form in his mind and to shape its course.

Ever since he'd started working around Wall Street, one thing had been a puzzlement to Bill. That was why everyone—not just the amateurs, the little outside traders, but the big operators as well, the heads of brokerage houses, men who were supposed to know—why they would take such ridiculous chances and invest in companies they knew nothing about, when with a very little outlay of capital, a sensible research study could be made. In the past years Bill had developed certain investigative talents and he knew something about the market. The few shares he owned (they were mostly GE, purchased back in '21 at $180 a share) were now, through splits, worth four or five thousand a share.

Why not go out, make a study of various companies, evaluate their potentials? Then sensible decisions could be reached, based on facts, on a diagnosis and a scientific prognosis. At this point in his career Bill's conversation was so studded with Wall Street jargon that when he first presented his plan to Lois it was a little difficult to follow. But he still had the knack of putting a complex matter in simple Vermont terms. Before his grandfather bought a cow, he would look at the cow, feel its legs, discover how much milk it produced, what its antecedents had been, etc. So why shouldn't they go out and apply the same principle to the purchase of stock?

Curiously, this scheme, which was certainly one of the most madcap of his life, came not from a sudden flash of insight, as had been the case when he entered law school, but evolved slowly, only after very careful consideration of the situation, weighing his own assets and weighing them for their true worth.

But once the spark had been ignited, nothing could stop him. Even before presenting the plan to anyone for possible financial backing, he borrowed three hundred dollars from Mrs. Burnham and bought a Harley-Davidson motorcycle, complete with a large sidecar; he bought sets of Moody's *Manuals* and every available

146

book on market analysis. For weeks he studied the locations and histories of various industries that he believed warranted investigation.

To Lois, once she understood the idea, it appeared to have many advantages; it would keep them together and it would keep them away from cities, away from bars. They were so together on this, so carried along with their own momentum, that when Bill finally presented the proposition to Frank Shaw at Rice, and to several other houses, and was met in each instance with a startling lack of interest, it in no way discouraged him.

In fact, the lack of support for his brainchild seemed to provide the final incentive, the exact stimulus he needed. They would be moving out into uncharted seas. Of course cautious brokers and bankers, whose businesses had hundreds of years of tradition, reaching clear back to the goldsmiths and moneylenders of the Middle Ages, of course they would be skeptical of such an idea. He was suggesting a business with no ancestry.

The more his advisers said no, the surer he became. The more they suggested that he was giving up everything and taking his wife across a desert with no compass to guide him, the more appealing it sounded. If there were no rules for such an enterprise, he would make his own.

Perhaps nothing could have stopped him at this point. They gave up the apartment, put what furniture they had in storage, studied and mapped itineraries, packed and repacked the sidecar to see how much it would carry, then, counter to the advice of everyone, they set off on their motorcycle to investigate American industry. Bill was his own man now.

3

The motorcycle trip which began in the middle of 1925 had all the elements of a great adventure: danger, an endless series of surprises and, above all, an encounter with the unknown.

If, as had been pointed out to him, his venture had no connection with the traditional procedures on Wall Street, still it was to Bill a natural thing to do. It was part of the oldest American tradition; something in the blood, something in the air; Americans were always busting loose, running away from home. Had he and Lois lived fifty years before, and had he found himself trapped in an irksome city job, there is no doubt they would have set out in a covered wagon to explore new territories and push the frontier a little farther west. They set forth now with the same pioneer innocence, the same resilience, ingenuity and hope. And once again as with all great adventures, the final outcome of this odyssey came not through any outside forces but through a contradiction deep within the adventurer, within Bill himself.

A psychiatrist might find it of interest that when their sidecar was finally loaded and they at last started off to conquer new worlds, Bill headed first for East Dorset, Vermont. After a considerable stay at the Burnham camp, after several late-night talks with Mark and some hilarious evenings drinking with the

Thacher brothers, especially with Ebby, who was spending the summer in the family home in Manchester, they were again ready to move on. Everything had been strapped into place the night before—the explorer's tent, the cookstove, the army locker with their clothing and Bill's set of Moody's *Manuals*—and early one July morning, they were on their way: a Don Quixote towering above the handlebars and an unlikely Sancho Panza in the sidecar, in knee-length knickers and a chic cloche hat.

The plan was to stop where night found them, cook supper, sleep and start out again at daybreak, and for a time they stuck to this. The Harley-Davidson was a powerful machine and Bill not the most careful driver. Down in the lowlands of New York State they raced along, a roar across the countryside. Farmers put down their hoes to stare. Chickens, geese and small children ran for cover, but the only sound the Wilsons heard was the wind in their ears, cheering them on.

Their first destination was the General Electric plant in Schenectady, New York, and as they leaped toward it, Bill was as happy as he had ever been, filled with the glorious belief that he was now in control of his destiny.

On the outskirts of Schenectady, they camped at the edge of a pleasant farm and the next morning Bill called on General Electric. Here he made his first mistake, or rather learned his first lesson about dealing with management. He had put on his good suit and had presented himself as a small stockholder eager to find out about the company. He was received courteously, but perhaps his incisive questions baffled the men he spoke with— how much had he a right to know, how little could they tell him? When he left after a few cordial hours he'd learned no more than he could have learned in New York.

There was another delay at this point, because one of the rules they had set themselves was never at any time to dip into their savings. They had started off with a hundred dollars, and the plan was that they would stop when they began to run low, find

149

jobs and work until they had earned enough of a grubstake to move on to another factory. The detour to East Dorset had made a considerable dent in Bill's wallet, so in Schenectady they studied the local paper and discovered that a man on a nearby farm needed extra help. In the midst of a downpour they packed and raced across Schenectady to a small farmhouse near Scotia. It wasn't much of a place and Bill could see at a glance that it was far from prosperous. It was run by a couple named Goldfoot, and whereas the wife seemed capable enough, Goldfoot himself was no farmer. He'd spent most of his life as a coachman for Samuel Insull, had served for some time as a turnkey in a local jail, and the problems of crops and cattle overwhelmed him. Still it took a while to persuade him that Bill was the assistant he was looking for, and that Lois was really an experienced cook who could take care of the house and prepare three meals a day for a lot of farmhands. It was late afternoon before he agreed to hire them for seventy-five dollars a month.

In a way this was a strangely idyllic month, and it certainly gave no hint of the extraordinary events waiting just ahead. Up at 4 A.M., Bill was busy milking, haying, and on rainy days repairing the mowing machine, horse rakes and other dilapidated bits of equipment. There was little talk of drinking and perhaps because of the strenuous new life, little thought of it even, and each night after supper he managed a few free hours to study his manuals.

There were, however, two aspects of this month that were special and Lois feared one of them might become worrisome. Adjacent to the Goldfoot farm was a large expanse of land that was owned by General Electric, and in several nondescript buildings on the property, they were told, GE conducted experiments. Naturally perhaps, Lois felt this might be a reminder to Bill of his missed opportunity, but as time passed and no reference was made to the subject, she relaxed.

The other element that made the month special for the Wilsons, special and a little painful, was an eleven-year-old boy named Robbie, whom the Goldfoots were bringing up. Robbie was a thin, wide-eyed youngster with a manner both wistful and cowed. From their first day on the farm the boy never left Bill's side, and the change that slowly began to occur in his attitude, his whole outlook, was remarkable. Bill could kid the child unmercifully, he would giggle and then roar with laughter, and he plied Bill with a million questions. For Bill it was a new experience, watching the boy's huge young eyes light up with enthusiasm on discovering he had done something right, and with a powerful passion, of the sort Bill could remember, to keep on doing it right. Looking at them through her kitchen window, seeing them going everywhere together, Lois began to wonder if it might not be wise to think about adopting a child of their own when they got back to the city, when finally they settled down.

One evening toward the end of their stay with the Goldfoots, Bill wandered off into the little town of Scotia. There he fell into conversation with several young men and after discovering that they worked for GE, he bought them some beers. When they learned of his great interest in electronics, they bought him some beers, and finally late at night they drove him out to their research laboratory to show him the sort of thing they were working on.

This was a night Bill would never forget. For stretched out before him was a kind of wonderland, a display of equipment and special devices like those he'd read about in H. G. Wells's fantasies of the future. He saw the first experiments that were being made in sound motion pictures, the work being done on console sets, magnets, all sorts of shortwave communications. In a few hours he was given a complete preview of what General Electric was to become.

It was not only a night to remember; it was a beginning and a confirmation of all he had gambled on. By sheer chance he had stumbled upon top-secret information it might have taken others months, even years to acquire.

The next morning he sent a report to Shaw, at Rice & Co., but it was only a partial report. Some of his information he would hold until he could present it in person.

The next company Bill decided to investigate was Giant Portland Cement. Ever since talking with Mark at the end of the war, he'd been aware of the tremendous amounts of cement going into the new concrete roads that were spreading across the country, and in New York State he'd seen how much the farmers were beginning to use. He had made a study of every cement manufacturer mentioned in his manuals, and finally hit a small company whose stock was listed on the Philadelphia exchange. So from Schenectady he headed the motorcycle toward Egypt, Pennsylvania.

But here, instead of confronting management in their offices, he got a job in the plant. In time this was to become a key factor of Bill's method; by "walking the rails," as he put it, and going in at the employees' entrance, he was able to find out everything he needed to know. At Giant Portland he discovered how much coal they were burning to make a barrel of cement; he read the meters on their power input, and saw the exact quantity they were shipping out each day. He also noticed the amount of new equipment—super synchronic motors and the like—that was being installed and, figuring out what this would mean to future production, he estimated that they would be able to make cement for less than a dollar a barrel. Yet for some reason their stock was dawdling on the Philadelphia market at only fifteen dollars a share.

Armed with this information and a few shares of stock he'd bought, he put on his good suit, marched into the front office and confronted them with the facts. It was an absurd situation. The management apparently had no faith in their potential. Indeed, having seen their stock shoot up from three dollars a share to fifteen, the officers of the company were convinced it was far too high, and individual members of the firm were actually sell-

152

ing out as fast as they could. To Bill it was incredible, and feeling like a man who had fallen into a gold mine, he sent a signal to a Philadelphia broker to buy Giant Portland.

At this point there was one of those benign ill winds. While Bill was still in Egypt, a letter came from his brother-in-law in Tarrytown telling him Dorothy and the baby had been in a serious auto accident. There was no question, the Wilsons had to get to them, so they headed east. In Tarrytown, while Lois nursed and tended, Bill was able to get into the city.

He went immediately to Rice & Co. and described the situation at Schenectady and Egypt. It was a brilliant presentation and resulted in Rice's buying five thousand shares of Giant Portland and carrying Bill for a hundred shares. This was his first experience with a hundred-share lot of anything, and of course, with the sudden flurry of buying, it quickly jumped to nearly twenty-five dollars. Eventually Giant Portland was to wind up at seventy-five dollars a share.

Within only a matter of months the attitude of Rice & Co. was totally reversed. Were there perhaps some other companies they would like him to look into now? There were. A great many. They wanted to know more about the Aluminium Company of America, the American Cyanamide Company, certain power companies that had been behaving oddly on the board, and one of the partners suggested that if it interested him, he might investigate the Florida real estate situation.

A time to remember and a beginning.

There is one other ingredient in all great adventures, and one that the adventurer seldom acknowledges: that is the role played by chance. Like most men when life goes well for them, Bill was able to take the credit to himself. It wasn't luck or any combination of events that had changed his world; it had come about because of his unique ability to assess a situation, his own acumen. Suddenly all his old doubts and fears became part of the past.

With their family in Tarrytown on the way to recovery, he and

Lois picked up the motorcycle and, with winter coming on, headed south.

Bill—once again like all true adventurers—had believed that he was born to be free, born to wander. Americans, he said once, had to be taught to settle down, to stay at home and work. No one could now criticize this side of his nature, just as no one was now in a position to question his drinking. After all, hadn't it been through buying a few drinks that he'd unearthed the secrets of General Electric? At long, long last, he saw himself as his own master, a free and confident man.

The next segment of Bill's story, indeed the next four or five years of his life, might be described in terms of one of those silent movies that were becoming so popular. For although he and Lois were never pursued by Keystone Kops, the weeks and months rolled by at the same frenetic pace. Once he had thought of himself as a character in a family novel. Now the events of his life seemed more those of a short flickering film, in which episode followed episode, getting nowhere in particular—nowhere except the accumulation of more money, more reports to Shaw, more stock certificates in the portfolio.

Two wild riders, they raced through Virginia into the Carolinas and on across the corduroy roads of Georgia, camping at night, pausing to investigate a factory, a cotton mill, then on into Florida. Everything seemed to unfold in a series of cuts and quick dissolves: breakdowns and flat tires, four blowouts in one day, the frantic waving of arms to attract the attention of passers-by, skidding around corners on just one wheel, accidents and near accidents. Once when Lois was driving, and the full six foot two of Bill was squeezed into the sidecar with only his arms and legs hanging out, an unexpected curve sent the Harley-Davidson onto its side, shooting them both into the air, breaking Bill's collarbone and injuring Lois's knee.

At Fort Myers, Florida, they gave themselves a brief hiatus while visiting Bill's mother and her new husband, Dr. Charles Strobel, who were spending the winter on a houseboat. While there, they took an afternoon off to wander along the beach at Sanibel. Soon after arriving on the island, they noticed a huge yacht anchored offshore, and two figures dressed in dusters busily collecting shells along the beach. There was no doubt about whose yacht it was, or indeed who the two figures were. They were Henry Ford and his wife.

Scenarios of old movies always dealt with action, there seemed no time for reaction, but here on the beach at Sanibel, a camera might pause a moment and move in for a close-up of Bill. For as Lois joined the Fords, introduced herself and went into what appeared to be an animated conversation about rare shells, Bill stayed back. What might be revealed in such a close-up, as he stood watching the great tycoon relaxing, talking with his wife? Bill never wanted to be an observer of great men or of great events; he wanted to be center stage. At this point in his career he was already gaining a little reputation, on his way to becoming a Mr. Big in certain sections of Wall Street, but wasn't he still obsessed with the notion that someday, somehow, he too would be a number-one man? Whatever his thoughts that afternoon, he watched and made no move to join the group.

From Florida they headed north and the film began to roll again. They examined the phosphate mines outside Coronet, raced up through Alabama—doing a hundred miles a day—camped on the shores of the Tennessee to study the wondrous new developments around Muscle Shoals, were ferried across rivers on old stern-wheelers—there were times you could almost hear the piano in the pit of the movie theater, beating out its tinny, staccato accompaniment. He prepared voluminous reports on coal, iron and rail companies owned by U.S. Steel. Then on north—they were never still—to Holyoke, Massachusetts, where he and Frank Shaw were developing a great interest in American Writing Paper, and later still—there was no sense of sequence—on into the wild lands of Canada and the Aluminium Company of America.

And as in all good movies, there were frightening sequences

too, scenes of danger and a maiden in distress. Once in the South they stopped for the night close to what turned out to be a chain-gang camp. For some reason Bill wandered off that night and as Lois settled down with their one small electric lantern, a huge black in striped prison uniform suddenly appeared out of the darkness and demanded to know what she was doing there. It was a night of near panic—Bill was forever getting back—a night of strange inexplicable sounds, animals drawing too close to their tent, and always in the distance the clank of chains as the prisoners moved about.

Another night, some months later, as they were coming back from Canada, just as they approached the International Bridge Bill drew to a sudden stop, jumped down from the saddle and said he needed cigarettes. They were cheaper in Canada, he explained, and locking the motorcycle, he disappeared. Lois waited. There was nothing else to do. She waited and waited. Then as the chill of midnight settled over the plaza, she began to worry. Bill had taken the keys with him and he had all their money in his wallet. Then slowly but very clearly, Lois understood. Cigarettes were not cheaper in Canada, but liquor was.

Leaving the cycle where he'd parked it, she began to make the rounds. She went from bar to bar, saloon to saloon, knocking on doors, peering through windows, like Lillian Gish searching for her man. Finally she found him stretched out across a table in what must have been the last bar in town. He was happy that she had come for him, but for the life of him he couldn't remember what he had done with all their cash.

The spring of '26 found them back in Brooklyn for Kitty Burnham's wedding. There were also some business conferences with Frank Shaw, who at this point was doing so well he was considering branching out on his own. At these meetings there were open and frank discussions about Bill's drinking, but Shaw was a man with a keen eye for "the long haul situations" Bill was unearthing, and their arrangement was proving so profitable for

156

them both there was no serious thought of changing it. Besides, when he was around the Street, Bill rarely drank until the bell sounded at 3 P.M. Then, realizing the magnitude of some of the deals he was involved in—he had a twenty-thousand-dollar credit with which to buy any stock he chose—he would head for the nearest speak, and from there gradually make his way uptown. He'd often be pretty much out of commission by Fourteenth Street, and completely lost by Fifty-ninth. Starting out some afternoons with five hundred dollars in cash, he'd blow it all, and by midnight have to crawl under a subway gate to get back to Brooklyn. All this Shaw knew, but he also knew Bill Wilson was not the only man on the Street who enjoyed tying one on.

Indeed, looking back at this latter part of the twenties, it is easy to believe that the whole city, the whole country was getting drunk along with Bill.

This was an odd time in our history, a curious way station in a country's development. Fayette and Mark had sensed the change that was coming, but no man could have seen how it would alter the face of a nation, revolutionize our manners and what seemed our very philosophy of life. In the course of a few years established patterns had broken down everywhere. Men who before prohibition never thought of drinking suddenly took it up with no concern about breaking the law; it was simply the thing to do. And with this the underworld moved in. Everyone wanted his share of the good things—bathtub gin, plus fours, new cars and membership in the country club—and everyone wanted them now. The old frontiers might be disappearing, but business and industry with its incredible technologies were opening up new territories that everyone could explore.

If it can be said that any single force ever motivated a generation, surely in the twenties that force was our will to succeed, and succeed through selling, selling ourselves or our product. Having fun and making your fortune became a mass movement. Other nations might have done the same, but what made Europe watch us in awe was our production, our promotion and our talent for creating great wealth. We went after this with all our cocksureness, our wit and resilience, laughing, as Sandburg said of his Chicago, "as an ignorant fighter laughs who has never lost a battle."

Everything was accepted now. And everything was accepted in the same way as the great new advertising campaigns that inundated the country, all of them done up in the bright, gaudy colors with which the whole U.S.A. seemed to be painted. Bank loans and installment buying paid for the show. In his travels Bill was meeting businessmen who admitted they had borrowed ten times more money than they owned to speculate in the market and pyramid their profits. Anything went, and everything fed the great miracle machines of American prosperity.

Perhaps someone, especially someone in Washington, should have read the signals and given a warning, but after twelve years of the Democrats the country was back in safe Republican hands. And hadn't our first Vermont president himself declared that "the business of America is business"? You could call it a debauch, a fool's paradise, but no one in '28 could deny that it worked, and besides, as the governor of the Federal Reserve Bank said, "How are you going to stop a million people from doing what they want to do?"

The carnival spirit didn't of course touch everyone. There was poverty and there was savage injustice. Bill and Lois camped near the shack of one Robert Lee Brown for their first Christmas on the road. Brown was a sharecropper who was trying to raise tobacco. He invited the Wilsons to share Christmas dinner with his family, sons, daughters-in-law, and six younger children. Dinner consisted of turnip greens and sweet potato custard, the only presents a package of jelly beans and a knitted cap for the baby. (At this point, when prosperity was nearing its peak, it was calculated that a family needed two thousand dollars to provide the basic necessities, yet 60 percent of our families lived on less.)

The signs were there. But the simple faith, the blind confidence

158

was there too. Destiny was on the side of America all the way. Bill believed this in his heart. And things would improve still more, they were already improving, and didn't a rising tide lift all the boats?

Besides, he knew what his role was now. His immediate concern was investigation and investment, which meant assessing situations, understanding and dealing with the status quo. Later, when he had made his place, when he was secure, there would be time—and he hoped he would use it—to do something about the Robert Lee Browns.

Meanwhile the trick was to keep going, ride the waves, and this in the U.S.A. in the late 1920s was no small accomplishment. There were times when it seemed enough just to keep abreast and adjust to the whirling sense of change. And wasn't this all that really mattered? He and Lois had grabbed themselves two fine front seats from which they could view the giddy show racing by.

In much the same way Bill rationalized his drinking.

He was not a drunk, he told himself, he was a man who drank badly at times. What he must do was cut down a little, and always remember to eat when he drank; then when things simmered down he'd be all right. He was sorry his drinking upset Lois, and he knew that it did, that it worried, embarrassed her, and on occasion had been a real humiliation.

We can interpret only by experience, and Lois could understand the tensions and some of the conflicts, but she could not understand the changes. And Bill was changing now. Some nights it was difficult to see any trace of the easygoing Vermonter everyone had loved. It was as though old snubs he'd received, either real or imagined, still riled him deep inside, and with a few drinks he felt a compulsion to even scores. The backwoods boy had come to town and beaten them all at their own game. He was making as much as any of the Burnhams' friends, and for some reason he needed to point this out in words.

In '28 they moved into a new apartment on Livingston Street, but even this wasn't grand enough, and when an adjoining apartment became vacant, Bill rented it, paying for two years in advance and having the dividing wall knocked out to make one huge apartment. He needed the sense of spaciousness, he explained.

Curiously, during this period when he was making such financial strides yet because of his drinking was sinking into a sump of hostility that could poison all his relationships, there was one couple he never fought with, his sister Dorothy and her husband, Dr. Strong. Bill liked and respected Leonard Strong, and Leonard was able to point out to him the progressive nature of his kind of drinking; he might stay on the wagon for several weeks, but when he started in again it was as though the compulsion had actually grown during his abstinence and he needed more and still more. All of this Bill listened to, and much of it he understood.

Leonard also made an appointment with a young colleague in New York for Bill to have a complete physical examination. Bill had a bad hangover the morning of the exam; his ears were ringing, but the young doctor couldn't hear that. He found him to be in perfect health and saw no reason why with a little of "the old will power" he shouldn't be able to drink in moderation. Bill thought the doctor an ass, but now the words "will power" and "moderation" had been planted in his mind.

A definite pattern was beginning to develop. For weeks he would stay completely off the booze, then he would have a few, just a few in the evening, then there would be a party out on Long Island or with some Wall Street friends up in Connecticut, and suddenly his drinks would hit him. He would have to have more and more. Someone would say something then, perhaps just a casual remark, but he would sense a certain implication behind the words. The arguments that followed were often grim and always out of hand. For the one talent Bill seemed to have at such times was the ability to recognize an opponent's weak spot and move in on it. The next morning he might be a little vague about some of the details, but he remembered his feelings. He would apologize, claim that someone else took over when he'd had too much and that he wasn't himself.

For a long time Bill said this and in a way believed it. But only in a way. He knew that the words that came out of him during these drunken fights emerged from some very deep emotion. They were part of him. The realization was profoundly shocking at first, but it had happened so often and the feelings were so genuine, he knew it was a truth he could not brush aside, and he made a serious effort to look at it and understand it.

He reviewed the list of symptoms Leonard had pointed out, admitted that he did need a drink to fortify himself for any important occasion, that he needed one to relax his nerves after work, and he agreed that he did sometimes sneak them now, even that he lied about how many he had. But this was only to others; he never lied to himself, and there was a difference.

Long ago, when people had first started talking about his drinking, he'd made what he called his list of "nevers." These were the things he'd never done, and as long as he never did them, he knew he was not and could not be an alcoholic. For example, he had never stolen, never let himself go so far as to beg for a drink. He'd never been violent with a woman, never intentionally cruel. These were his criteria, rules he had made for himself, and at the top of the list was the matter of honor. Old Fayette's statement that a man's word is his bond was of supreme importance to Bill. To break his word would indeed be breaking a golden rule.

Of course, it was true he had gone back on pledges, but the point was they had been made to another, not to himself, and to another who really didn't understand. Only in trivial things did he ever lie to himself; saying, for instance, when he thought a subway would be crowded, that he would stop in a bar for just one drink, knowing full well that he would have three or four. But that was more in the area of a comfortable half-truth, or kidding oneself.

There were so many things about drinking that others didn't

161

understand, just as they didn't understand about his kind of work and the way the two things often combined. There was no way to explain the tensions, the constant need to be alert or the necessity to relax. It was not to escape, it was quite the opposite, but there was no way of explaining that it was important to get away in the evening after the racket of people, of sounds and ideas—exactly as he had had to get away as a boy—to find out what he himself thought. At these times, with his first few drinks, as he felt the mysterious glow creeping through his body, he became sharper, keener, he opened out. He could assess a situation because he was freer to consider all sorts of improbabilities he would never have dreamed of during the day. With a few drinks he knew he was a clearer, brighter man. And—why not admit it?—in a bar with men he liked, with the world relaxing around him, he was a gentler, more loving man.

But then—and he knew he had to look at this too—something could happen, someone could say something and the world could change. He realized that what was behind this, what caused the sudden shift, was important too, and that he should stay with it, examine it; that situation was occurring much too often now. But he didn't want to think about it, just as he did not want to think about that other thing, the attacks, which he knew had some vague connection with drinking.

There was no way of describing these attacks. They'd been going on for only a matter of months, but they seemed to be increasing and he had discovered no way of coping with them. He'd not mentioned them to anyone because he had no words to and because he kept thinking they would go away. But they didn't. They had something to do with fear, but it was no fear his rational mind could label. They usually came in the morning and he thought they were connected with hangovers, but one could hit him with no warning in the midst of an ordinary business conference and he'd be powerless to shake off the terrible floating anxiety he couldn't pin down, the great nameless fear. And the only thing that would quiet it was a quick shot of whiskey.

162

But more important than the fights, or what caused them, more important than the attacks of nameless fears, was what happened to him after he'd taken his first few drinks. If he was ever to make peace with his drinking, or with himself, he knew that he would one day have to look at that, at that first warm, loving interval, and he would have to look at it straight. And about this he was of two minds.

Here, he knew, he was completely on his own. No matter what others said, what kind or wise advice they might offer, no word from an outsider could help him here because he knew that what happened in those brief hours did not represent, did not derive from anything evil. It was a feeling his whole being craved, as though all the warring sides of his nature, mental, physical, spiritual, were in harmony then, functioning at their best and on a slightly higher plane than usual. The world in the evening with a few quiet drinks was the world as it ought to be, as he had always wanted it to be.

His mind seemed to stop at the word "wanted." Was that it? Was there some direct connection between wanting and the answer he was seeking? Did he truly want more than other men? Once a bartender had told him, "Trouble with you, Bill, is you want double everything—double Scotch, double laughs, double sex and double loving. Double everything." He'd laughed and he'd tipped the man too much that night, but although he felt he'd been paid a compliment, he also felt there was some seed of truth in what had been said.

Again, on a winter night when he was alone—it may have been the January he sent Lois and Dorothy to Bermuda for a little break, or it may have been the time Lois took off to test him, leaving a note saying that when he'd gone six days without a drink he was to let her mother know, she would get word to her, and she would come back—he awoke in the night still a little drunk, reached out and found only the emptiness of the bed. He got up then, he remembered, stumbled across to the window and stood looking out at the moon-white streets of Brooklyn. Then he held out his arms in the dark apartment and said, as he had said before, "I want, I want . . ." It was a sentence that had no end, a pronoun and a verb with no object.

Was this some curse, something inherited from his father? Or were there other men alone in the dark with their arms stretched out, wanting, wanting in the night?

His hands were spread up and out, his fingers open. There seemed something familiar in the gesture, but at first he could not place it. Something connected with dawn, with the ship at dawn, or the feeling in Winchester . . . ? It seemed to go way back and he searched for a glimpse of the past, the innocent years, but they were too distant, and all he could recall was the more recent past, the restless, angry past. Then he remembered—another night, front porch steps and a pair of hands reaching up beside his, and Bertha Banford in a long white dress, Darwin and evolution. Always from the earliest times men had wanted life to be more, to break through into another dimension. And from this wanting had come the doing, from the doing the means with which to do. "Then," she had said, "it means man will always want to break through . . . always want more."

Alone in an empty apartment, he let his arms drop to his sides, but he stayed at the window, stayed looking down at his hands. He and Bertha had believed that if they didn't go on, didn't want more, they would be letting down all those who had gone before. It was more than sex, this wanting in the night, though sex might be a part of it; more than a desire for peace, or a sur-cease from compulsion. It was part of life in him, in his father, in all those men out there in the night. It had been here always, before there were men to give it a name.

For one moment then he understood. He knew as a fact that somewhere in this idea lay the reason for all the striving, all the hunger and desire everywhere. But as soon as he turned from the window, the moment the feeling became thought and he tried to put it into words, it was gone from him. All that remained as he poured himself a drink was a sense of having been close, very

164

close, to his answer. In the morning there was only a sense of having failed again.

Since he could not recall what it was that he had lost, he tried to push all thoughts of it from his mind, and there were many ways of doing this. The main thing, as he'd said before, was to keep rolling. This procedure had seen him through before. When he found himself plagued with questions, when there were personal problems, often the best method of handling them might be simply to ignore them and not indulge in what he began to call juvenile fancies, childish speculations, He was doing all right, and he was determined that at any cost he must keep moving.

If there is a line, as Bill came to believe, an invisible line that every alcoholic crosses, it may be that he crossed it at that point, late in '28 or early in '29. He began to drink as he never had before, and he drank his booze straight now, with no chasers, drinking as an antidote to confusion and in order to dream, as he put it, dreams of greater glory. He began to envision himself as an independent operator, sitting on this board or that board, graciously giving advice to Morgan and Company.

At times he felt himself a man moving through enemy territory, for he had not simply entered the competitive world but had indeed been taken over by it. But he believed that he was winning and during this time it never occurred to him that success and happiness were not the same.

If he sometimes needed booze to ignite the spark of his dreams, well, that was all right too. He had money to pay for his drinks, he was healthy, he lived well, was respected and he had the support of a devoted wife.

In fact, at the start of 1929, Bill Wilson was living in what many would call an alcoholic's paradise.

4

An alcoholic's paradise, as every drunk knows, can become in no time at all an alcoholic hell.

For Bill this began to happen in '29. He could no longer deny the truth of what Leonard Strong had told him about the progressive nature of his drinking. Also he was now doing many things on that list of things he had sworn he would never do—yet he could still find an excuse, a justification, for each of these.

But much worse than this were the attacks that would suddenly descend and overwhelm him. He had believed they would disappear with more financial security, a more regulated life, but they only increased and by the fall of '29 his apprehensions were specific, the fears no longer nameless.

It had probably been an attempt to combat these attacks and at the same time restore his physical health that made him decide to spend some time in Vermont. By then he had broken all connections with Baylis, Shaw, and Rice & Co. He was a free agent and saw himself as a big-time operator, the lone wolf of Wall Street.

In many ways Bill loved this image, and he enjoyed his stay. He took up golf, playing three rounds a day—determined, of course, that by the end of summer he'd be better than Ben Hogan. He enjoyed partying with those he considered the elite of Manchester, the people, he was still convinced, who had looked down on and despised his kind when he was a boy. Most of all he enjoyed the attitude of local bankers when they'd discover the size of the check he'd stopped by to cash or to send as a money order to a New York broker.

His portfolio was extensive. Most of it, as was the case with the stocks of almost everyone he knew, had been bought on margin. Some time back he had grown concerned about the fantastically high prices of certain auto, radio and utility stocks and, searching for something more conservative to balance his holdings, he had hit upon Penick and Ford. This was a small molasses business that had combined with a corn products plant, and after one of his inside inspections, Bill had begun buying it up. By 1929 he was pretty much in control of the company, selling great blocks of its stock to friends and relatives or anyone else who wanted to come along for the ride. In this way, all on his own, he was able to oversee its ups and downs and peg it where he wanted it to be—always, of course, protecting his own investment. It had become his pet operation and, more perhaps than anything, gave him the sense of power he had always craved.

Late in the summer he grew worried because the market seemed a bit wobbly, and thinking it might be time to unload a little Penick and Ford, he returned to the city. But after a few consultations with men he considered specialists, and more than a few drinks in his favorite speak, he changed his mind. Everything was rosy, they told him, everything was high, but it was going higher. American Tel and Tel was over 310, General Electric 403. It was a time to have confidence. It was a time to enjoy. A time to get drunk.

Then it happened.

On October 23, there was a tremendous drop in the last hour of trading and the following day, Black Thursday, thirteen million shares changed hands. The worst had to be over, everyone insisted, and Bill hung on, but on October 28 and 29, sixteen million shares were thrown on the market for whatever they might bring. Within a matter of weeks the paper value of common stocks had dropped thirty billion dollars. Bill was in a hotel lobby, quite drunk, the night of the twenty-ninth. He reached into the ticker-tape basket and pulled out the long streamer of tape. "Penick and Ford—32." That was it. It was all over.

It was the end of the big bull market. The end of normalcy, and from this there would be no recovery. The merry-go-round had come to a stop, the structure broken down.

Leaders in Washington and on the Street tried to combat the collapse. Conditions were still fundamentally sound, they said. It was a natural readjustment. . . . The nation's business would make steady progress from now on. . . . But the leaders had lost all touch with the realities of the country.

For a while most Americans went on with their usual jobs, but there was a sense of false calm everywhere, and many men wondered how much what had happened on Wall Street would touch them directly. In that winter of '29, America waited, anxious, a little stunned, as if somehow crippled by an enemy it could not see and did not understand.

Bill Wilson sensed this, but there wasn't time to digest or examine it. Only later, years later, would he be able to look back and discover the curious parallel between what was happening to him and what had happened around him. It was not in his nature to admit there was anything wrong with the system, with his country or with himself. With the kind of superhuman power he and the country had, they would prevail. He would keep going and somehow he would show them. He would show them all.

This first reaction was typical and in a way it was even gallant. On October 29 he was a man sixty thousand dollars in arrears, with a wife to support, a grand double apartment they could sublease only at a loss and practically no ready cash. Yet his initial response was one of almost boyish excitement; he saw it all as a personal challenge. "Back," Philip H. Sheridan had said, "We will go back and retake our camps!" And why not? By rallying his forces, by carefully watching his step, he might—who

168

knew—not only recoup his losses and the losses of those who had trusted him; he might also at such a depressed time make another killing.

This may have been a gesture, a crazy bluff, but he was determined to give an impression of total confidence, and if this meant more drinking than some thought wise, that was all right too. He'd show them.

His first move toward rallying his forces was to contact Greenshields and Company, a brokerage firm in Montreal. He had done business with them in the past and several deals had proved quite lucrative for all concerned; besides, Canada had not been quite so hard hit. By the middle of November he had received a wire from Dick Johnson, an old friend at Greenshields, telling him to come on up, they would give him a job. It was a golden opportunity and he and Lois set off for Canada. He was going to prove that he had weathered the storm. He was on his way again.

But it was later than Bill Wilson realized.

The Canadian venture began modestly, except where Bill's drinking was concerned. With no money behind them, they moved into a small furnished apartment on Gerard Street. But by the end of winter Bill had struck up a friendship with a young remittance man from England, who appeared to have plenty of ready cash. In the slight upswing of the market that occurred in the spring of '30, Penick and Ford showed some signs of recovery and Bill was able to sell his new friend a considerable block of P. and F. He also managed to get from him a five-thousand-dollar credit with which to buy any stocks he considered sound.

Due to this and a few other deals that seemed to be going particularly well, he was once more filled with dreams of financial omnipotence and by May he had rented a handsome apartment on Côtes des Neiges and immediately sent for all their furniture to be shipped up from Brooklyn. They joined the country club and dined in only the finest restaurants. Penick and Ford was continuing to go up and up—and so was the drinking, despite Bill's resolve to be careful and watch his step this time. By now he had started nipping in the morning. There was always a bottle stashed away in his desk at the office and one behind the bookcase at the apartment. He had to know there was a drink at hand just in case he needed one.

In the summer Mrs. Burnham visited the Wilsons and while she was there Bill managed to keep some sort of lid on his drinks. Bill loved Mrs. Burnham. She was about Lois's height and her face wore the same happy yet serious expression. It was true that Mrs. Burnham's expression seemed quieter now, more satisfied, while Lois's seemed to be growing more intense, more inquiring, but both had a look about them that he admired, the look of someone not always broken up and distracted by unimportant details, and both carried themselves regally. He loved standing beside them at the windows of their apartment, looking down at the St. Lawrence just below and across at the expanse of Vermont hills stretching to the south. Yet during that visit he and Lois were concerned about Mrs. Burnham's health and before she left they made her promise that when she got home she'd have the doctor give her a thorough examination.

In the early fall, the partners of Greenshields had several meetings with Bill. It was true that he had made them some money, but there were too many stories about his drinking, too many fights at the country club or in various bars around the city, and often with potential customers. But somehow Bill seemed unable—perhaps he did not consider it necessary—to curb his life style. Finally it reached the point where the partners agreed they had no choice: they had to let him go.

It was unbelievable to Bill and Lois. After working for ten months, after being connected with so many big operations, there was nothing to show for it. Lois had to write her mother for bread-and-butter money and Bill borrowed five hundred dollars by putting up his life insurance for collateral.

The word from Clinton Street was far from encouraging. Mrs. Burnham's condition had originally been diagnosed as a low-grade infection but now it was feared a cancer might be involved and she was undergoing x-ray treatment. Feeling she had to be with her mother, Lois took off for Brooklyn, leaving Bill to close up, sublease the apartment if possible, put the furniture in storage again and sell their one real asset, a Packard touring car.

Being fired from Greenshields marked another ending and another beginning. With Lois gone, he drank around the clock, and his memories of this period, the next month, the next year, were always vague and unconnected.

They were vague as to detail and the chronology of certain incidents—how, for example, he got from place to place. But memories of other events, encounters with various individuals, etched themselves on his mind, and these he never forgot.

There was a fight with a hotel detective; a night spent in jail; being let off next morning by a lenient judge. Somewhere in here he met an elderly confidence man, told him about the Packard and apparently learned from him that they could get a good price for it in Providence, Rhode Island, because somehow—Bill never remembered how or indeed where they finally disposed of the Packard—the two of them drove off together. He remembered awakening at the Burnham camp on Emerald Lake with a terrible hangover and still in the company of the stranger. It took every cent he had to get the man back across the border.

If earlier his life had been like the scenario of a silent movie, his memories of this period resembled a rough cut that a director works with while a picture is still in production. A rough cut may contain a group of scenes, beautifully photographed, clear and perfect in every detail, and then suddenly all will go blank on the screen or a title may appear, "Scene Missing," and after that only bits and pieces, fragments complete in themselves but unrelated to anything that has gone before; or the camera may have moved in on a tight head shot and remained fixed on it for what seem endless minutes.

171

One close shot that was to stand out above all others in Bill's memory was of Lois and Lois's eyes. It was Christmas 1930. He'd got back to Brooklyn; they were staying on Clinton Street, and Lois was looking into his eyes, telling him her mother was dead— that woman who was all love, who had a capacity for loving greater than that of any soul he'd ever known—and Lois was saying she was dead. Then nothing. A scene missing and the terrible knowledge that he'd got drunk, too drunk even to pay Mrs. Burnham the tiny respect of attending her funeral, or offering her daughter any kind of support.

That look remained, superimposed on a thousand details of the winter, of endless subway rides into the city to see what friends still had jobs or what new contacts he might make. It was there, on top of the uncertainty and fear he met when he talked with men in offices and passed the crowds on the street, crowds that seemed to be going nowhere, just standing about and waiting. And it was there when he saw his first bread line. These lines were not on Wall Street, but in front of municipal lodgings and churches on little side streets, so that at first it was easy not to notice—but only at first. As the months passed and the heavy pall of the depression settled over the city, the lines grew longer and one was increasingly aware. In the year he'd been away, everything about Manhattan had changed. The great crash which he had tried to override had severed the twenties from the thirties with the sharp efficiency of a guillotine, and as he walked about New York he wondered if what had been lost would ever be replaced.

He and Lois were alone with the doctor on Clinton Street now, the family scattered. Even young Lyman had married and was practicing medicine out in Jersey, and once again Bill found himself a guest, a permanent guest. This was no easy role for a man who prided himself on being the great provider, especially since he knew the doctor had suffered heavy losses in '29 and suspected that most of his patients were being carried on credit.

There had been talk of possibly selling the camp, if there was an advantageous offer, of course, and possibly even breaking up the house and renting out apartments, but his financial situation was not a subject Clark Burnham could ever bring himself to discuss with his family. Then one evening Lois asked if, with no money coming in, they didn't think it would be a good idea if she got a job, she was sure she could, and it would only be temporary, of course, until Bill got hold. . . .

It was not the sort of question Bill knew how to answer, but some weeks later, when he was offered a job at Stanley Statistics, a humiliating job that paid only one hundred dollars a week, he knew he had no choice; he accepted.

One night not too long after he had been hired, he got himself involved in a barroom brawl. At the time this didn't worry him, it was so like many other fights he'd been in recently. He remembered a pair of sinister-looking thugs in the melee, and he remembered that somewhere in the course of the evening he had mislaid his briefcase, but most of the details were blacked out. A few afternoons later he got a mysterious phone call at the office. He realized it was one of the thugs, wanting to know if Bill recalled everything that had been in his briefcase. There were a few other veiled remarks before the man said he would call back the next day and maybe they could work a deal. He called the next day and the next, and each time his remarks were more insinuating, not only about the contents of the case but about certain information they had picked up on Bill, and each time Bill's panic grew. Finally he could do nothing all day except sit at his desk and stare at the phone, terrified it would ring, terrified it would not—for the true horror of the situation was that he knew that whatever the man was suggesting could very well be true. He had no memory of where he had been that night, or what he had done. A policeman could walk into the office and accuse him of any crime at all; he would have no defense; he would have to go along with anything that was said. A voice on the

173

telephone and what it would say next became the only things he could think about.

Even years later he could not remember if this threat of blackmail had been the cause of his dismissal from Stanley Statistics. All he remembered was the cold terror of those days, and the feeling that at any moment, sitting at his desk, he might lose complete control of himself. Then came the Friday night when he was told that the job had ended and he need not report for work on Monday morning.

Lois began working at R. H. Macy in May; her job was in the furniture department demonstrating a new kind of collapsible card table. She enjoyed it, she said. The pay was nineteen dollars a week, and now Bill sat in silence each evening at the supper table as Dr. Burnham turned to Lois and asked, "How were things on the job today?"

Bill's days were hardly days a man would care to be asked about. The mornings were spent in some brokerage firm, often trying to master a hangover, lolling back in one of the leather chairs in an outer office, his inevitable brown hat pushed back on his head, the financial page of the *Times* open on his lap. Occasionally he would rise and study the ticker tape, hoping to give the impression of being involved in some stock deal, but all he was doing was waiting for the three o'clock bell; then possibly he'd be able to cadge a few drinks in a local speak. His chances of bumming drinks, however, like his chances of getting a job, seemed to grow slimmer each week as word of his Canadian escapade began to spread along the Street.

Every so often he'd spot a stock, follow it for a while, do a little research on the company, and then, if it showed signs of health, he'd sell his idea to a small-time operator, borrow enough to buy a few shares. Sometimes he might make a hundred or a hundred and fifty in the course of a week.

When this happened he would immediately pay up his speakeasy bills. First things first: he knew the importance of fresh

174

credit in these establishments. But such windfalls were rare. Most afternoons he left the Street alone, stopping at the rear of a little delicatessen he knew and buying a fifth of gin, always remembering to tell the clerk to put the bottle in a brown paper bag. Then he could relax and nip from the bag on the long subway ride back to Clinton Street.

Occasionally, too, there would come one of those inexplicable, beautiful lifts of the spirit and his whole being would be filled with hope. One afternoon Clint Frazer, a drinking companion from the old, good days, introduced him to Joe Hirshhorn. Hirshhorn was already a legend on the Street. A dynamo who'd come up the hard way, he had an uncanny trading flair and even in these desperate times he had money and was daily making more. He took an immediate liking to Bill and seemed fascinated by his yarns about GE, Giant Portland Cement, and his handling of P. and F. He was sure they could work together. Sometimes he would tell Bill of a line of stock he was buying and add that he was carrying him for a few shares on credit. Sometimes when they'd run into each other, Hirshhorn would beat him on the back and then reach into his wallet and hand him a small check.

On one occasion—and in the whole long rough cut of Bill's memory this sequence remained clear and complete in every happy detail—Hirshhorn gave him a check for one thousand dollars. Bill knew exactly what he would do. He stopped first in a florist's shop, then in a few neighborhood speaks, then he headed for Macy's. With the check in one hand, a vast bouquet of chrysanthemums in the other, he wove his way through the aisles of the furniture department. Lois saw him coming. When he reached her he spread the flowers at her feet and with a great sweeping bow he dropped to one knee and handed her the check.

Next morning, of course, he had to ask her to return the thousand dollars, but he promised that by investing it in a small trading company he would be able in no time to pyramid it into ten times that amount. Somehow this didn't work out.

175

In time he lost touch with Joe Hirshhorn, whose interests seemed to have more to do with the Canadian market now. At this point Bill didn't think it wise to try Canada again.

If Bill would have found it difficult to describe to Clark Burnham and to Lois what he did each day, he knew it would be impossible to share his thoughts and feelings or any of the strange questions that absorbed him as he made his way along the Street.

When he first got back from Canada he'd been shocked by what he'd seen and not only by the uncertainty and fear he sensed everywhere, nor by the growing lines of unemployed. He understood the economic consequences of the crash—the decline in sales and the decreased demand for goods forcing curtailment of production, wage cuts, firings. He had read that unemployment had tripled in 1930, would double again in '31, and would probably go on up to twelve or thirteen million. He knew the facts. But it was those who did not know, or pretended not to know, who disturbed him, those chairmen of boards, presidents of banks, whom he watched stepping from their limousines each morning, sailing into inner offices as though everything were the same, as though their position and their right to enjoy their wealth were ordained by the Almighty. These men had a way of smiling and then driving off to their clubs as though nothing in their world had changed or would ever change.

But Bill was beginning to see that something had changed irrevocably. He saw it in the quiet dignity of men standing around the street, waiting. These were not always the unemployed; they were the partially employed, those who worked one or two days a week. He saw it in the offended eyes of men who slept on park benches, in bus depots and railway stations, men with newspapers for blankets, boys with no shoes to change. As the months passed and the winter grew sharper, he knew that some of these boys were spending their nights curled up on the dank floors of subway lavatories, and in time the acrid stench of urine worked its way in to become a permanent part of his memories.

Sometimes the lines on Whitehall Street appeared endless, yet he knew that each day more freight trains were arriving over in Jersey, and each train carried its load of men riding deadhead; in time they would make their way across to the city to join the others. And each day he seemed to be struck by the number of very young and very old in the lines, boys not out of their teens, elderly gentlemen who had clearly spent their lives in the certitude that a decent life and hard work would bring them security and, if they had families, even an honorable old age.

Some days Bill would fall into talk with a man he'd find standing on a corner or resting on a bench; he'd take him into the delicatessen, buy him a beer and listen. After a while all their stories seemed the same story—each had a sister or an uncle and if only he could get to them, out West or somewhere in the South, then everything would be all right, all problems solved. Their disasters became inseparably confused with those of other workless wanderers and he knew that what he was watching and hearing was a fragment of a saga unfolding in every town and city in the country. In time, too, his buying them beers, worrying for an hour, seemed an idle, footless gesture.

As a man with certain advantages, he felt a kind of guilt, almost as if he owed them a debt, for he was learning now that the difference between a gentleman with fifty thousand a year and a man whose wife worked and gave him beer money was negligible in comparison with a man who had nothing. He wanted to help, to find some answer, yet at the same time he felt isolated, as if his few advantages disqualified him. He felt a part of these lost, hapless men yet in a way separate from them.

For to Bill they were lost. Young or old, they had no ability to adjust to circumstances and so were forced into indifference and detachment, both of which were totally alien to him. By not being bosses, as some of them must have dreamed of being, and by no longer being workers, they evidently saw themselves as victims, and Bill did not yet see himself as a victim.

He did not understand the meaning of what was happening around him and to him. It would take a long time before he would realize its true significance and be able to fit it into place, but at least what he was seeing had shocked him out of his total absorption in his private, self-centered world. He knew that something was crucially wrong. There was an aching pain across the land and one day he knew it must be tended.

Many of these ideas he was only dimly aware of that winter. Too much else filled his mind, primarily the necessity of finding a job and thereby proving to Clark Burnham and to Lois that he was still capable of staying sober and making his living and doing something they would consider important.

Often in the evening now, when the supper dishes had been washed and stacked away, he would wander out for a little stroll, always under the pretext of wanting some fresh air or needing to pick up a late edition, and he'd stop in a small speakeasy he'd discovered that sold whiskey for twenty-five cents a shot. He would take his place at the far end of the bar and, over what was to be just one little drink, he would begin to organize a plan and develop a new approach.

He would sip his shot very slowly and try to look at the situation realistically. He would start out tomorrow—he was sure this was the right way to begin—go into town when Lois went to work, and—perhaps he should lower his sights a little now—perhaps see Frank Shaw, or Baylis, and be completely honest with them, admit he'd been foolish and had perhaps drunk too much, and then remind them that he had done some important investigative work for them and confess that he wanted to start again; he was still an honorable man, they could trust him, no one would question that. . . .

After what seemed no time at all—it was almost an hallucinatory experience—still on his first drink, all the details of the next morning became clear in his mind. He knew what suit he would

178

wear, he could see the Street, the office, the way he would walk in; he knew the way he would greet the secretary, the sort of smile he'd give and the sort of smile he'd get back. This picture became much more real than the reality of the bar. Frank Shaw was much more vivid than the men around him. This would happen. Tomorrow morning. At ten o'clock.

He would stand then and look down at his shot glass. Since all this was true, since there was no doubt anywhere about what he would do, everything was settled—why not have just one more little drink? Tomorrow was a certainty.

So he would have one more. And one more . . .

And soon, before he knew it, it was closing time and there had to be one for the road. Just one.

Next morning the alarm would go off and there'd be the shakes. Lois would leave, and he would have to find the fifth he'd stashed away behind the laundry bag.

Finally, when he was together and on his way to the subway, he would have to stop by the speak to find out what had happened, what he'd done. "Was I pretty bad last night?"

"No, Bill." The bartender was a good man. "You were fine. Maybe a couple too many, but you were fine. . . ." And he'd give him one on the house.

Yet through it all, night after night, morning after lost morning, he never was without hope or his sure belief that for him there would be one more chance. And curiously, about this at least he was right. There was to be another, a golden, chance.

179

5

Lois's sister Kitty was married to Gardner Swentzel, who, despite the continuing decline in the market, was still doing extremely well at Taylor, Bates and Company, a firm closely connected to all J. P. Morgan's enterprises. Gardner liked Bill; he respected many of his theories about the market, and it was through him that Bill first met Arthur Wheeler.

Artie was the only son of the president of American Can Company, a hard drinker, although nowhere near Bill's league. As the two talked and got to know each other, it was evident they had a great deal in common. Artie made up his mind that Bill had many ideas he could use, and Artie, with his great Wheeler connections, certainly had the capital Bill could use. In time Artie introduced Bill to Frank Winans, a banker from Chicago. Winans also was attracted to his theories, and early in '32 these three formed a long-term speculative syndicate, based on the notion that if one could overcome the present timidity of Wall Street and had enough capital and enough patience, there was a vast fortune to be made out of the recovery that was bound to come.

Wheeler and Winans, however, were conservative, and they were cautious. Before drawing up the contract, they investigated Bill's background and discovered his drinking history. They

180

faced him with it frankly. Winans was frightened and insisted on an addendum to the contract, which stated in the clearest possible terms that if ever during the life of the syndicate Bill took so much as one drink of alcohol, he would thereby forfeit his entire interest in the enterprise.

On April 8, Bill signed the agreement with no hesitation. The other two would of course continue to operate on the side with their own cash, but with the money they were putting up and with his third interest in the deal, the great comeback he'd been dreaming of was practically assured. As to the addendum about his drinking, he knew it offered the motivation he needed. To this he would be true. He was Fayette Griffith's grandson. A man's word was his bond.

Spring came early that year, and it was an extraordinary, beautiful spring. It was extraordinary because Bill did not drink and did not want to drink. He was totally absorbed in his prospects, buoyed up, almost high on the change in himself and in his world. He told everyone he was not drinking and why, and for the first time Bill used the word "alcoholic" about himself, as if, by admitting it aloud, he believed he was somehow firming up his commitment.

And it was a beautiful, happy time in Brooklyn. At 182 Clinton Street they had not realized the tension they had been living under until that tension was lifted. Lois had her hair done. She took a day off and bought new dresses. Privately she reprimanded herself for doubting; she should have known, had more faith. She was younger than she had been in years, pretty and chic again.

But it wasn't only the Burnhams. People everywhere heard the news and were delighted. A man Bill hadn't spoken with in months called one afternoon to ask if he'd care to do a little moonlighting. It was an investigative job; he'd go with a group of engineers to the Pathé studios in Jersey and look over a new photographic process they were developing. The pay was quite good and Bill accepted.

On the way to Jersey, in the middle of May '32—a date that coincided almost to the day with the lowest point in our economic history—Bill knew he'd never felt better. Five weeks without booze, a corner had been turned, the long night was ending and he was free to make plans: possibly a trip with Lois, maybe even some sort of gift for Clark Burnham . . .

In Bound Brook, New Jersey, he and the engineers checked into a small hotel. After dinner a deck of cards was brought out, but Bill, although he was fascinated by all forms of stock market gambling, had no interest in cards. He sat at the side, read, kibitzed a little. After a time one of the men produced a jug of applejack, but no one was offended, no one even noticed when he shook his head and said no, he figured he'd had more booze than he needed for one lifetime.

The game continued. He sat and watched. The jug moved around the table. It was something special, the men insisted, this was real applejack, Jersey Lightning, and they held out the jug to him again. But again Bill shook his head and was amazed at how easy it was to refuse. He'd been right, he guessed, he had had more than he needed, and sitting at the side of the little room, he began to think back over just what he'd had in his thirty-seven years. The Bronx cocktail in New Bedford at the beginning, then brandies on the ship and the wines in France. It became a kind of game, listing them all, and he wondered if there was anything, any kind of alcohol he hadn't tasted in the long road between 1918 in New Bedford, and May 1932.

"Bill"—the jug was being held out to him again—"you ought to try it."

There was indeed one thing he'd never tasted. Jersey Lightning. He considered this. Then, "Why not?" he said. What harm could one taste do? He smiled, reached out for the jug and took a swig.

The men were right. There was nothing like it. He took another long, long swig. Then when the jug had gone around again and come back to him, he took another.

And it was then, that night, in that room in New Jersey, that he learned there was not, and never would be, such a thing as just one drink.

He had no memory of the rest of the night, of how long the card game went on, of getting to his room or going to bed. The next thing he knew, it was morning and the engineers had gone off to Pathé without him. His room was flooded with blinding sunlight. His head was spinning and he was sure he was going to be ill.

On the bureau across from his bed he could see a jug with an inch of applejack still at the bottom. He did not want to drink. He was still too close to last night to want the sharp raw taste of applejack, but he knew he would take it. He rose, staggered to the bureau, lifted the jug to his lips and, with great determination, swallowed what was left in one long gulp. But it did no good. The shakes were still there, worse than before. He rang for a bellboy, gave him ten dollars and ordered another crock of Lightning.

There must have been other calls to other bellboys, other jugs, other bottles. He never knew. He knew nothing until what turned out to be three days later. The room was dark again and as from a great distance he heard a bell ringing and gradually woke to the fact that it was a telephone. New York was calling. Mr. Wheeler. And Arthur Wheeler said what Bill knew he would say. He'd heard all about it. The contract was canceled.

The contract was canceled but there was something worse, something he had known in some far corner of his mind for three days now, and from which he'd been running—something he had done to himself and now could never undo.

He didn't remember getting back to Brooklyn, whether by bus, car or train, but he remembered Clinton Street and the dozens of eyes pinned on him as he stumbled along. There were voices too, but their words were far away and didn't reach him. At one point someone's arm was behind his back and as he let himself be guided, he clenched his jaw and tried to stop shaking, but he could no more stop the tremors racking his body than he could halt the waves or the terrible gray sick feeling that was making everything sway and shimmer before him.

Somehow he reached 182, but there everything suddenly went wrong: the light turned into blind, gray motes, the waves continued to pound all around him and now the steps, the door, the whole house seemed to be withdrawing into some vast roaring distance and only the little railing by the stairs rose and drew nearer with the waves. As he leaned forward to let his head rest on the railing, he realized that if he didn't lower himself to the steps, he would fall, and fall into a space that was opening out before him, huge and dark and every minute growing darker.

This was not the worst or even the longest drunk in his career, but more than anything that had happened, the experience with Jersey Lightning changed Bill's thinking as well as his picture of himself.

He could never again think of himself as a man of honor. His word was not his bond.

Now for the first time he drank simply to escape and to block from his mind what he had done. He was unemployed and unemployable, his life blown apart, and in the weeks that followed he felt no inner strength to reshape or formulate new plans. What he had done represented the antithesis of everything a man reared as he'd been reared consciously believed in.

Yet at the same time he felt a kind of personal hurt as though some outside force he could not see and could not label had betrayed him. This new notion of a force working outside himself began to intrigue him. He wondered if there indeed might be forces over which a man had no control. And with this thought there was an immediate and frightening corollary. By admitting that there could be forces more powerful than he, a door was opened to the idea that such forces might win out. They might conquer him, and with this came another secret terror—the terror of insanity. He could already be on his way to complete loss of control.

But he was still Bill Wilson, still a man of pride. Bill's pride, however, was of a special order. Throughout his life he was never proud of accomplishments. The fact that he had succeeded in a particular area meant little to him. His pride was based only on what he believed he could do—and for this reason perhaps he was always forced to find new challenges.

In the summer of '32 the challenge was alcohol. He was going to prove he could control his drinking, and by doing this he would repudiate what everyone had been trying to drive home to him—namely, that he could *never*, with any safety, take a drink. He managed to stay sober for weeks, through fear and through constant vigilance. Then—it was the old pattern—he would try just a few, and having started, nothing could stop him.

Still it was his challenge, he would find his way of mastering it. When he failed now, when he wound up passed out, unable to get home alone, he saw it as bad luck—he'd forgotten to eat before he drank, or his drinks had been spiked, or he'd gulped them too fast. More and more it was due to some specific factor outside himself.

In time his thinking about powers greater than the individual began to color his views on all sorts of subjects. In the winter of '32 there was a sense of foreboding everywhere in America. One out of every four workers was unemployed. Yet even the fear of hunger wasn't always drawing men closer. We were becoming a nation of strangers, and the faces Bill noticed on bread lines were no longer bewildered; they were angry, desperate faces. People listened to radios, they heard the news and they were perhaps better informed than ever before about the great events of the world, but these were events they could neither understand nor control. And as he walked the streets, Bill was filled with a sense of men biding their time, waiting for a leader, and the sort of leader who might emerge to guide them was something that troubled him profoundly. For Bill had been brought up by Fayette Griffith to carry steadily in his mind an image of independent democracy, and this was a legacy that, drunk or sober, he could not easily forget.*

But now even Fayette's words seemed quaint and far in the past. And as he pondered these matters wandering alone through Brooklyn or sitting in the little back bar of the delicatessen, Bill tried to accept the fact that he lived in a world where dreams die or are betrayed, just as with most of us love must die, or in some rare cases like his Lois—refuses to die.

But love was a thought he was becoming adept at putting from his mind. Whenever a picture of Lois threatened, when an image of her going off to work and remembering to leave a few dollars on the bureau rose before him, he knew the trick of immediately ordering another drink, concentrating on another subject, or making a joke if there was someone near. By now their relationship had passed through every phase classic to the drunk and his devoted wife: uncontrolled fury, despair, resignation. There had been times when, remembering how alive and beautiful she had been at the start, he literally could not accept what he had done. Yet they had always gone on, Lois sustained by some passion to survive and master every situation. He knew that she had probably, and often, turned to him with needs he could not satisfy, just as he had gone to her with hungers she could

* Curiously, when a leader did appear on the scene, FDR, Bill opposed him vigorously. Perhaps this was a holdover from the old Vermont belief that nature should be allowed to take its course, and the less governmental interference the better. Shortly after Roosevelt's inaugural in March 1933, Bill began a correspondence with the White House. A study of these letters gives a remarkable picture of alcoholic progression during the course of a single evening. Often they start off lucidly, respectfully, and are extremely well expressed, but as they continue they turn into gibberish and quite often are peppered with four-letter words. Bill would tear these up or crumple them into a ball and toss them in a basket. Lois would retrieve them, put them together with sticky tape and save them. When, forty years later, she was asked why she had done this, her only answer was that she knew they must be of value. Such was her faith even then in Bill's importance.

not satisfy, could not even sense. Above all he remembered the look when he'd failed again, the look that told him these hurts were nothing new, that they were as old as her love for him. Then somehow their positions had shifted and she had begun to represent authority. There were times—usually after a horrendous fight—when she seemed to understand nothing and control everything, and he felt on these mornings that the very essence of himself was threatened, and that the atmosphere at home had become that of an armed camp—two people watching, waiting to see what the other's next move would be. Now, in the winter of '33, they had arrived at a quiet period. There was solicitude and kindness. Lois treated him almost as if he were an invalid, gently encouraging him, and both of them always avoided any mention of what was really wrong.

Bill was living and doing his thinking in a strange twilight area between fantasy and fact, between fear and loneliness. After a drinking spree and the emotional beating that always followed, he was a man half awake, his mind so befogged that only a couple of quick shots could clarify his thoughts; or, as sometimes happened, a sudden inexplicable outburst of rage would brush away the confusion and make him, for the moment at least, wildly articulate about what he believed was taking place, about the murder of the dream.

Yet even his deep bitterness at what he saw happening around him was nothing compared to his despair when, after weeks of total sobriety, he'd find himself lost in a wild drunken haze, at dawn, stretched out in the vestibule, bloodied, with no memory of how it had happened. Lois would have to get him into the house and up the stairs to bed. Fortunately Dr. Burnham had remarried early in '33 and had moved from 182, so there was no one except Lois to witness these scenes—the pitiful bravado, the childlike attempt to explain how it had occurred, the unspoken plea that she sense his unbearable humiliation. For one thing must be made clear. At this point, while Bill's view of the world was undergoing such a change, he was involved as he had never been before with his own inner struggle, his battle to master alcohol.

Once he grew quite encouraged because he thought he had recognized a pattern in the way he handled challenges. He saw that he had a tendency to relax after staying on the wagon for a time, to think that he had it made. In a way staying sober destroyed the challenge. He had done it so it no longer represented anything to be proud of. His pride now needed to believe he could accomplish something that was more demanding, that implied more of a risk—now he needed to prove to himself that he could handle a few drinks.

Yet a pride—if that is what it was—that constantly needed to be tested was close to suicidal. To try and to fail a few times might be one thing, but to go on again and again with all the odds against you was a kind of insanity.

Still he tried. When Leonard Strong insisted that he was in such poor physical shape he had no resistance, even though he knew Leonard and Dorothy were hard pressed he allowed them to put him in a hospital not once but several times, until finally they had no choice but to ask Dr. Emily for some financial help. He underwent the regulation detoxification, took vitamins and listened to the doctor's advice about will power.

When Lois suggested that he get away from the city and spend some time in Vermont, he went to a farm the Strongs owned near Green River junction. He would be up at dawn, chopping wood, tending the farm, but it took no more than a chance meeting with a local fisherman who just happened to have a flask, and the good intentions, the months of outdoor living, went for nothing.

He studied everything written on the subject of alcohol, all the self-help books of the period. He even spent hours reading Mary Baker Eddy—perhaps he misread her—but much of *Science and Health* fascinated him. He knew, however, that in the end Christian Science could work only if he had faith, and faith, he had decided, was not something that could be reached by thinking alone.

He was on a subway going back to Brooklyn one night—and what was shocking about this experience was that he had had nothing to drink that day and knew he was completely sober. The car was almost empty, but across from him sat a father, a mother and three young boys. They sat quietly, huddled together, and in one glance Bill felt he knew their story. There was about them not only a look of poverty and of silent pride: he saw in their pale, thin faces, in their large, dull, staring eyes, the unmistakable look of hunger. He knew they were in the subway not because they were going anywhere, but because it was dry and relatively warm.

There was one other passenger, an elderly priest sitting near Bill, but Bill could not draw his eyes from the family, from the softly whimpering boys. Then, as the train rattled on through the tunnel, he saw that the mother had unbuttoned her blouse and was nursing one of the children, a child he would have thought too old for breast-feeding. Immediately he dropped his eyes and slowly turned and looked at the priest. The priest had obviously been watching the family too. Now their eyes met and, uncannily, he appeared to be reading Bill's thoughts. But what was even more startling was the soft, almost beatific smile that moved across his face. Then, in a voice Bill was never to forget, he said quietly, "Do not worry, God will provide."

Suddenly Bill was on his feet. "When?" He towered above the priest. "What God?" he demanded. "And what will he provide?" He was like someone possessed, his words pouring out with a fury completely beyond his control.

The pious shit this man was passing out, asking these decent people to believe, didn't come from any faith, from any caring, and how, he wanted to know, could a God of love, a God who cared, watch innocent children starving? Then, having found himself tricked into using the priest's vocabulary, his fury mounted. He didn't believe in his God, he declared, or in his

189

God's begotten son. They were not facts. Heaven and hell were not facts. He and his church were making people believe through fear, and medieval superstition, and he gestured toward the family, poor, suffering bastards who were afraid not to believe.

He had never felt such cold hatred as he felt at that moment, and when the train stopped at the next station and he got off, he was embarrassed but he couldn't be sorry, and the mood didn't lessen as he walked along. There was also a kind of righteousness in his emotion. He might be a poor sinner, he might have done everything he'd sworn he would never do, he might not be a man of honor, but God damn it, he refused to be solaced by religious cant or ever to believe anything his rational mind could not accept.

In a way, it represented a part of himself, a part of his pride. He was, he told himself, and he always had been, a seeker after facts, after truth. Only facts, looking at facts, could save anything, and he'd rather go on holding that belief than accept the soft comfort of religion.

6

Of those few who still tried to talk and reason with Bill in this period—doctors, members of the family—only one man spoke to his condition, Dr. William Silkworth. The Silkworth experience must be recorded. It was recorded permanently in Bill's mind and is part of his story.

Four times in 1933–34, Bill was a patient at Towns Hospital, a drying-out establishment on Central Park West, and it was probably during his second visit that he had his first talk with Dr. Silkworth. What was unique about this interview was that the doctor showed no condescension. He was a medical man speaking to a patient he knew to be very ill. He made no bones about this. And Bill felt that this slight little man with compassionate blue eyes peering out from beneath a shock of pure white hair was speaking from profound scientific knowledge. During their initial encounter Silkworth used two phrases which Bill latched on to instantly and recognized as indisputable medical facts. The doctor said that Bill's drinking had become an obsession that condemned him to drink against his will. There was no question in his mind that Bill wanted to stop, but there was an additional complication: he had become physically allergic to alcohol, his body could no longer tolerate it—hence his hangovers, his strange mental deviations. Their job, and he used

191

the word "their," was to break the obsession. He didn't theorize, he didn't preach; he presented Bill with this double-pronged bind.

Bill's first reaction was remarkable. Instead of being depressed, he experienced an immense, indescribable relief. He had found someone who understood him, and he now believed he understood himself. And with such a man as Silkworth, who made a patient feel that his recovery mattered tremendously to them both, he was convinced that they could handle it.

When he saw Lois again the change in him was immediately apparent. The seeker after truth had been presented with empirical, scientific fact which he could not and did not want to deny. What was more, he was filled with hope, and he was learning that hope was the first requisite of courage.

He stayed at Towns until he believed the poison was completely removed from his body, his mind and his emotions. The homecoming at Clinton Street was an evening such as they had not known for years, the house filled with flowers, all the foods Bill loved to eat. Lois had bought little tricks, gags and jokes, even a miniature golf green so Bill could practice putting across the parlor, and there were plans for trips, they'd go hiking again. Most important of all, he'd keep in touch with Silkworth, who had told him he didn't know if there were deep psychological problems that caused alcoholism but was convinced that alcohol caused psychological problems. Together they would go into those.

This was it. Of that they were absolutely sure. In their wild high hopes they could be lovers again. He could be a man again.

Even years later, no matter how hard he tried, Bill could not remember the circumstances of his next drunk, or even when it started, whether it was a month or a couple of weeks after leaving Towns. He knew only that it was one of his worst and one that seemingly was impossible to stop.

In fact, his memories of this entire period, from '33 until about

192

the end of '34, were totally disordered. Yet strangely he remembered the shameful debilitating weakness, the black terror that would suddenly engulf him, when, for example, he was trying to think, to clear his mind. Coming out of nowhere, a small, cold ball of fear would start in his stomach, then it would surge up and spread so that he could feel its chill in the marrow of his being, until the fact of his terror blocked out any other thought and only a drink could soften it or perhaps enable him to sleep for a while. Then morning, Lois leaving for work, and the fear of other fears taking over the day. For the rest of his life Bill could relive those mornings with what seemed total emotional recall.

Now there were fewer and fewer things he would not bring himself to do for a drink. It was almost as though he felt a need to strike every item from the list of nevers. He begged drinks now, and did it, as others said, shamelessly, which of course was the impression he tried to give, but the truth was that some bit of him withered every time he had to beg.

He stole, at first just a few bills from Lois's purse when he needed to buy a fifth of gin. Then he began taking small objects from the house to a pawnshop on Atlantic Avenue. He became cagey, conniving, and soon he did not even cringe when he was called an out-and-out liar.

Also at this time he was convinced he was the only man alive with this problem.

His moral feelings had no anchorage now and daily he watched his physical health disintegrating. He ate very little. For two or three days after a drunk he literally could hold nothing on his stomach and when he had to look in a mirror he saw only his unsmiling grin and the knobby skull that seemed to be waiting beneath his tight, pale flesh.

Still he continued drinking, often against his will now, often starting out toward a bar saying, "I won't go in. I won't," knowing with every step he took that he would go in. And this evil pendulum continued to rule his life on into the summer of '34.

Drunk, sober, sober, drunk, days of tenuous sobriety, days of blacked-out drunkenness, a man forever driven and forever blocked.

In July he was put into Towns Hospital again, and again there was a memorable session with Silkworth. But this time the interview was held in a small office on the ground floor and it was between Lois and the doctor. Bill was upstairs in bed. When, however, he learned what had been said—and when later he learned more of the doctor's history and got to know him as a man—the cruel reality of what took place that hot summer evening became so vivid, so horrifying, that forever after he could believe that he himself had been there, hearing and watching them both.

To the doctor these interviews had become very much of a type, with the reaction of the wife often as baffling as the drunkenness of the patient upstairs: gallant women always believing he had some magic words that could bring their lives together into one piece, when actually the words he had to speak would lead them into another, deeper labyrinth. Women who went on hoping when there was no cause for hope. They were the strongest people God ever made. Yet he did not overlook the threat they represented. He knew they might be part of the cause and, if not that, that they often went on feeding the flames of destruction—and all of it in the name of love. They needed miracles to save them, and who could furnish miracles now?

As he fumbled with his papers, Dr. Silkworth felt painfully aware of his inadequacies. For one thing he never knew how to begin, how to present the words that could signify the total failure of all a wife had worked and prayed for, for ten, fifteen years. But there was no escaping the intense blue eyes that looked up at him that evening, or the questions Lois forced herself to ask—"Why? What causes it?"—questions he knew had been asked since the beginning of time. Perhaps the A.M.A. was right, such obsessive drinking was a moral weakness, a defect of character, and as such should not be the concern of medical men.

"What," she asked, "do we do? Where do we go now?" And he answered as gently and as truthfully as he could: He had hoped that Bill might prove one of the exceptions, one of his few successes, because of his real desire to stop, because of his character, his intelligence. But he saw now that the obsession was too deep to overcome and the physical effects were too severe. He was already showing signs of brain damage, and if Bill went on in the same way they would have to fear for his sanity.

"And"—Lois never took her eyes from him—"and what does that mean exactly?"

"It means you will have to confine him, lock him up somewhere if he is to remain sane. He cannot go on for another year. . . ."

When he left Towns Hospital Bill had been told some of Silkworth's prognosis, in part by Lois, in part by the doctor himself. At any rate, it was enough to frighten him into staying sober for a period of weeks, perhaps for more than a month—again his memory was not too clear.

The fact that this medical man whom he respected had warned of brain damage placed a solid foundation beneath the terrible suspicion he'd been living with for years, and from now on the thought was never far from his mind. In addition, the idea that Lois and Silkworth could actually have discussed the possibility of incarceration brought on such terrors and caused such unbearable physical tension that he was forced to reach out for the only relief he knew.

When he was a boy his grandfather had driven him past the state asylum in Brattleboro, a large red brick building by the river. It was midday, he remembered, the exercise hour, and they had drawn up at the side of the road to watch the patients through a metal fence. There had been rows of unpainted park benches on which the guards sat, as the inmates stumbled, shuffled around and around, bumped into one another, or just stood mumbling to no one, or staring out across the trodden yard with huge blank eyes. Bill noticed several who kept trying to pull their robes up over their heads as if they wanted to hide, or block out the sun. One old lady—though they all seemed ageless to Bill—his grandfather said, came from East Dorset. She was a schizophrenic and no one had visited her for ten years. Another patient had his arms strapped to his sides because if he wasn't strapped, he tried to play with himself.

Whenever he was alone now, a picture of those faces would flash across his mind, and they were as clear as if they were standing across the room. He could see the haunted eyes, even the spittle on the chin.

Bill was alone now most of the time, because Lois had to leave each morning by eight and didn't get home till after six. In the past years he'd watched his wife going off to a series of jobs, mostly at Macy's. Then she'd taken a leave of absence to go with him to Vermont. Now, in the early fall of '34, she was working in the drapery department of Loesser's in Brooklyn.

Most mornings he didn't mind seeing her go. He'd even get up and have coffee with her. Then, when she'd close the door behind her, there was always a kind of relief, a kind of excitement, too, in the empty house—a child with the whole place to himself: he could do whatever he wanted. But some mornings, from what he knew were the best of intentions, Lois would turn in the bedroom doorway and smile lovingly and say, "Why don't you just go back to sleep?" as if to imply, Bill, you don't have to get up for anything.

The best of intentions, but how could she, how could anyone, say it? Those words would fill him with a wild rage for which there seemed no possible outlet, and often on such days he'd stay in his bathrobe well into the afternoon. "You don't have to get up for anything."

First off, after knowing she was gone and that it was safe, she wouldn't be back because she had forgotten something, he would make a systematic check of his supplies. He had bottles, half bottles, pints stashed away in every part of the house—in the coalbin by the furnace, behind certain books on the library shelves, underneath his shirts. Whether it was a day when he was drinking or one when he was coming off a drunk, he had to know a bottle was there, had to actually feel the cool glass against his fingers. For the fear of being without a drink in case he had to have one and the challenge of always keeping one at hand was becoming as obsessive as his terror of the "crazy house."

His world was gradually narrowing, and he was acutely aware of it, but he made few objections. In the evening he no longer had to excuse himself. He had only to keep peace with Lois and handle the problems of the day, and each day seemed to have enough of these.

His concept of self was narrowing, too, as he grew more conscious of the forces operating beyond his control.

One problem he never seemed to solve was when to get up, when to go outside. If he rose and left the house with Lois, the streets were filled with men and women hurrying along to their jobs, all seeming very important. He didn't belong with them. If he waited and went out at noon, he seemed to see nothing but idle old men or nursemaids airing babies. He belonged nowhere.

Fortunately—and he knew this was a true blessing, for without it he would have been completely lost—a visit to a bar or a few drinks of gin at home could still restore him, could still give him that sense of exaltation and the feeling that he was still an authentic part of life. That this happened now in more and more disreputable dives and that nothing ever came from these fine feelings—he indeed seemed to be living in a kind of gray, inane vacuum—he also recognized as true. But he was careful

197

to avoid anyone who might point it out. If he happened to run into an old acquaintance from Wall Street, he was ready with excuses for hurrying on. If, entering a bar, he sensed there might be someone there who'd recognize him, he'd immediately turn and move on to another place. And all of this, he told himself, was because he was now in his natural state, what he had started out to be, a complete loner, when in reality he was a man with an almost desperate need for any kind of friendship.

On Armistice Day 1934, there was no problem about when to get up or when to leave the house. It was a handsome, crisp fall day and Bill had had nothing to drink for some time—days, weeks, it no longer mattered. He felt fine and decided he wanted to go to Staten Island and play a few rounds of golf.

After getting off the ferry at St. George, he boarded a bus and found himself sitting beside a pleasant enough man who was carrying a target rifle. They fell into easy conversation, and Bill talked about his old Remington. Halfway across the island and still a good distance from the golf course, their bus suddenly broke down, and to kill time they went together into a nearby restaurant. Bill's new friend wanted a drink but Bill said no and ordered a ginger ale. In fact, he said a great deal more than no. He explained that he was an alcoholic and gave a brief outline of his history; he even described Silkworth's theory of an obsession combined with an allergy, and was quite pleased that he'd made his points so clearly.

It was past noon when a substitute bus picked them up and carried them on to the golf course. By now they figured it was lunchtime and, still together, they went into the Club Inn, a large, congenial spot that was already filling up with the holiday crowd. In a corner by the bar a group of early drinkers were gathered round a piano singing happily but not too obtrusively. While his friend with the gun ordered a Scotch, Bill again asked for a ginger ale. He liked the place—it had an atmosphere he understood and could be comfortable in—but in a few moments a large, hearty bartender placed two Scotches before them. "On the house," he announced in a cheery Irish brogue. "It's Armistice Day. Drink 'em up, lads." And Bill reached out for the Scotch.

As he did he was aware of his friend staring at him. "After what you've told me," he said, "if you drink that you have to be insane."

Bill returned his look. "I am," he said.

He did not know what happened to his friend after that—he must have got lost in the crowd—but Bill stayed on at the bar. In time the singers quieted down and let a young fellow who'd been playing their accompaniment move into a medley of World War melodies—"Mademoiselle from Armentières," "Over There," "A Long, Long Trail"—and with every new song the fellow played, Bill's mind drifted farther back to other times, other places.

It had been a different world then, and he a different man. There had been nothing unusual in having drinks handed out then, just because of who he was, what he represented—in France, in little cafés with other officers; even when they first got back to the States. What they represented had been something noble, something everyone believed in.

Men of his generation, men of good will, had answered a call, and in doing this they had turned back a night of barbarism that might have lasted a thousand years had they failed. They knew it and the world knew it, and for a time the simple problem of survival had been common to all men everywhere. *But we were the men of action then and the world looked to us. And when the great killing was over, the world still turned to us, and in that moment anything and everything was possible. Doors could have been opened for all mankind, people in all nations could have moved into a larger destiny. There had, in that brief moment, been a chance.*

But then this too had ended. America turned her back on the world's hope. The League was someone else's business. We handed it over to the confused, empty men in Washington. We were too busy getting back to normalcy, too busy making a buck. And with this had come the total breakdown. Individuals had become hopeless, helpless to do anything but watch. Caught up in a dream of bigness, they took freedom for granted.

Bill at least had seen what was happening; at least he had looked at the cause, at the heart of our defeat, our failure. He had not been fooled. He had watched a country moving a century out of place.

As these thoughts took shape, fed and inflamed by the beautiful glow of the Scotch the bartender kept serving, he sat on a stool talking to no one, staring straight ahead at a small section of mirror he could just make out between the even row of bottles behind the bar. He studied his own face in the mirror and as he did a simple question, then a series of rapid-fire questions, shot across his mind. Who? Who did all this? Not the presidents of banks, not the chairmen of boards. And who chased the buck? Who saw the world as a great competitive arena and had to win at any cost, succeed by whatever standards prevailed? Who had to be the number-one man and show them all? Who was the enemy of the dream?

He sat hypnotized, staring into the patch of mirror, his jaw set. His eyes sparked back into his own as the answer came. It was he who had stepped aside. He, Bill Wilson, was the enemy!

And it was that one word that finally touched off the panic button.

Always, even as a small boy in Sunday school, he had been taught that one must forgive, even try to love, the enemy, as one did unto the least of these—and this he had believed. But, as he struggled to look at the fact that he himself was the enemy, he found no loving, no hint of forgiveness. He felt a total reversal of all he'd been taught. There was no question now of acceptance, of love or charity or forgiveness. He thought only of ways to hide the fact, hide this man from the world and from himself.

The panic that seized him as he stumbled from the bar, somehow found a bus, the ferry and subway back to Brooklyn, could be described in many ways, but for Bill it was the panic of a man driving a car, believing he has control of the vehicle, then discovering the car has run away with him. Any pressure on the brakes, anything his conscious mind can think to do, only makes the car go more wildly out of control.

In some way he reached 182, but there he stopped, unable even to ring the bell. His body had been goaded into action, but his mind could no longer function. He dropped to his knees, stretched himself out and slept all night in the vestibule.

Lois found him there when she left for work in the morning.

7

A man with an active and naturally curious mind who suddenly finds himself a recluse can be distracted by any living thing. A group of boys playing in the street, even a dog stopping to sniff a tree, can rivet his attention. Ever since his night on Staten Island Bill had been in total seclusion, venturing out only to replenish his supplies, then sitting for hours at a kitchen table, alone with a fifth of gin. For this reason, perhaps, he experienced an extraordinary lift when, late in November, Ebby Thacher phoned and said he'd like to stop by. Immediately Bill was a kid again, wildly excited by the prospect of a session with his old friend.

To Bill, Ebby Thacher had always been a rare one. A man with an inexhaustible capacity, Ebby had not only been thrown out of bars and out of hotels, he'd been asked not to return to certain cities. Still, in the years since Bill first knew him at Burr and Burton, nothing had downed his verve. Bill had sometimes envied Ebby, wondering what it would be like to play in his league, with his freedoms and the glorious irresponsibility of the moneyed drunk. But no one could harbor ill feeling toward Ebby; even now, in his early forties, growing a little heavy, a little soft, somehow he'd preserved his youthful attitude, as if he'd managed to pickle in booze his boyish outlook on life. It was this, plus his smile and the straightforward kindness in his eyes, that always drew people to him.

As Bill tidied the kitchen and brought out a fresh bottle of gin, he began to go over some of the times, some of the great laughs they had shared. It had been well over a year since he'd seen Ebby, but he'd heard the rumors. One of these was that his family, discouraged by his recent escapades, had threatened to lock him up, but Bill was sure this hadn't happened. As he found two tall glasses and placed them beside the gin, he remembered a weekend in '29. He'd been on the road that year and had planned to spend a few nights with the Thachers in Albany, but when he and Ebby learned that the town of Manchester was constructing an airfield which was scheduled to open in a few weeks, there was nothing for it: they must charter a plane, fly up that very afternoon to test the field, and thereby become the first men ever to land in Manchester. And this they did. Without much effort they located an alcoholic young pilot who was all for the idea, and they sent word that they were on their way.

It was quite a flight. They were well equipped with flasks, which kept passing from Ebby to the pilot to Bill. It was quite a flight in the view of the townspeople too. News of their imminent arrival had spread everywhere. A delegation had been organized to greet them and they'd even called out the high school band. All these good people stood waiting at the edge of the unfinished field to watch the approach and honor the historic event.

At first they appeared to be dead on course, but then they veered off and, after grazing the pines on the side of Mount Equinox, dipped several times, circled and finally came to a stop near a large open ditch. The band immediately struck up, the official delegation rushed forward, and Bill and Ebby realized that it was up to them to do something befitting such an occasion. Unfortunately they were in no condition to do anything. Somehow they managed to slide out of the cockpit, but the moment their feet touched ground they fell forward, and there they both lay, spread out and immobile, the first passengers to alight in Manchester, Vermont.

Of course they had sent letters of apology to the town, even attempts at an explanation, but they'd had some laughs about it too, and in memory it remained a warm and happy time.

The last of Ebby's capers Bill had heard about concerned his driving off the road and through a small frame house. He'd been in his open touring car that afternoon and it hadn't stopped as it plowed its way through the parlor. Indeed, it did not come to a halt until it was in the middle of the kitchen. There Ebby stepped out and, addressing a completely dumbstruck old couple, he asked if he might have a cup of coffee with just a little cream and only one sugar.

It would be good to see such a character again. Bill hurried toward the stairs, deciding he'd shave for this reunion, he'd even get out of his pajamas and put on a shirt and a pair of pants.

At the foot of the stairs his eye happened to fall on a large, folded-over mattress at the side of the hall. In an instant—it was as though a thundercloud had passed across the sun—all light disappeared from the hall. The night before last, Lois had helped him carry the mattress down to the first floor, and for two nights he'd tried to sleep down here because she had been afraid that if he stayed upstairs he might try to throw himself out a window.

He stood looking down at the mattress, one hand resting on the stair rail, feeling a pale weakness rising from his knees. Suddenly his whole body was swept by a wave of panic and deep, indescribable shame as he remembered every detail of those nights.

Until Staten Island—until the realization that he himself was the enemy of all he had thought he believed in, that he himself was everything he had vowed he would never be—booze had been his friend. No matter what happened, he'd always known that if he took enough and kept on taking it, booze would block out anything and finally bring him a kind of glorious dark oblivion. But since that night the opposite had been true. Now not even alcohol could help him. And knowing this had created a panic all its own.

Now at night, as it grew later, as he drank more and more, even sneaking a bottle upstairs to place under his side of the bed, so that it would be there and he could nip throughout the night, instead of calming him, it only seemed to make him more awake. Instead of blocking out memories, it opened doors so that all manner of horrors, fears and doubts were free to enter and sweep through his reeling brain.

Only it wasn't his brain now—that was the hell. As he lay stretched out beside Lois, as the room grew darker and he listened to her even breathing, as he prayed for sleep, just a snatch of sleep, and no sleep came, he was tortured with new terrors that rose from subconscious depths over which he seemed to have no control. These demons had no connection with conscious thinking. They were the fears of a timid child he didn't know or recognize, and did not want to know: a bird shot down by a .22 rifle flapped its wings in agony beside him on the bed; a circle of schoolboys laughed down at an object he couldn't see, and laughed so wildly, so uproariously, he had to bury his head in the pillow to shut them out; when he looked up again they were no longer boys, but guards in an asylum, and they went on laughing, even when the walls behind them became infested with snakes and long dark wormy things he could not place and could not make go away. Even when he reached under the bed, found the bottle and took another swig, still the sound of crazy laughter went on and on.

At Towns he'd heard other men, other drunks, describe their d.t.'s as wild hallucinations that took over and became the only reality. They said there was nothing you could do. But there had to be something, something a man could do.

Often in the past when he had not been able to sleep, Lois, as if sensing it, had stirred beside him, reached out a hand and placed it on his shoulder, and then she had drawn him to her, taken his head in her arms and rocked him against her breast like a baby—the baby he knew he had become—and then after a time they had made love. But now even this no longer worked.

Suddenly his whole body would seem to freeze, to shrivel at the thought of how long this had been the case. A man with no job, a man completely dependent on a wife, who would not—could not—make love to that wife, was an abomination to life.

Unable to think of this, unable not to think and thereby give himself over to the demons that hovered in the darkness ready to pounce if he relaxed his mind, he would pull himself out of bed and stumble to the window, wondering if all desires had left him, if he ever would desire anyone again, searching for some answer, some way out, some way to sleep, to sleep now and forever.

At one such time, two nights before, when he stood at the window gazing down into the empty street, his body trembling, covered with sweat, Lois had awakened, seen him and, as if reading a thought before he actually reached that thought, asked him to help her carry the mattress down to the ground floor.

Waiting for Ebby, he stared at the mattress. Then he turned suddenly, went back into the kitchen and poured himself a drink. He swallowed the gin straight, screwed the top back on the bottle, then rubbed the back of his hand across his mouth and shook his head, filled once again with the sensation he'd been aware of often in the last two weeks, the sensation that over everything, behind the fears and humiliation, there was a sense of movement now, a blind tumbling forward of everyone and everything.

If once life had seemed a crazy merry-go-round, now he knew it was a high greased slide, going straight down, and as he pictured the slide, he also knew there was nothing he could do about it. His descent would proceed rapidly, inexorably.

He could not live if he went on drinking. He could not stop drinking. And he was terrified at the thought of death.

He turned and again started upstairs. Possibly—it was a slim hope, but a hope, and he would cling to it as he tried to shave and not cut himself with the razor—possibly if he drank with Ebby, with someone he knew and trusted, if he could laugh again, it might somehow make the difference. Afterward he might, he just might sleep again.

As soon as he opened the door for Ebby he knew something about him was different, but it took several minutes to understand what it was. Ebby was sober.

Ebby Thacher was in New York and he was cold sober. It was an unheard-of situation. And yet, when Bill led him into the kitchen and pointed to the bottle and glasses lined up before them, Ebby shook his head.

"No?" Bill studied him.

"No."

"Why not?"

Then Ebby answered and Bill was never to forget his answer. "I don't need it anymore."

It was a shock. Along with that it was a disappointment, a terrible letdown. Bill tried to cover his reaction with a little joke as they sat at the table and he filled just one glass. All the more for him, he said. They both laughed, but it was clearly not a subject a man could pass over.

"What's this mean?" he asked finally. "What's it all about?"

Ebby answered very simply and very directly. "You see, I've got religion."

At first Bill wasn't sure he'd heard him, but in the silence that followed, when he looked into Ebby's eyes, he knew that he had heard and had heard correctly. "Well . . ." he mumbled, and he realized as he did that he was feeling all sorts of conflicting emotions. He was startled and he was certainly as uncomfortable at the mention of the word as he was at finding himself drinking alone. He felt not exactly insulted, but embarrassed and somehow strangely betrayed.

"What brand of religion have you got?" he asked, and Ebby smiled and said he didn't think it had any special brand name.

207

He'd simply fallen in with a group of people, wonderful people, the Oxford Group. Maybe Bill had heard of them.

Bill nodded. He vaguely remembered having heard of them, but it was his impression that they were a bunch of Christers, rich folks mostly, all very chic and high-minded, so he said nothing and let Ebby go on. Ebby said that when he'd been arrested on one of his sprees three men from the group had come to his rescue. They'd talked to the judge and promised to work with him. . . .

As Ebby continued about the group and about his own history, Bill found himself listening almost as two men, one nodding, trying to appear interested, the other sitting back making comments to himself. It seemed they'd started off on the Princeton campus, but then had moved on to Oxford—so he'd been right, it was a lot of fancy Ivy League nonsense—then they had worked for a time in South Africa, where they discovered that many of their precepts, such as taking stock of oneself, confessing one's defects and being willing to make restitution, were truly international. . . . These words were merely words to Bill now. He would have thought Ebby Thacher the last man on earth to be taken in by such easy salvation.

Then Ebby smiled a little apologetically and said he guessed Bill would gag at this, but the group had asked him to pray to whatever God he believed there might be.

It wasn't that Bill gagged; it was more as though when Ebby said this, a door closed between them and for the next few minutes he literally did not hear what his friend was saying. Then he began picking up half thoughts, fragments of sentences. . . . As soon as he'd tried praying, and keeping an open mind about it . . . his drinking problem had been lifted from him. . . .

It had nothing to do with being on the wagon, he said; that had always been a struggle. When he succeeded for a few days, he'd felt noble and puffed up about it, and when he failed he felt—Ebby paused, then he went on: He guessed he didn't have to tell Bill; Bill knew about the hells.

As he said this their eyes met and held. And in that moment there was no judgment, no opinion even. They were two drunks looking at each other with total understanding. In those few seconds each had moved from collecting and assessing information about the other to a true communion. Ebby might have been a clown, but he was also a drunk and when he used the word "hell" they both understood as no man who had not been there would ever understand.

After that nothing Ebby could say would block out or even veil that contact, that thing that had existed between them, that light that had shown for a moment. And Bill did find much that Ebby said extremely hard to take. Still he listened.

This wasn't like being on the wagon at all, Ebby insisted, because now he felt completely released from his desire to drink. The result was that he had not had, nor had he wanted, a drink in months.

It was simply a matter of admitting you were licked, he said, of throwing in the sponge and finally accepting the fact that booze was more powerful than you. Then—and if this was by chance or the conscious result of a well thought out plan, Bill never knew—instead of using the word "God" again, Ebby began speaking of "another power," a "higher power." And as he did, Bill was no longer pretending to listen; his full attention had been won.

It was actually much more than his attention he was giving now, for as Ebby spoke of powers that existed beyond the individual, Bill experienced a very definite and a very curious physical reaction. As he leaned forward in his chair, he felt a chill run up his arm, and suddenly he was listening not so much to what Ebby was saying, but *for* something, some intimation beyond his words, and he was filled with a strange sense of expectancy, as if he was drawing nearer, hovering very close to some new understanding, some further dimension of perception or a higher state of consciousness than any he had so far known. He was sure he had had this same feeling before, this sense of approaching a truer reality, but at the moment he could not place it.

And at that moment Ebby stood up.

Had Ebby by some deep intuition guessed at and then understood Bill's despair? Had some sixth sense been responsible for the words he had used? Is that why he had gone on despite what he must have recognized as Bill's skepticism? And did that same intuition guide him now to say he was sorry, he must be getting back to Manhattan, but that he would like to call again? Whatever his motivations and despite the fact that he had been there such a short time, with no further ado, with no preaching or evangelizing, having planted what he hoped might be a seed, Ebby picked up his hat and was gone.

Just as earlier Bill had seen himself as two men, one participating, the other sitting back silently and commenting, now alone in the kitchen this strange dichotomy continued. Part of him kept remembering the look of Ebby and somewhere in this there was an implication of hope such as he'd not felt in months. But another part kept resisting, dismissing almost everything that had been said.

For all Ebby's efforts to make his group sound different, its religion unconventional, when you looked at what he had been giving out it was nothing new. There was nothing novel in knowing thyself, in admitting you were hopeless and confessing sins or making amends. And up to a point he could see that this made sense, psychologically speaking—obviously it was working for Ebby—but if in the end it all depended on the God bit, and giving oneself over to that, it had to be the same old malarkey. And yet . . .

And yet Ebby Thacher was sober.

He stayed in the kitchen and alone drank on into the night, and the debate continued, the seesawing back and forth from hope to total rejection of all he'd been offered.

If only Ebby had said more about forces that operated beyond an individual's control, or even about powers greater than oneself, he was sure he would have gone along with him. But when he put the emphasis on prayer and some kind of divine guidance that had freed him, it sounded like all the sentimental garbage religious nuts handed out on the street. Brooklyn was filled with wild-eyed fanatics who were always passing out pamphlets haranguing people to come to Jesus and renounce the world. But if you read their tracts you saw they had little to offer in exchange for this world except some pious pap no rational man could ever accept.

In the end—and this inner argument was to go on well beyond one night; for days he remembered Ebby everywhere he went and remembered that he was in New York and sober, while he, Bill, was once again on his way to getting soused; he remembered the clarity in Ebby's eyes and that look that had passed between them when they had wordlessly confessed the hell their lives had been—still, in the end, there was this one point he could not swallow. Ebby was asking him to accept something his thinking mind had to reject. The very idea of a personal God, a Great Somebody, who looked after things and cared about each little sparrow, each shot of gin he swallowed, this was intellectually insulting. And he resented it.

His resentments mounted and seemed to come to a peak when Ebby phoned again a few days later and said he would like to stop by with a friend from his group.

The man he chose to bring along was Shep Cornell. This was a mistake. Cornell was handsome, well built and well born, a young fellow whom Bill immediately pegged as a socialite. He was cheery and outgoing and ready to confess to having had quite a drinking career himself. But about this Bill had his doubts. As a drunk he was sure Cornell was a pantywaist, a man who'd probably gone wild one night on too many sherries at a Junior League cotillion, but God knew he was sober now and God knew they both seemed to be enjoying their sobriety. They talked incessantly, discussed the serenity of their new life and their new-found sense of purpose. They touched on the power of prayer and the rewards of meditation. But most of the conversation that afternoon had to do with love, a new kind of loving, a complete giving of oneself that had no price tag on it.

Fortunately they did not stay too long, and again Ebby said if it was all right with Bill he'd like to come back.

When they were gone Bill went straight for a bottle and this time the drinks he poured himself were stiff ones. His initial reaction to Cornell didn't bother him; it was an ancient reflex whose origins went back to his resentment of rich Burr and Burton boys in belted jackets. But the change in his old drinking pal was another matter. For he could tell that Ebby was more than inwardly reorganized; he was on a brand-new footing, his very roots seemed to grasp new soil.

And as he drank into what was to be still another night of arguing and debating, of struggle between two desires, his sudden swings of mood seemed to increase and they were increasing in intensity as well. From his certain knowledge of the change in Ebby and the bright hope that if Ebby could get hold, he could do it too, he would fall back to rebellion and his deep abhorrence at the whole idea of a man handing his life over to a god.

They had suggested he pray to any god he believed in or to anything he'd ever had faith in, and this he was willing to admit might work for some people, certain visionaries perhaps, but he was by training and inclination a materialist. His nature bent toward connections. If an equation was faulty in its premise, then all that followed had to be in error. Still, and although he knew his mind was already befogged with gin, he decided he would try to take a clear look at the record of his beliefs.

Christ he believed in as a moral leader, probably the greatest of them all, but he had certainly not been too closely followed by those who claimed him as their master. As for the organized religions that had been established for him, the wars, burnings and obscenities that had been perpetrated in his name, these were too easy a target to go into now.

As a boy he knew he had believed in Fayette's dreams, and he smiled over his gin, imagining old Fayette's responses to an Oxford Group. His grandfather had believed in the "music of the spheres," he told him once, but his Yankee independence denied any preacher the right to tell him how he must listen. But Bill had once had faith in his America and his view of democracy. On a cliff in Newport long ago he'd known he'd be willing to die for that, but America had become bread lines now, timid and greedy, and democracy was supported by government hand-outs.

As for love, he would not let himself think of love, of Lois, of what he had done to her. His mind literally could not accept the picture of a drunk lying in bed, hopeless and impotent.

Beyond and above it all he knew that if he had not believed in men, at least he had believed in man, the spearhead of evolution, the rebel spirit who always wanted more and had to reach out into a new dimension. (It didn't occur to him that the rebel reaching out for other dimensions might be Ebby Thacher.)

As a student, if he'd had any God it had been the God of Science, of facts. At Norwich he had learned that there were laws governing the cosmos; some of them were known and the others would be discovered. But did that knowledge imply that the laws had an author, some czar of heaven to whom he was expected to pray?

Ebby and Shep Cornell were now asking him to give up the one attribute of which he was most proud, the one quality that set a man above the animals—his inquiring, rational mind. And they wanted him to give this up for an illusion.

Finally—and he knew he was pretty drunk by the time he reached this point—he had to look at the fact and admit it: what they were asking him to do represented weakness to him. How

213

could a man so demean himself as to surrender the one thing in which he should have faith, his innate, inquiring mind?

He was willing to concede religious comfort might be all right for some—for the old, the hopeless, for those who had passed beyond loving, beyond any hope of really living, but, by Christ, he was different.

It might be the last arrogant gasp of alcoholic pride but, miserable and terrified as he was, he would not humble himself here. On this point he would go out swinging.

The next morning, surprisingly—surprisingly because he'd been convinced that he'd finally settled the argument—he decided he'd do a little further investigating. Immediately on awakening he'd thought of Ebby, thought of him in the city, sober, with no trace of a hangover, and once again there was the plaguing question: What had really happened to Ebby? Had he tapped some inner resource, truly made a connection with a power he believed greater than himself? Did he honestly believe in God, or did he, as so many men do, only long to believe?

Bill had been an investigator, a professional who had earned a reputation for being able to get at the facts of complex situations, so by midday it appeared logical that if he wanted to know about the source of Ebby's sobriety he should take a subway into New York and make an investigation of the Oxford Group and their headquarters in old Calvary Church.

With a few shots under his belt he started off for the church, which he knew to be on Fourth Avenue, and to have a look at their mission, which he believed to be in the vicinity, somewhere along Twenty-third Street.

At that time Twenty-third Street was abloom with bars and as he headed east he managed to hit most of them. By late afternoon he'd reached one near First Avenue, and there he found himself in an animated conversation with a young Finn named Alec. Alec had been a fisherman and a sailmaker back in the old country and Bill considered him a splendid fellow. Then suddenly he remembered why he was in the city and after explaining to Alec, he somehow persuaded him to come along to the mission.

As they hurried down the street, they seemed to be leaning against each other. Bill's feet moved straight ahead but his center of gravity kept shifting so he traveled on a kind of bias. When finally they reached the mission they were both staggering and their conversation was probably still animated. They were greeted at the door by one Tex Francisco, a huge ex-drunk who ran the place and who immediately informed them he was capable of running them out. But at that moment Ebby materialized from the shadows and suggested that they all go upstairs for something to eat.

After a plate of beans and a great deal of coffee, Bill appeared a little more sober and Ebby asked him to join a meeting in the main hall. This was a large room lined with rows of hard wooden benches and filled now with men in every stage of decay. These were the discards, the rejects of society, men who existed beneath the lowest rung of Mark Whalon's ladder. As he took a place in the last row, Bill studied the faces around him, the bedraggled waste of a city. They had all, he was sure, made their separate peace with reality, and now amidst the stench of alcohol and sweat they were kept going by such places as this. They were sad, even tragic figures, he could see, but like the boys on the bread lines long ago, they all looked upon themselves as victims, and Bill did not, could not, see himself a victim.

The meeting was the usual, hymns and prayers. Tex spoke, mostly about Jesus and the possibility of a new life. Then a few rose from the benches and gave brief testimonials, and as they did, it happened again.

Exactly as he had across the kitchen table from Ebby, Bill found himself listening without judgment. There was no denying that he was with his fellow drunks. When these sick ghosts rose

215

and for a moment or two spoke in their stumbling inarticulate way about their private hells, they were telling something Bill understood, a part of his own story.

Then Tex called for penitents to come forward and Bill watched a few of those who had spoken begin to go forward, then a few more, a few more. In all probability ten or twelve shuffled up to Tex, and suddenly, impelled by he knew not what, Bill found himself rising, starting up the aisle.

At the front of the hall he stopped and stood at a railing surrounded by sweating, stinking penitents. The man beside him was shaking with a palsy that anywhere else would have been frightening. Tex mumbled a few words, then they all headed back to their seats. But now Bill was filled with a wild and uncontrollable impulse to talk, to speak out and tell about himself.

And he did speak then, for several minutes. Later he had no idea what he had said. He could no more remember his words than he could analyze what had made him go forward. Perhaps, he thought afterward as he wandered through the mission dormitory and talked with several of the men, he'd been in a mood, had been operating in an area made up partly of penitence, partly of showmanship. He knew that there in the hall there had been an audience. He had to speak to them.

And he knew that when he left and walked back across Twenty-third Street to the subway, in that whole long trip he never thought of stopping in a bar.

In the morning, instead of the bad hangover he'd expected, he had only a mild headache and a slight case of the shakes. But this was enough to make him take a quick drink as soon as Lois was out of the house. "To taper off," he told himself. Then there was another, and another, and instead of tapering off, he tapered on.

By the time Lois got back he had stopped thinking about the night before. Indeed, he had stopped thinking about anything. She found him upstairs, passed out across the bed.

216

So the incident of the mission was to remain a mystery. It fitted no pattern. It was an interruption, a baffling momentary pause on that greased slide that destiny had created for him, and over which he knew he had no control.

For three days he never left the house and seldom left the bedroom. These were days of struggle and days of bleak futility. No questions led to satisfactory answers now, nor did he any longer believe they would. He was doomed to the intolerable alternatives of dependence on some spurious faith or an alcoholic death or incarceration in an institution.

He drank now as he never had. He could eat nothing and he drank simply to stay alive.

Now he seemed to be existing in a strange twilit zone of time. There was no passion, no conviction in his thinking. Indeed, all rebellion seemed drained away. Thoughts did not come in any particular sequence but as a parade of images that would drift into his mind, remain awhile, then disappear.

Still he struggled. At times he fought with what strengths he could muster to find a solution, a way out, and to see it through on his own terms. Images of Ebby and his new happiness continually returned and he went over and over his simple formula. He knew Ebby was trying to lead him to some new ground of belief, but perhaps, he decided, he was one of those who could never be led, who must always make his own discoveries.

At times he seemed a creature more of feeling than of thinking. He understood that the truer reality, that absolute nature of things the simple mention of which had so excited him when at their first meeting he had thought it was what Ebby was referring to, must of course exist independently of his senses. Yet his senses were all that a man had to perceive with, with the result that whatever he saw, whatever he perceived, had to be a reflection of his own sick mind, his own twisted psyche.

For now there was no question that he was ill. Silkworth's pronouncement about brain damage was always with him during these days and he finally was beginning to accept it. Once his mind had been lucid, proportioned and able to use whatever materials were pertinent to the problem he was examining. Now all that was gone. Now he could not sustain a thought, much less develop one to its logical conclusion, and this was not just the dimness of gin. Back of the fog something was no longer functioning. As he went over his rational arguments about Ebby's God, his thoughts were constantly interrupted and distracted by his picture of the new Ebby. And as he tried to consider those forces he could admit were greater than he, they invariably narrowed down to memories of the demons that rose from the subconscious to torture his nights. And his terror of once again being faced with a sleepless night, tormented by phantoms, snakes, d.t.'s, left him spent and totally incapable of any rational thought, any action except pouring another drink.

Filling a glass, then immediately emptying its contents, he felt himself in a strange paralysis of thought and will, as if in some feverish dream he was forced to watch himself do the one thing he knew he did not want to do. Alone in a house in Brooklyn, he not only watched himself drinking but also watched the slow, deliberate progress of some monstrous thing he could not exactly see but could feel moving toward him, blindly, stupidly, crushing everything along its way. In Vermont once he'd been shown a house razed by termites. Termites were always there, they had told him, waiting, nibbling away in different directions, but it was only a matter of time till they joined forces. Then havoc reigned.

In college he had learned of particular cells of the body that sometimes rebelled and set up their own warlike states, and these were labeled cancerous. It seemed they too were always there, waiting, a kind of nibbling menace, a distant murmur, until one day under certain circumstances the murmur grew louder, the cells joined together and mass movements began. Then chaos ruled, swept through the individual. This dread procession was coming now. The storm would break about him without mercy and he would be open to its blows as he had always been.

Finally on the morning of the fourth day after his visit to the mission—as he took his first drink he knew he could no longer trust himself, he could not trust his mind. If he went on drinking throughout the day he'd have no control of his actions, or of his thinking. Somehow he'd have to find a way to stop, if only temporarily, if only in order to think.

"The alternative to government is anarchy." He recited the schoolboy maxim aloud. Now his life was in a state of anarchy. His mind had become unmanageable.

If he had a cancer, if he knew he were dying of it as he knew now he would die of booze, he would do anything, any-thing—he half smiled at the thought that he would even be willing to pray out loud at noon in Macy's window—if it would arrest the disease. And surely the first thing he'd do would be to find a physician, the best one in the city, and have him destroy or cut out the consuming cells.

On a sudden impulse, then—though it didn't seem an impulse at the time; it was the only thing he could do—he dressed, scribbled a note for Lois and left the house, heading for Towns Hospital and Dr. Silkworth.

On the street he discovered he had only a nickle, the subway fare into the city, so stopping by a grocery where he remembered Lois had some credit, he talked a clerk into giving him four bottles of beer. One of these he drank in the street, another in the subway, and feeling somewhat better, he offered the third bottle to a fellow passenger, who politely refused, so he finished that one on the platform before going up to the hospital and arrived at the door holding the last bottle by the neck.

Silkworth greeted him outside his office—Bill had to look away to avoid the hurt he knew would be in the old man's eyes—and then the good doctor placed an arm across his shoulder and said

219

quietly, "Well, now, boy, isn't it time you got upstairs and went to bed?"

He was home now.

In a small room with a bed, one chair and a bureau, he was safe. He would be cared for and comforted. He need make no decisions. He had no responsibilities. Back in the nursery—even further back, in the nirvana of the womb—he could do what he liked.

If he wished to put on his slippers and wander down to the end of the hall, he could talk to other recovering drunks who'd be sitting there in pajamas and robes, listening to a radio. Or if he wished just to lean back, his cheek against the clean cool pillow, that was all right too. Occasionally from down the stairs he would hear a clock striking, but whether it was three in the afternoon or three in the morning, it didn't matter. Soon a nice nurse would be in with a cup of broth or his little tray of food.

This was not the worst drunk he'd been on and after a few days of sedatives, belladonna and a massive quantity of vitamins, his physical being seemed restored. His mind cleared, but as the boozy fog lifted, a great black depression, the worst one of his life, gradually settled over him.

On the way to the hospital he'd pictured himself a cancer victim seeking a cure. Now, alone in the tiny room, he began to feel and to think as a child. Here for a time he knew he was safe, because he was being treated as just that, a helpless child.

His first night in the hospital, he overheard two nurses talking by his door. He picked up only one phrase of their conversation, ". . . incontinent in bowel and bladder . . ." and although he knew they could not be talking about him, his instant reaction was one of terror and shame. He had been bathed, he was in clean pajamas and between fresh sheets, but he knew that once and not so long ago, they could have been talking about him.

One afternoon, only a few weeks back, his bowels had turned to water and gushed down into his pants. And now, for the rest of the night, despite the sedation, all his thoughts and memories, even his strange disjointed dreams, were stained by his own terrible stench, his own unspeakable shame.

For a man with so little control of his thinking, his reactions or even his physical being, a room in a drying-out hospital, with its protections and its complete isolation from the rest of the world, was perhaps the only, the inevitable place to be.

He saw now that he was reacting to everything not as a man of thirty-nine, but as a maimed, dull child. When, on the second evening, Ebby stopped by for a visit and, after a little general talk, again repeated his pat formula about realizing you were licked, admitting it and being willing to turn your life over to the care of God, Bill nodded. And it was not just his head that was nodding now—he'd been listening to these words with a blank, almost stuporous expression—it was as though his whole being nodded in response. He was so lost he was willing to believe anything. Anything could be the answer. He had no mind with which to argue, no energies to fight with.

When Ebby left he did not get up from the side of the bed or make any move toward seeing him out. He sat with the passivity of a six-year-old who knows he has done wrong, but cannot understand what he is supposed to do.

He stayed in his room now, never going down the hall, often not even going to the window, for the view of the city streets with cars driving past, people hurrying along through the winter night, was a reminder of what was waiting. Tomorrow or the following day he would have to leave, and at this thought a sudden chill would sweep over him, his whole body would be covered with a cold sweat; he could not go home. Out there were three choices. Only three. He could stop drinking. Or he would go insane. Or he would die.

Alone, lost and terrified, he saw no place to turn. He needed, every particle of him hungered for, someone, something to tell him what to do, someone to take care of him.

Finally, unable to stay on the bed, unwilling to go down the hall and join the others, he began to pace the tiny room, from the bed to the door, from the door to the bed. He would do anything; anything now. But what was there to do?

Now he was less than a child; he was an animal caught in a trap and held. Yet part of him still lived, was still crying out, thrashing about insanely, flailing himself murderously.

He must leave the hospital. He knew it. Silkworth would come into the room and tell him he must go. And what then? What was strong enough to stop his drinking? Past experience would not do it; will power could not; nor could reliance on Ebby's God. Pride? His pride had always been based on what he could do. Now he knew he could do nothing. So—he halted by the foot of the bed—he was hopeless. This was his ending. Still he would not, could not accept the word, because in some far corner of his being he did not want to die. In spite of the terror, in spite of the agony, the strain and the unending tumult, he wanted life more than he wanted an end to the striving. That was a belief and a desire. He wanted to live.

His hands clasped the footboard of the bed. *But how? How?* The cancer of alcohol had already killed his mind, his will, his spirit, and it was only a matter of time before it would kill his body. Yet at this moment, with the last vestige of pride, the last trace of obstinacy crushed out of him, still he knew he wanted to live.

His fingers relaxed a little on the footboard, his arms slowly reached out and up. "I want," he said aloud. "I want . . ."

Ever since infancy, they said, he'd been reaching out this way, arms up, fingers spread, and as far back as he could remember he'd been saying just that. But always before it had been an unfinished sentence. Now it had its ending. *He wanted to live.* He would do anything, anything, to be allowed to go on living.

"Oh, God," he cried, and it was the sound not of a man, but

of a trapped and crippled animal. "If there is a God, show me. Show me. Give me some sign."

As he formed the words, in that very instant he was aware first of a light, a great white light that filled the room, then he suddenly seemed caught up in a kind of joy, an ecstasy such as he would never find words to describe. It was as though he were standing high on a mountaintop and a strong clear wind blew against him, around him, through him—but it seemed a wind not of air, but of spirit—and as this happened he had the feeling that he was stepping into another world, a new world of consciousness, and everywhere now there was a wondrous feeling of Presence which all his life he had been seeking. Nowhere had he ever felt so complete, so satisfied, so embraced.

This happened. And it happened as suddenly and as definitely as one may receive a shock from an electrode, or feel heat when a hand is placed close to a flame. Then when it passed, when the light slowly dimmed, and the ecstasy subsided—and whether this was a matter of minutes or much longer he never knew; he was beyond any reckoning of time—the sense of Presence was still there about him, within him. And with it there was still another sense, a sense of rightness. No matter how wrong things seemed to be, they were as they were meant to be. There could be no doubt of ultimate order in the universe, the cosmos was not dead matter, but a part of the living Presence, just as he was part of it.

Now, in place of the light, the exaltation, he was filled with a peace such as he had never known. He had heard of men who'd tried to open the universe to themselves; he had opened himself to the universe. He had heard men say there was a bit of God in everyone, but this feeling that he was a part of God, himself a living part of the higher power, was a new and revolutionary feeling.

And it was as feeling that he wanted to hang on to it now, to whatever it was that had happened; he wanted only to feel it. In time, when the rational mind began to take over, the floodgates would open to words, thoughts, explanations. Now, for a brief moment, he fell back on the bed and refused to allow himself to think.

Gradually—and again there was no awareness of time—he pulled himself up and permitted himself to think as well as feel, and as he did, little by little fears began to return, to reenter along with his rational thought. Was what had happened some form of hallucination, some phenomenon a doctor would spot as a natural symptom of a damaged brain?

As he recognized the first signs of approaching panic, he stood up, walked into the hall and did a very sensible thing. He asked a nurse to find Silkworth.

He told the old man everything that had happened, every detail he could remember. Then he waited for his answer.

Silkworth had some questions first, probing questions, and Bill replied as best he could. When he was finished he watched the doctor sit back in his chair, his brow knitted. And as he did, as Bill waited, everything seemed to stop. Finally Bill could stand it no longer.

"Tell me," he asked, "was it real? Am I still . . . sane?"

And Silkworth answered, "Yes, my boy. You are sane. Perfectly sane, in my opinion." Then he went on to explain that Bill had probably undergone some tremendous psychic upheaval. He'd read about such things, and sometimes they had been known to produce remarkable results. But he was a simple man of science, he said, and he didn't begin to understand what some would call conversion, or a conversion experience. He knew that it could happen and something obviously had happened to Bill. "So . . ." he said, and he looked deeply into Bill's eyes when he said it, "whatever it is you've got now, hang on to it. Hang on to it, boy. It is so much better than what you had only a couple of hours ago."

It was shortly after leaving Towns that Bill heard for the first time the line of an old spiritual: "Young man, young man, your arm's too short to box with God." In a way this said it all for him.

To Bill there seemed nothing supernatural or supernormal in his experience. It had happened. That was all he knew and, at the time, all he needed to know.

Those who were close to him were interested to see what would happen next, where he would go now that he was sober, and few understood the look of bafflement on his face when they asked about this, or why it seemed to him an irrelevant question. Where was he going? He didn't have to go anyplace. He was here.

He was here now.

8

"When the pupil is ready the teacher appears."

This was another saying Bill latched on to after leaving Towns, and for him three remarkable teachers now appeared: Silkworth, Sam Shoemaker, rector of Calvary Church, and, perhaps most important of all, a small group of ex-drunks who met each week in Stewart's cafeteria.

There was no doubt about Bill's being ready. His physical health had been restored; he was standing straighter, his step was more resilient, his eyes constantly smiling, and often, for what seemed no good reason, he found himself wanting to laugh aloud. All his tremendous energies were back. His senses were sharpened—the sky was bluer, the lights of the city more vivid—and with this he felt a new capacity for the sensual and sensuous pleasures alcohol had all but destroyed.

There were times that winter, rushing to catch a subway or hurrying across the park to a meeting, when he felt so alive, so new, he could honestly believe he had never lived before.

Talks with Silkworth often went on late into the night and the little doctor contributed so profoundly to Bill's understanding of himself that it would be difficult to imagine what the next years would have been if he had not been there. Bill once said that Silkworth had explained the mechanisms of the lock that held the alcoholic in prison, but he did more. In the winter of 1934–35 Silkworth was a necessary safety valve. He kept bringing Bill down to earth.

The doctor had many ideas about alcoholism but—and this should be remembered—he was not a psychiatrist, he was a neurologist. As a young man he had wanted a hospital of his own and had saved and aimed his life toward acquiring one, but all his dreams crashed in the upheaval of '29, and in 1930 he had to go to work for Charles Towns at forty dollars a week. Still, the conviction never left him that one day there would be a cure for the insidious malady that was wrecking the lives of millions of men and women, and the hope of contributing his bit to the cure guided his life.

At Towns he had developed his theory of a mental obsession combined with a physical allergy, and Bill would listen entranced as the old man outlined the histories of various patients, knowing that these were never cases to Silkworth; each of them was a trapped human being.*

His method of treatment—and from a psychiatric point of view this was the rankest sort of heresy—was to direct an alcoholic away from any deep or morbid examination of the past. He went straight at the problems that were obvious and conscious, willing to let the unconscious take care of itself. By charging a great deal of behavior to the illness itself, he was able to take a patient off the hook so far as guilt, shame and morbidity were concerned. Then doctor and patient together would search out those defects of character that were blocking recovery. And Bill knew Silkworth was able to do this because of his extraordinary talent for spotting the good in people and his pointing out how these fine qualities had been run over and obliterated by the obsession.

Through the years he had of course discovered and analyzed

---

* It has been estimated that during his life, William D. Silkworth treated over 50,000 alcoholics. Bill wrote that his compassionate attitude toward alcoholism would have been remarkable at any period in medical history, but in the year 1934 it had struck him as unique, and "Silky" well deserved the title he is remembered by: The Little Doctor Who Loved Drunks.

many stages of the progression of the illness, many forms of alcoholic resistance. Bill could identify with most of these and they would discuss them endlessly. But of all the tools in Silkworth's kit two impressed Bill most deeply and were to become a vital part of his future work. First was the doctor's rare capacity to engage the confidence of a drunk. As if by some miracle, he seemed able to step into and stay with a drunk in the special cave in which he lived. The second tool was Silkworth's constant reiteration of the fact that alcoholism is an illness, an often fatal illness.

As to the changes in Bill himself, his ability to look at and root out certain defects, especially those that might threaten his sobriety if they got out of hand, they were able to discuss some of these, but Bill was beginning to believe much of his own inner revolution was now the province of Sam Shoemaker and the new friends he was making in Ebby's Oxford Group.

If Bill had met Shoemaker at any other point in his life, he undoubtedly would have been impressed, but the timing of his introduction to this dynamic leader of the New York group always struck Bill as more than coincidence. For if Silkworth had described the mysteries of the lock that held the drunk in prison, Shoemaker—or so Bill believed—was offering the keys by which he might be freed.

Sam Shoemaker was a tall, handsome man, somewhat heavier in build than Bill, but in many ways very like him; both seemed to possess a special extra dose of life. Shoemaker was perhaps more intellectually inclined than Bill, but his erudition was tempered by tremendous eagerness, enthusiasm and honesty. Like Bill, he could always bring himself down to any man's size, and unlike any other clergyman Bill had ever met, Sam Shoemaker appeared more willing to talk about his own shortcomings than anyone else's. People invariably turned to him as if sensing that here was a man who could make things happen.

The spiritual principles underlying his belief—self-examination, acknowledgement of faults, restitution for wrongs done, and above all constant work with others—were the principles upon which the Oxford Movement was based, and they seemed to create an atmosphere in which Bill believed he as a recovering drunk could not only survive, but might begin to grow and reach out along new lines.

Perhaps the most important contribution Sam Shoemaker made to Bill's life was in giving him a new interpretation of prayer. Prayer, Bill came to see, could be more than a listing of personal needs and desires, more than an attempt to influence the will of God. It could also be a method of discovering that will, and for this reason he began to believe that it was as important to listen as to speak in prayer.

If to some it seemed strange that a man who had built up such a powerful resistance to prayer, indeed to the whole vocabulary of religion, could now find himself so receptive, so totally willing to accept, Bill had one simple answer. Remembering his night at Towns, he said, "A dying man can become remarkably open-minded."

(And this was not just a saying. He never forgot the frantic animal that had faced death and had then, by some intervention, been allowed to live. From that night on he felt no hint of embarrassment in discussing in whatever terms a man might care to use the power that had returned him to life.)

If also some of the disciplines of the Oxford Group were a little beyond his grasp, if some of their special tenets, such as their absolutes—absolute purity, absolute honesty, etc.—were eventually to prove too strict a diet for a drunk, none of this bothered Bill. He was sober. He was staying sober. That was the fact of his life.

Then, too, he knew now exactly what he was going to do.

Within ten days of his release from Towns, Bill happened to run across a small group of ex-drunks who had developed the habit of sticking together and going around to Stewart's cafeteria after regular Oxford Group meetings.

On the first evening he was with them, he sensed a feeling, a special communion among the little group which, in the beginning, he couldn't quite place. But it was a feeling he had experienced before, not unlike what he had felt at Clinton Street when he and Ebby had looked at each other and known they wouldn't have to describe the hells they'd been through. And possibly he had felt it one other time, that night at the mission when he had realized he was surrounded by his fellow drunks.

At Stewart's they were never more than a small handful—Grace McC., Roland H., Ebby, of course, and perhaps one or two others —but Bill knew immediately and instinctively that these were his people. He could say anything to them, they anything to him, and it would be all right. Around a little rear table, over mugs of coffee and too many cigarettes, they would talk for hours, often until the proprietor had to close up for the night, giving one another the most horrendous accounts of their drinking, after which they would laugh unashamedly at and with each other.

At first their communication seemed so beautiful and so complete he could not analyze it. Was it a kinship of suffering? They had all admittedly at one time or another hit bottom; each had been beaten into complete defeat and each by the same thing— booze. Could that be it, or was it that they had found a common means of escape? He knew only that these people had been drunks, were now sober and obviously having a hell of a good time. To him they were living proof that it was possible.

It was with them that Bill learned that even his experience at Towns was not unique. He could never recollect if it had been Ebby or Roland who gave him a copy of William James's *Varieties of Religious Experience,* but he remembered the impact of the book. It was James's theory that spiritual experiences could have a very definite objective reality and might totally transform a man's life. Some of these experiences, James believed, arrived with a sudden burst of light, while others developed more gradually; some, but by no means all, came through religious channels— there were indeed many varieties. All, however, appeared to have one common denominator and that was their source in pain and utter hopelessness. Complete deflation at depth was the one requirement to prepare the recipient and make him ready for a transforming experience.

"Deflation at depth." These words leaped from the page as Bill read them. For what else was hitting bottom except deflation? Wasn't this what had happened to him when Silkworth had condemned him to insanity or death? Wasn't it the story of every ex-drunk he knew?

Roland H., the man who had come to Ebby's rescue, was the son of a prominent Connecticut family. He'd drunk his way through a fortune and in 1930 had wound up in Zurich, a patient of Carl Jung. For over a year he worked with the great psychoanalyst, then, when all his hidden springs and the warped motors of his unconscious had been revealed, he believed he had a full understanding of the cause of his obsession and could therefore go on and live a sober life. But in a matter of weeks after leaving Zurich, Roland H. was drunk, unaccountably drunk. When he returned to Jung the doctor was frank. There was nothing more that medicine or psychiatry could do for him. There was only one hope: occasionally alcoholics had shown signs of recovery through religious conversion. Jung had no advice about where or how Roland might prepare himself for this, but he would first have to admit his personal powerlessness to go on living. Then perhaps, if he sought, he might find.

And this was precisely what Roland had done. Upon leaving Jung the second time, he fell into the hands of the Oxford Group. With their evangelical eagerness, they were organized to bring about the exact sort of change Roland was seeking. Some time later, returning to America, Roland had carried the message to Ebby. Ebby had carried it to Bill. Powerlessness. Deflation at depth. Then, only then, was an alcoholic made ready.

As he read William James, as he reviewed Roland's story, his own story, Bill's mind raced ahead. He saw what had happened: one drunk taking the word to another; and now he began to envision a vast chain reaction that someday would encircle the globe—a chain of alcoholics passing these principles along, one to the other. And it could begin here. Now. With this little group he had found in Stewart's cafeteria. And he knew now he wanted to work with alcoholics more than he had ever wanted anything in his life.

And Bill Wilson worked with them. With the compulsive dedication of the twelve-year-old boy challenged to make a boomerang, he set off to sober up all drunks everywhere. There was no besotted derelict who staggered into the mission he didn't buttonhole, no fine executive wanting a quick drying out at Towns he didn't try to reach. Some would nod blank-eyed, appearing to listen; others would go screaming to their rooms. Nothing stopped him. He was all over New York, at all hours, indefatigable and incorrigible, totally convinced that if *he* could do it, could find a way out, they could do it. And he was spectacularly unsuccessful with everyone.

Later he was to describe his behavior at this time as twin jet propulsion, part genuine spirituality, part the old power drive to be number one. If he sensed a certain coolness and lack of support on the part of the bigwigs of the Oxford Group, he simply ignored it. If they weren't able to share his vision yet, he would just have to work harder and eventually show them. There was a kind of young madness in this new and magnificent obsession.

The reaction of the group shouldn't have been surprising. They had had extremely bad luck with drunks. Only recently, Shoemaker, in an effort to rehabilitate some local alcoholics, had housed a small group in an apartment near Calvary Church, but one of them, still resisting salvation, had hurled a brick through a handsome stained-glass window. Also it had become a practice of the Oxford Group to hold meditation sessions. Members would sit, pencils in hand, waiting to jot down any guidance that might come through during their silences, and it was extraordinary how many times that winter the message from on high would indicate that Bill Wilson should get himself a job and leave his drunks in peace.

Then, too—and this may well have affected Bill—no one seemed to share or even understand Silkworth's idea about alcoholism being an illness. To the Oxford Group drinking was a moral issue and should be treated as such. In an effort to please, or at least show his gratitude to the people who had done so much for him, Bill undoubtedly began to shift his approach and put less emphasis on the physical aspects of his story, more on the mystical awakening. But the effect on potential recruits was exactly the same.

Occasionally he would think he'd found a live one—Ed W., a former sales manager for a paper company; Walter P., a writer he'd contacted at Towns. He would take them back to Clinton Street and never leave their sides, but after a few days, or a week at the most, they'd invariably slip away. During this whole period only Lois seemed to understand and approve. She would get home from her department store never knowing what she'd find, whether she was to cook supper for three or ten, go off to a meeting with Bill or sit up half the night with some stranger who was trying to sweat it out. There was, however, one thing she knew: their efforts might not have brought about any recoveries, but no one could deny the work was keeping Bill sober.

As spring came on and Bill could not honestly say he had helped one man, he began to think of these months as a time when he was learning nothing except how not to communicate with alcoholics.

In April he had another session with Silkworth. The doctor had gone out on quite a limb for Bill; in fact, he'd been risking his professional reputation by letting him talk with patients. Now when Bill asked what he was doing wrong, what had gone so amiss with the deflation technique, the old man decided to give it to him straight.

"For God's sake stop preaching," he said. "You're scaring the poor drunks half crazy. They want to get sober, but you're telling

them they can only do it as you did, by some special hot flash.
. . ." And he went on to point out that religion usually filled a man
with guilt or rebellion, two things guaranteed to send a real alcoholic running for a drink.

"You've got the cart before the horse, boy. Hit them with the
physical first"—he kept saying this—"and hit them hard. Tell about
the obsession and the physical sensitivity they are developing
that will condemn them to go mad or die. Pour it on. Say it's
lethal as cancer." Coming from Bill, another drunk, Silkworth
believed this might crack their rugged little egos and crack them
in depth. Maybe then, but only then, would they be ready to listen to his God talk; maybe they'd even buy some of his lofty
principles, because they'd see they had no other place to go. "A
drunk," he said, "must be led, not pushed." Over and over he
begged Bill to shift his emphasis from sin to sickness.

He gave it to him straight that afternoon and Bill listened, but
how much he agreed, how much he was able to accept on a conscious level, is a question. He had surrendered, admitted total
defeat, and in the moment of doing so he had been given what he
believed to be divine guidance. Possibly this appealed to the
evangelical side of his nature. Or possibly, as his grandfather
would have said, a man always has faith in the horse that gets him
across the river.

At this point, other problems were beginning to fill Bill's mind.
There was very little money coming in at Clinton Street. Lois had
her salary and, it's true, they were able to stay on in the house by
paying the bank only twenty dollars a month against the mortgage, but hints were beginning to arrive from every direction that
the time had come for Bill to start earning some money.

In April he returned to the Street, and almost immediately
found himself involved in a complicated proxy fight over control
of a small machine-tool factory in Akron, Ohio. By joining forces
with the secretary of the company and two other men, who had
started buying and selling stock in the company, he managed to
get hold of quite a packet of proxies. However, another group in

New York were out for the same thing and claimed to hold the balance of power, at least 40 percent of the company. By May it seemed a wise move for Bill and his new friends to get themselves out to Akron for the annual stockholders meeting, but they had underestimated their opposition. They had got there first. And after spreading stories about Bill's drinking history, his power drive and probable ambition to be president of the company—all of which were plausible—they pooled their shares with management's and at the meeting produced well over 50 percent of the necessary proxies.

Bill's new friends retreated. The deal and all their fine expectations had fallen through, and they took a train back to New York, leaving Bill stranded in the Mayflower Hotel on a hot Saturday afternoon with exactly ten dollars in his pocket.

There was no way he could think of to report his failure to Lois or to the Oxford Groupers, who'd seen him off with such high hopes. For a long while he sat considering his next move, then he rose and began to pace the lobby, from the elevators past the manager's desk to a row of telephones, then back along the same route.

Directly across from his path of march was the entrance to the Mayflower Bar, and with every step he took he was growing more aware of the cool inviting darkness just beyond the entrance, the low din of male voices, occasionally interrupted by a girl's happy laugh, or the sweet crackling sound of ice in a cocktail shaker. Then came—as he may have always known they would—the words: Why not? Who would know? And what harm could one drink do?

Instantly he panicked. He felt his knees go weak; a cold sweat ran down his arms. For the first time fear overrode his rationalizing alcoholic mind. But even as he noticed that his hands had actually begun to shake, he felt a small, strange sense of relief. Maybe sanity could be restored. Maybe. He turned.

There was one thing he knew he had to do—and do immediately. As he'd been pacing out his beat, he'd been aware of a glass-enclosed sign, a sort of bulletin, beside the telephones. His eye had passed over this, hardly noticing it, but he had the impression it was a church directory. He walked back and stood for a long moment, studying the names of churches, ministers and times of services. Then choosing one name at random, Reverend Walter Tunks, he stepped into the booth and made a call.

Reverend Tunks answered and Bill began his story: he was an alcoholic from New York and it was vital that he find another alcoholic to talk with. Later he wondered what must have been going through the good reverend's mind as he listened. Tunks had had some experience with drunks and had always worked on the theory that one drunk at a time was quite enough, but as Bill went on he seemed to understand, enough to give Bill a list of names before he rang off.

There were ten names. Some turned out to be Oxford Group members, some were not. Bill decided to start at the top and, if necessary, go right down the list. A few were out; a few others were busy; a few said they would be happy to see him in church tomorrow. The last name on the list, a Mrs. Seiberling, sounded familiar. Back on Wall Street he'd heard of a Seiberling who'd been president of Goodyear Tire. He didn't see how he could tell this man's wife about his problem, so he stepped out of the booth and again began to pace.

The bar was still there and it seemed to be filling up. The laughter was louder as a happy Saturday-afternoon crowd began to arrive. He stood and watched a young couple wander in, arm in arm, then he turned, went back to the phone booth and called the tenth and last name on his list.

A soft Southern voice answered—not Mrs. Frank Seiberling, but her daughter-in-law, Henrietta—and after only a few sentences she interrupted to tell him that she understood perfectly, and she proceeded to give him specific instructions for getting to the gatehouse of the Seiberling estate, where she was living with her two small sons.

Nothing had prepared Bill for the charm, the warmth or the

236

understanding of Henrietta Seiberling. After he'd arrived at the house and told her a little more of his story, she saw the situation clearly. She was not an alcoholic, she explained, but she had had her troubles in the last years and had found many answers in the Oxford Group. What was more, she was sure she knew just the man for Bill, a prominent surgeon, one of the finest in Akron, but his drinking had got so out of hand few of his colleagues and practically none of his patients could trust him. He'd tried all sorts of cures, but nothing had worked, and she gathered he was now in dire financial straits.

When Henrietta tried to phone Dr. Robert H. Smith, she got his wife, Anne, instead and learned the doctor was in no condition to see anyone. Completely undaunted, Henrietta made a date for the four of them to get together the following afternoon at five o'clock.

Next day, a little after five, Bill met a man some fifteen years older than he, a man who'd clearly cut an impressive figure once and who still tried to carry himself with dignity. But there was a stoop now, his eyes were red and at times his hands shook uncontrollably. And his first remark was one that any alcoholic in the world would have made under these circumstances. He said he could stay only a few minutes. So with no ado, Henrietta ushered the two men into her library and left them alone.

There were two completely new elements in Bill's approach to Dr. Bob. One came from a conscious decision on his part to follow Silkworth's advice for once and hit the physical side of the illness first. The other welled up from a deep emotional need that may have always been there but that he had not recognized until this trip to Akron. Alone in the Mayflower lobby, he had known with a desperate certainty that he needed to be with, to talk and work with another alcoholic.

He started the conversation in the library by admitting frankly that he was not there, as Dr. Bob might suppose, to help *him*, but because he, Bill Wilson, needed help. Then he told his own story, playing down his spiritual experience and describing, as he had never done to anyone the horror of the suicidal obsession that had forced him to go on drinking and the physical allergy his body had developed. He quoted Silkworth frequently about the progress of the illness and its obvious prognosis, insanity or death.

From Bob's point of view, this was undoubtedly the only thing he would have listened to that afternoon. He did not need, as Bill was to learn, any spiritual instruction. He had been a member of the Oxford Group much longer than Bill and was far more versed in such matters. He thought he had heard everything there was to hear about alcoholism. Yet, ironically, as a doctor he had paid little attention to the physical aspects of his own case, and it was the obvious scientific soundness of Silkworth's statements— those twin ogres of madness and death—that finally delivered the telling blow. For Dr. Bob could not deny that here before him was something new: another alcoholic holding out hope in one hand and stark hopelessness in the other.

They talked on for hours. Soon Dr. Bob had opened up and was speaking as frankly, as unashamedly, as Bill. When they parted after eleven o'clock, they knew something had radically changed in them both. Although they could not be specific about what it was, a spark that was to light future fires had been struck.

For Bill it had been a unique, wondrous and totally engrossing experience. After admitting his deep need to share his problems with another drunk, he had not felt the slightest desire to preach or in any way judge the other man. With a sense of incredible freedom, relief and, yes, joy, he'd felt the two of them growing closer, their talk becoming a mutual thing, and he knew they had both felt this. Two drunks had found a new, mysterious and loving kind of communication, a new language of the heart.

The link he had been seeking was located that night in Henrietta's library.

They had dinner together the next evening and after a few days Bill moved in with Anne and Dr. Bob in their house on

238

Ardmore Avenue. He sent word to his proxy associates in New York that he'd be staying on in Akron, and, to his surprise, they wired him some cash and suggested he might hire a lawyer and investigate the possibility of fraud at the stockholders meeting. Thus he was no longer penniless, but his primary interest now was his work with Dr. Bob and the uncanny parallels they were discovering in their stories.

Both were Vermonters, Bob the son of a judge in St. Johnsbury. Both had taken up drinking at an early age, Bob while still a student at Dartmouth, even before medical school, and from the beginning they had both gone at booze heavily. Each, except for the hells created by drinking, had had a happy marriage and each admitted he must have been born with an iron constitution to have withstood the beatings he had given himself. And each of them had wrecked a career that had started out brilliantly.

These were the external parallels. The interior ones were equally striking, the guilt and remorse, the defenses they'd constructed, the passionate desires and the futile efforts to understand and be in control, and finally, after seeking so many other solutions, they had both wound up trying to give shape and meaning to their lives by adhering to the excruciatingly high standards of the Oxford Group.

Until talking with Bill, Dr. Bob had been willing to describe his own case as that of "a man who just loved his grog." Together they began to dig deeper, to take the first tentative steps toward self-examination. They had, of course, both given tacit approval to this as well as to the other tenets of the movement—admitting faults, attempting to make amends and working with others. They'd even nodded to the religious absolutes. But now two pragmatic Yankees were working in tandem to make these lofty concepts part of the real world and to apply them, in a practical way, to their alcoholic natures.

As they talked on night after night, they were struck by the fact that they were speaking more openly than either had ever

239

spoken to another person. They discussed quite freely and frankly Bill's failure in the five months he'd been storming around New York trying to reform drunks, and they decided it was his ego that had got in the way. He'd concerned himself too much with being successful and, whether he realized it or not, with trying to prove himself worthy of the Oxford Group's approval. His fear of failing had made him less than himself and this, of course, had made failure even more likely. Whereas when he had met Bob at Henrietta's there had been no question of ego or of impressing anyone. He had needed Bob, he'd told him so; therefore they had been able to talk as equals, almost anonymous equals.

They learned many things in their nights together and one of them, one they felt they should have known was this: *You can never talk down to a drunk.*

As time passed, there seemed to be two issues involved in their discussions. The immediate issue was how they could survive. The other, the ultimate issue, was one they may not have stated in words, but they both were beginning to sense that in the things they were talking about—in their new way of life—there might be implications that could reach far beyond the two of them holed up together in a house in Akron, Ohio. And sensing this, Bill Wilson felt his dreams once again begin to take fire.

But again life wasn't to proceed along the straightforward lines Bill always expected.

One morning after he had been sober about ten days, Dr. Bob mentioned quite casually that the following week the A.M.A. was holding its convention in Atlantic City. He had always made a practice of attending these gatherings and wondered what Bill thought about his going this year.

From the corner of his eye Bill had noticed a look of dismay shoot across Anne's face, but he tried to ignore it as they went into the pros and cons of such a trip. Finally they reached the conclusion that since they wanted to live in the real world, and conventions and drinking would always be a part of that world,

240

they'd have to face it. Perhaps, therefore, he should go to Atlantic City and test himself.

He went. And for days they heard nothing. For the first two days Bill and Anne tried to go about their normal lives and not give any indication of their mounting apprehension, but by the third day, when there was still no news, Bill was filled with conflicting and contradictory emotions he didn't know how to handle. Surely he told himself, they'd grown close enough so that Bob would know his concern, his natural fears. But then came the question: How many times had he, had any drunk, stopped to call home?

Pictures of what might be going on in Atlantic City became more real than anything happening around him and with it all there was the terrible feeling that it was his fault. They had been safe when they were together, and he had encouraged Bob to go. Still he refused to give way to fear and he would not let himself admit how much of his own life seemed at stake in Bob Smith's safety. And the worst of it was he couldn't mention his feelings; he knew Anne was as anxious as he. So they talked, told stories, made feeble jokes, but each knew the other was thinking of only one thing.

It was this way all through the third day and the fourth. Then, on the morning of the fifth day, there was a call from Bob's secretary-nurse. Bob had phoned from the station about 4 A.M., dead drunk, and she had picked him up. He was at her place and she wished Anne would come and get him.

They got him, brought him home, and as they put him to bed Bill's heart sank, only to sink still lower when Anne reminded him that the following Monday, just three days away, Bob was scheduled to perform an operation. It was a complex, intricate operation and they'd hoped it would be his chance for a real comeback.

As a team then, working around the clock, Bill and Anne Smith decided they'd sober him up. They started by tapering him off.

They used a few sedatives, masses of vitamins, even a special diet Bill had heard sometimes worked with hangovers.

They never left his side and for the first two days it was discouraging work, but just before dawn on Monday morning, Bill, who had moved into the doctor's room and was sleeping on a cot, happened to look across at Bob and saw that he was wide awake. He was still shaking miserably. but he was sitting up in bed, and as he turned his head toward Bill he said, "I'm going to do it, I'm going through with it." Thinking he meant the operation, Bill said of course he would, but Dr. Bob shook his head. He didn't mean that, he meant the things they'd been talking about, he said, the thing they'd been working on. Then he leaned back against the pillow and slept for another hour.

Bill drove him to the hospital about nine o'clock, and the sight of the surgeon sitting beside him and every now and then holding out his right hand, testing to see how steady it was, was a picture Bill would not forget.

In front of the hospital, Bill reached into his pocket, took out a bottle of beer and handed it to Dr. Bob. Then he leaned over, opened the door and let him out. After watching him move slowly up the steps and into the building, Bill drove back to Ardmore Avenue, and again he and Anne waited—hour after hour, far beyond the time the operation should have taken; still no word. Finally they could bear it no longer; they phoned the hospital. The operation had been completed and had apparently been successful, but Dr. Bob was not in the hospital.

This was early in the afternoon. There was nothing they could do, so they sat—trying not to think, again trying to talk—and they waited. It was almost five-thirty when they heard his key turning in the door.

After leaving the hospital he'd had a few calls to make, he said, a few amends that needed tending to, several doctors he'd wanted to apologize to, several tradespeople he had owed some money.

This was June 10, 1935, a date they wouldn't forget. After the beer Bill had handed him in front of the hospital, Dr. Bob Smith never had another drink.

The next morning Dr. Bob said there was another part of the program that he and Bill should get going on—working with others. And that afternoon they went together to City Hospital, where they knew there was always a healthy crop of alcoholics.

When they went in, Dr. Bob explained to a receiving nurse that they wanted to talk with a patient and then introduced Bill as a man from New York who had come across a cure for drunks. The nurse, knowing Dr. Bob, listened politely, then said she hoped he had used it on himself. He promised her he had and she led them into the ward and pointed to a young fellow she described as "a *very* tough case." He'd been there many times and when he'd arrived last night with a bad case of d.t.'s, he had proceeded to blacken the eye of the nurse who had tried to put him to bed.

This was Bill D., and he was indeed in poor shape. As they sat, one on either side of his bed, and began to tell him their stories, he listened with what they could see was some interest, but at the first mention of the word "God," Bill D. shook his head. It was no use, he said. He believed in God, but he was convinced God no longer believed in him. It wasn't an encouraging visit. But before they left they asked if they could stop around again, and Bill D. made no objection.

When they arrived the following afternoon, Bill D.'s wife was with him. These, he said, were the two men he had been talking about. Then, before they could say anything, he told them about his night, how he hadn't slept but had been thinking about them all night long, and he wanted them to know that he had decided that if they could do it, maybe he could do it, maybe they could do together what they couldn't do separately.

Bill D. was an attorney at law. Within three days he had

checked out of the hospital. Within a week he was back in court, sober, and arguing a case.

Although it would be four more years before Alcoholics Anonymous would have a name, it had been founded by Bill W. and Dr. Bob in Akron, Ohio, and now it had a third member, Bill D.

BOOK FOUR

1

The years immediately following Bill's visit to Akron were the happiest in his life. He discovered this long afterward when he had a chance to look back and see that, despite the disorder and uncertainty, it had been a period of tremendous activity, of constantly working with others and a continuous sense of growing.

They were years of education and training. In many areas he knew he was still in an anteroom of fulfillment, but he was moving, he was on his way. The newness, and the feeling of living completely in the here and now, which had been such a part of him after leaving Towns, had not worn off, nor had he lost his true gut-level gratitude for having been given a second chance. But more and more as the months passed he had begun to see that this awareness could become a now and then thing.

There was, however, one experience that could invariably bring it back. Whenever he was talking with a potential recruit and caught that sudden flash of recognition, the first faint spark of hope in a drunk's eyes, then the full wonder of who he was and what had happened would wash over him and he'd be totally alive, totally aware.

He and Dr. Bob had talked about this awareness and its peculiar relevance to drunks. They'd even come up with a handy phrase to describe it, one that in its simplicity covered an entire canon of belief: they called it their twenty-four-hour plan. They had stumbled across the phrase almost by accident while working with new men who were still drinking. Neither of them would ask a drunk if he wanted to stop forever. They knew that the vision of a world stretching on with no booze ad infinitum was impossible for any drinker to contemplate, so they asked if he thought he could stop for one day. All men at some time or other had been dry for a day. And if this seemed too rough a proposition, they would bring it down to just one hour.

In the last years of their own drinking they knew they had lived only in the past or in the future. Haunted by memories of what they had done the night before, terrified of what might happen tomorrow, they had had no present tense, and they discovered the same thing was true of every alcoholic they met.

In time they came to see that their little phrase—their little trick, if you wanted to call it that—could work for other problems as well, for by thinking only in terms of twenty-four hours, a man was able to concentrate on the job at hand instead of concentrating only on results, as was the alcoholic tendency. And there was no doubt that there would be many problems to cope with besides just staying away from a drink.

Some men, such as Bill D. and one other fellow they'd found, Ernie G., seemed able to latch on immediately and, with no trouble at all, go right back and take up their old lives. Others, and these were the majority, could grope their way back to life only gradually. With them it seemed a matter of time or luck, because as soon as their minds cleared, and they were starting to live again, an obstacle would inevitably turn up. These obstacles would grow, would become life itself, and of course, when they became overwhelming, a man would look for answers where he had looked before, in booze. For them, Bill and Bob knew, there had to be some plan, some program.

248

Fortunately, as the summer of 1935 raced by, there had been no further developments in Bill's proxy fight, so his time was his own. In July Lois came to Akron for a two-week visit, and seeing how absorbed Bill was, how much he seemed to be learning, she was able to give this new project her full support. By the time she returned to Brooklyn, all four of them, the Wilsons and the Smiths, were agreed that their efforts to find a practical program of recovery must be given top priority.

They were agreed, but it was not an easy project. Still, it was the only thing Bill wanted to do. He knew that few men forty years old find a vocation that can totally absorb their energies. And he was right in thinking that few vocations could have proved more fascinating—or more insanely frustrating—than trying to understand an alcoholic.

But fortunately again—or so Bill and Bob believed at the time —there was the Oxford Group with its dynamic course of action all mapped out. They tried to base everything they did, every step they took toward formulating their program, on Oxford Group principles. And they both worked. They went daily to City Hospital, talked to drunks, brought some hopeful prospects back to live with them on Ardmore Avenue. They never stopped, and there were heady moments when their wildest hopes seemed justified. There were great laughs too, because some they brought home were born clowns, drunk or sober. But there were also moments of heartbreak and near despair. On one hot summer night the entire project almost ended when one Eddie R., who aside from being alcoholic was clearly manic depressive, threatened to kill Bill and Annie Smith with a carving knife.

Still they kept going, day and night, until the end of August when Bill had to leave for New York. By then there was a nucleus of five, possibly six men who were staying sober, sticking together and trying to carry their message to others who were still drinking.

There had been mistakes that summer, big ones, but, as Bill

wrote Bob, he was leaving Akron with a little more humility, a little more understanding, and considerably more experience.

Back on Clinton Street, Bill was somehow able to arouse enough interest to begin holding a series of meetings every Tuesday night. Usually, at this point, there'd be two or three drunks staying in the upstairs rooms. Most of the time they caused little trouble, but there were occasions when, with no warning, the house would be overrun with six or eight men in various stages of recovery. One of them would locate a bottle; then most of them would proceed to get royally soused. On such nights Bill would remember his times with the Smiths as downright pastoral, idyllic and innocent. Still his belief in what he was doing never waned. At this point too—the fall and early winter of '35—he began to receive some surprising support, and it came from a most unlikely source, from two brand-new men, Hank P. and Fitz M.

There could not have been two more contrasting personalities than Hank and Fitz, nor two men with more dissimilar backgrounds, but both caught on to Bill's ideas almost instantly, and both were convinced that every alcoholic could do the same. Hank was a dynamo, a redhead with the broad shoulders and stocky build of a football player, which he had indeed been. Fitz was thinner, quite handsome, with the chiseled features of a Southern gentleman. And their manners were as different as their appearances. Hank went at life with the hearty authority of a supersalesman, Fitz with the quieter, easier charm of the landed gentry. Yet even more remarkable than their differences was the fact that they both saw the infinite possibilities of the fellowship Bill was trying to establish. They not only shared his vision; Hank and Fitz fed it.

If throughout his history there seemed to be certain characters who entered Bill Wilson's life at the very moment they were needed, as though in answer to some silent call, this was never truer than with these two, who were to become his most dependable lieutenants—though Hank would not have appreciated the title. Hank P. always regarded himself as an officer of senior rank.

Primarily, of course, Fitz, Hank and Bill were three extraordinarily healthy males who never let themselves forget what they had been, what had happened to them and what they were now —men who had meant to live life passionately, but whose ambitions had been derailed. Now they had a new outlet and they brought to it a wonderful young exuberance.

One night the three of them were driving down Park Avenue in Hank's car with the top down, when suddenly Hank stood straight up. Grasping the steering wheel in both hands and with the wind beating against him, he yelled, "God!"—wanting God and all the people of New York to hear him. "God almighty," he cried, "booze was never this good."

They believed, these three, that a miraculous thing had happened and that they had the answers. They had heaven in their hands to give to others, and they traveled everywhere—to Towns, to the mission, out to Jersey, up into Westchester—if they heard there was a drunk who might be interested. Hell-bent that others should have what they had, they attended innumerable Oxford Group meetings, whenever and wherever one was held in the New York area.

It was in connection with one of these meetings that a small incident occurred on Clinton Street, which would have been remembered as an incident, nothing more, except for certain repercussions that eventually developed. It was in the evening. Bill had on his hat and coat and was ready to leave the house, when he noticed that Lois wasn't quite ready. He told her to hurry up or they'd be late for the meeting.

Suddenly, at that moment, Lois Wilson had had it. It had been a long day at the store, she'd cooked supper, washed the dishes. . . . In a towering rage, she reached for the nearest object, which happened to be a shoe, and hurled it across the room. "You and your damned meetings," she cried.

In the doorway Bill turned. Nothing more was said, but in the

251

look that passed between them in that brief moment, nothing was held back. Their two lives were spread out before them. For twenty years Lois had done everything possible to support and nurture Bill, always confident that through her love he would somehow get sober. And he had done it, what she had dreamed of and slaved for. But he had done it in a way she had nothing to do with and had no control over. She was no longer needed.

That is what happened that night. They stood looking at each other for a long moment. Then Bill turned and left the room and Lois hurried to finish dressing. These are the facts, not what legend would build them into—that Lois, shocked by the violence of her reaction, immediately took stock of herself and instantly decided on her future course. They were different people and moved at different tempos. But it is equally true that in that moment, in that exchange of looks, a seed had been dropped and it had fallen on receptive soil.

That evening, however, Lois simply picked up her shoe, put it on, grabbed her coat and went out through the door Bill had left open.

For the next six months, late or early, they continued going to meetings, but for Bill, and for Hank and Fitz too, the regular Oxford Group sessions were less important than their own Tuesday night meetings aimed solely at the alcoholic.

By mid '36, in spite of many failures, a small but very solid group was starting to develop on Clinton Street. Traditionally, of course—and the three of them realized this—men who get together for an evening do not go in for confessions, but the group they were collecting was hardly traditional. After a man had taken what they called the first step and had admitted he was powerless over alcohol, he began to see that what they were discussing might well be a matter of life or death for him. Staying away from a drink became more important than his wife, his job, his reputation, his sex life, more important than anything, for in the end everything depended on this one thing. And as various men recognized this, they would open up and begin talking about their lives and sharing their intimate experiences. When they did, each man in the room was struck by the number of things they had in common; not just curious little parallels in their drinking stories—although those were often remarkable—but the tremendous emotions that controlled their lives.

At these moments it was incredible to Bill that he had ever felt alone or believed himself the only man whose life had been ruled by the need to succeed, the terror of failure, or by his deep resentments.

Fears and various kinds of resentment showed up in all the stories and the men discovered that these feelings were often still with them—more under control perhaps, but still there—a living part of them, just waiting to flare up and take control again. And Bill began to sense a pattern here. It might not be true for the rest of the world—he wasn't concerned about them—but for alcoholics it was surely true that nine times out of ten their troubles were of their own making, arose completely out of themselves. Although they often wouldn't admit it at first, they all had been wildly self-centered. By definition, a drinking alcoholic was a prime example of self-will run riot, and so of course was always finding himself in a head-on collision with someone else.

They were so many actors wanting to run the show. This metaphor came to Bill at an early meeting and it struck such a responsive chord that he remembered it and was to use it many times. As an actor the alcoholic was forever trying to arrange everything in his own special way—the lights, the ballet, the scenery, as well as all the other players. Furthermore, he was convinced that if only others would do as he wished, the show would be a huge success, everyone would be delighted. But when things didn't work out exactly as he'd planned, he had a problem. Usually he decided that next time he would have to exert himself a little more. Then, if again it wasn't all he desired, he'd start blaming others; he'd grow angry, self-pitying. But always he remained convinced that he was capable of wresting happiness

253

and satisfaction out of life if only he was in charge and allowed to manage things *his way*. Naturally, others would sense what he was up to; they'd want to retaliate and get something out of the show themselves. Naturally, there would be confusion, conflict and pain and, for the actor-manager, deep resentment.

There was only one answer that Bill could see. They had to find some way to eradicate their self-centeredness, stop thinking they could run the whole production, stop trying to play God. And above all, they must rid themselves of resentment.

Resentments, he was beginning to think, had destroyed more good drunks than any other single cause. Again he didn't know about normal people: maybe they could afford them; they'd get angry for a while and then forget it. But for the alcoholic resentments were a poison, and in some cases a deadly poison. Drunks clung to resentments, nursed them with what seemed total emotional recall, and by so concentrating their thinking on the wrongdoings of others, they gave others power over their lives. Finally they built up such a degree of frustration that there was no other way out: they would have to take a drink. Even in the earlier stages—and Bill could think of many examples in his own case—resentments blocked off any hope of spiritual growth.

These were the things they talked about, openly, frankly, with no sense of embarrassment, and as they did Bill could feel a closeness, and sometimes, when three or four would stay on for an after-meeting meeting because they were so revved up it would have been impossible to stop, he even felt a tremendous lift to their talk such as he'd never experienced with other men.

Here were men who, for the first time, were recognizing themselves in another man's story, and as he saw this happening over and over, he would find himself startled into a smile. There was such an intensity of consciousness in the old Burnham parlor that watching it grow and become stronger gave him an almost animal pleasure. They were, all of them, drunks, "hopeless drunks," working toward freedom, seeking liberation from fear, from jealousy and from all the crippling emotions that had been blocking them, holding them in shackles. He couldn't help smiling from ear to ear at such an assertion of life.

For many reasons, the subjects they were going into, especially those touching on spiritual matters, were easier for Bill to discuss than they may have been for others. Ever since his night at Towns, Bill had had no argument with God, and the impact of this sudden change had been far more profound than even he understood.

He was no longer seeing the world as an arena or himself as a loner forced to compete and win. An example of the extraordinary turnabout was his attitude toward work. He was going at it wholeheartedly, twenty-four hours a day, and doing it with no thought of prestige or any possible financial gain. All he wanted was to feel himself part of the higher power he knew was running the universe.

He was also convinced that alcoholism was a three-pronged illness, mental, physical and spiritual, and that this was something no man could handle on his own, but that as soon as an alcoholic could recognize the spiritual side of his illness, begin tending it, and the spiritual malady was overcome, then the physical and the mental aspects straightened out.

Bill never questioned this.

The others, however, had not had his night at Towns. There were agnostics in the Tuesday-night group, and several hardcore atheists who objected to any mention of God. On many evenings Bill had to remember his first meeting with Ebby. He'd been told to ask for help from anything he believed in. These men, he could see, believed in each other and in the strength of the group. At some time each of them had been totally unable to stop drinking on his own, yet when two of them had worked at it together, somehow they had become more powerful and they had finally been able to stop. This, then—whatever it was that occurred between them—was what they could accept as a power greater than themselves.

Another reason the discussions may have been easier for Bill was that he realized how much the group meant to him and therefore was willing to overlook annoyances that might disturb the others. In Henrietta Seiberling's gatehouse he'd accepted his dependence on Bob Smith. On Clinton Street he knew he needed these men as much as, if not more than, they needed him.

There was also a special faculty of Bill's, a talent that had been present in the boy in East Dorset and the commander of enlisted men in France—a rare ability to sympathize with and immerse himself in another man's problem. A story about this passed around these early meetings. They said you could go to Bill Wilson and tell him anything, you could tell him you'd just pushed your old crippled mother down the stairs, and Bill would nod. "I know. I know." Then he'd put his hand on your shoulder and say, "But you didn't take a drink today."

He loved people and they returned that love, and meetings may therefore have been easier for him. But that is not to imply that this was an easy period in the sense of being comfortable and serene. There continued to be obstacles and constant pressures inside and outside the group. From outside there came mounting criticism from the Oxford Group. Their disapproval of Bill's concentrating on drunks had grown into more than harmless sniping. One evening Bill discovered that alcoholics from the mission had been forbidden to come to Clinton Street, and at the large O.G. gatherings it was bandied about that, after all, the Wilsons were not "really maximum," a phrase that was foreign to Bill and Lois, but nonetheless upsetting. Finally, what was referred to as the divergent work of this secret group became the subject of a Sunday-morning sermon at Calvary. Yet, in a curious way, instead of distressing Bill and his associates, this criticism stiffened their resolve.

Problems within the group were harder to handle.

When a member they had known for months, had had faith in, had loved, would turn up drunk, a kind of terrible apprehension would settle over the meeting. They'd look at one another and see the same question in each man's eyes: Who would be next? Everything they had striven for, everything they had believed in, was threatened. For days they would wander about, conscious of a death in the family. But, as at times of death, there was also a new and startling awareness of life, even an unspeakable gratitude for being alive themselves.

For Bill there was always one other problem, the old problem of his personal finances. Theoretically, men who stayed at the house were to contribute something toward their room and board, but this rarely happened. An installment against the mortgage had to be paid each month and at this point Bill was bringing in no money. He'd tried to connect with some Wall Street deals, but nothing had come of it. What made the situation even more difficult was that each week he was with men who had been sober a much shorter time than he, and most of them were back on the job, earning fine salaries, while he remained what he had been for years, a man whose wife was working.

Then with no warning his whole picture seemed to change. Bill was offered a job at Towns Hospital.

One afternoon Charlie Towns, who had founded the hospital some years back, along with a Dr. Lambert, asked Bill to stop by his office for a little talk. Charlie didn't have to explain the history of the place. Bill knew all about the lucrative enterprise Towns had been in the boom days of the twenties, when wealthy actors such as John Barrymore and equally famous playboys had been willing to pour thousands of dollars a week into Charlie's till for a little discreet drying out. What Bill didn't know was how gravely business had been dropping off in recent years, and nothing, not even Charlie's opening his books and showing him his financial statements, prepared him for what they were to talk about.

Charlie had been watching him, he said, and he wanted Bill to know he had the greatest respect for what he and the members of his group were doing. He'd seen some of the "cures" they had brought about. What he would like Bill to do now was to move the entire operation up to the hospital and make Towns his headquarters. He was prepared to give him an office, a very decent drawing account, plus a healthy slice of the profits. Bill would be a lay therapist and, if Charlie knew anything about it, in no time at all he'd be the most renowned and successful therapist in New York, the number-one man.

Bill's initial reaction was almost disbelief. He told Charlie he wouldn't need any time to think this over, and promised he'd give him an answer in the morning. Even as he said it, a hundred thoughts jammed his mind: what it would mean for Lois to be able to give up her job; what it would mean to all the creditors he still had on the Street; and to the group. Then he realized this was a Tuesday and he wouldn't have to put off telling them.

On the subway back to Clinton Street, he began preparing the speech he'd make at the meeting, choosing the dramatic words he'd use to break the news. What seemed a most apt phrase came to him: "laborers worthy of their hire."

They had waited a long, long time and he knew as he walked into the house and kissed Lois that he was more hopeful at this moment than he had been in years.

But if the offer from Towns had been a surprise, it was as nothing compared to his bafflement when he first spoke to the group. He'd told Lois before the meeting and her reaction had been somewhat calmer than he had expected, but he decided she was preoccupied, tired, or hadn't fully understood. So when he started to address the meeting—and there was a good crowd that night, the parlor was full—he tried to keep a lid on his excitement and present the facts exactly as Charlie had done. But as he did, and then began to outline all that such an offer implied, he found he was addressing a row of impassive faces that just stared up at him, and after a time he noticed that his voice was beginning to trail off.

When he finished, one of the old-timers held up his hand. He was sure he was speaking for the others, he said. He admitted how worried they had all been about Bill's finances and how they knew something would have to be done about them. But what Bill was suggesting didn't seem like the answer; he could foresee too many complications.

Bill let him speak. Then he told them what a splendid fellow Charlie was. He promised them that Charlie Towns could be trusted and that they would be totally independent.

Others began to speak, and they spoke with kindness, with real understanding of what such an opportunity meant. But as Bill's voice had seemed to grow weaker, less sure, theirs grew more confident. What was more, they were all agreed. They spoke as a solid body and they were amazingly articulate about the nature of the problems they were sure they would encounter at Towns.

Finally one man stood up, He was a short, squat fellow who hadn't been with them long, but he'd been sober some months and Bill knew his sobriety meant everything in the world to him. When he started speaking he apologized and fumbled for words, but he wanted to appeal to Bill, he said, and to appeal to something he didn't have the right words to describe. It was the "thing" that bound them together, one to the other, and he knew, he said, that if such groups as theirs were to exist and go on, this thing would have to prevail. And these feelings, as he called them, his voice growing surer, could not be bought and paid for. This had nothing to do with patients and therapists. Drunks were not cases. What they had here, what the whole thing was based on, was one poor drunk bastard coming eye to eye with another poor drunk bastard.

There could be no substitute for that, he insisted, almost shouting now, because nothing but the best would work. Bill himself had told them, and he reminded Bill of this, that the good was often the enemy of the best and what he was suggesting now just wasn't good enough. Drunks needed the best.

Others spoke up. They didn't shout, but their points were

clear and well taken, and Bill knew—or rather he sensed before he knew it—that they were right. But this didn't stop his arguing, not at first. He went on trying to hammer home his position. And then, abruptly, he stopped arguing.

There were to be no bosses in a group. The only authority would be the group conscience, and all decisions were to be made by the group. This was something he and Bob had talked about from the beginning. They had exchanged endless letters on the subject. In theory, of course, they had been right, but now he, Bill Wilson, was being asked to put this belief into practice.

In the morning he phoned Charlie Towns and told him he couldn't accept the offer.

2

That call to Towns marked a decisive step, not in Bill's own recovery perhaps, but in his understanding of the needs and nature of groups. The common welfare had to come first; individual survival depended on group unity, and from this point on it was clear they must remain forever nonprofessional.

Curiously, another decision had to be made almost immediately and he learned one more lesson.

For some time he, Hank and Fitz had realized that eventually a split with the Oxford Group would be inevitable. If Bill had been on his own, this undoubtedly would have been postponed because in addition to his gratitude he felt a tremendous fondness for Sam Shoemaker. It was Sam who had been there, who had opened doors and made him see that belief in a higher power would not only change his thinking and feelings, but could become a living force in the world. Indeed, all the principles, all the foundation stones of the structure he and Bob were trying to shape, had come directly from Sam Shoemaker's Oxford Group. Because he was so acutely aware of this, he knew that a split could never be accomplished without misunderstandings and harsh feelings.

But more important than Bill's devotion to Sam or any indebtedness to the O.G. was the well-being of the group. It was becoming apparent that drunks could not stand up against Oxford Group pressures. In the beginning they wanted only to get sober. Silkworth was right: drunks had to be led, not pushed, and the Oxford Group was too authoritarian for alkies. And this didn't apply only to the newcomer. Bill always had to keep an eye out for his friends the atheists and the agnostics. He himself might believe that certain steps were essential to spiritual growth, but this must not be made a requirement for membership.

Another thing they were discovering—and this was no small matter—was that drunks wanted and needed anonymity. When a poor shaking alcoholic, who was sure about nothing in his life, showed up at a meeting he did not want this fact broadcast to his neighbors, his boss; possibly he did not even want his family to know. They were also learning that anonymity worked for the group as a whole. If one of their more erratic members began boasting around town about his new-found sobriety, there was the danger that this character might slip and get drunk in public, which could play hell with their reputation and that small degree of confidence they were trying to establish with the outside world.

The whole notion of anonymity went against the grain of the Oxford Group. These were generous, loving people, and in theory their movement was democratic, nonracial, nonsectarian. In practice, however, the Oxford Group put great emphasis on finding and saving the "key men" in a community, heads of industry, etc. As a group they were oriented to high-pressure salesmanship, convinced that the only way to carry the message was through publicity and big names.

Finally, in mid '37, when Bill saw that these differences were basic and that the New York members were finding it more and more difficult to work with alcoholics under Oxford Group pressures, he was able to make the break despite hard feelings, despite his gratitude.

From then on his collection of nameless drunks operated as a small, fragile, but completely independent group.

Of course, not all the lessons he was mastering were on so grand a scale. At this point he seemed to be learning from everything and everyone, from his own daily mistakes and from the mistakes of others, from members of the group and from those who were with them only a few nights, from watching and studying their struggles, their little successes.

For a time in the spring of 1937 he worked out of an office in Newark, New Jersey, on several business propositions Hank P. had come up with, but nothing much evolved from them. However, since they were in Jersey, they decided to try to get a meeting started in Hank's home in Upper Montclair. Fitz, who had returned to his family in Maryland, was trying to do the same thing in Baltimore, and that summer they even made several abortive attempts to establish beachheads in Washington and Philadelphia.

Although their percentage of failures was still great, they were kept going by their awareness of the few individuals who had stopped drinking and were staying stopped. Then, too, for Bill, the old investigator, there was the awareness of how much solid information he was acquiring. The house on Clinton Street had become both a home and a laboratory, for there was always someone in some stage of sobriety waiting to talk with him.

A few of their more permanent lodgers, such as Ebby, were with them for months. Others, like Oscar V., who came from an old St. Louis family, would stay for a while, then disappear from their lives, only to show up at some later date, drunk and penniless. There was Russell R., who in his better days had been a partner at Time-Life and now, unemployed and apparently unemployable, still had a brilliant mind and to Bill's thinking was the most hard-headed atheist he had ever run across; and Bill C., a young Canadian alkie, a former attorney and a compulsive gambler. Then there was Florence R., the first female drunk to check in to Clinton Street. Bill had known Florence's husband on Wall Street; when he called and explained that his wife was in Bellevue, Bill and Lois got her out. Florence stayed with them for many months, and seemed to be doing beautifully. They finally sent her down to work with Fitz in Washington. After that there was no news of Florence, only rumors; she'd started drinking again, she'd taken up with a house painter and was living with him somewhere near the Capitol. Then one night Fitz was called to identify her body at the Washington morgue.

The list of those they knew, those they cared for and took care of could go on endlessly. So might a list of the lessons Bill was learning, or the patterns he was beginning to recognize. When the caring took the form of treating drunks like children—which was not unreasonable since they often behaved like children—they sometimes developed a tendency to become too dependent. Life at Clinton Street could be so comfortable, so different from what they had recently known, it could seem like a vacation from real life, and as vacationers—well, why not?—they'd sneak off and have just one little drink. In time, of course, they'd have to have another and another. . . .

Still he could not use the word "hopeless" about any drunk, even one who would turn up from one of the municipal lodgings, bleary-eyed and only half alive. These were the rejects he'd first known at Calvary, the bedraggled flotsam of a city. Some were too far gone to communicate at all, others were great talkers, especially late-night talkers. During the day they'd be willing to chatter with anyone, but in the small hours it was always Bill they had to talk to.

Often Lois would hear Bill's voice drifting up from the kitchen or from one of the little bedrooms down the hall as late as one or two in the morning. Sitting beside a cot or over a cup of coffee in the shadows of Dr. Burnham's old parlor, he would listen as they told about their lives, their fears, their waning ambitions. Worlds whose existence he had never suspected were thrust upon him, and he began to recognize the terrible need of these men to feel in some way important.

With a few—but only a few—he might think he had got through and made some contact. He'd spot a glimmer of hope in their eyes, but it was a fugitive glimmer and was soon gone. He'd urge them to participate, to become part of life again, but they preferred to cling instead to their private hurts, their brooding resentments, as if some instinct told them that the worst fate of all, the one thing they could never face, would be to discover that their sufferings had no substance, no real meaning.

Often in the morning men he'd spent hours listening to, pleading with, would be gone, never to be seen again, or perhaps they'd show up at the door to ask for just enough money for a drink. Over and over Bill had to remind himself that no matter what hopes he might have had, in the end he was dealing with alcohol—cunning, baffling and powerful.

These were three words Bill used many times in his talks at meetings and they appeared often in his letters to Dr. Bob. Apparently things were moving along in Akron at about the same pace: failures, more failures and then an occasional success, although in the summer there was a bit of encouraging news. The Ohio group was beginning to spread out and a regular meeting was being held each week in Cleveland.

In October Bill and Lois took a long weekend off. Leaving Bill C. in charge of the house, they borrowed a car and drove down into Maryland to visit Fitz's family. But on Monday Bill heard of a possible opening with a Wall Street firm and, persuading Lois to stay on a few days more, he returned to the city alone Monday night.

Even before he entered the house Bill sensed something was wrong and as soon as he unlocked the door he knew what it was. The hall was filled with the sweet stench of gas. Throwing open windows, trying not to breathe, he made his way to the kitchen. As soon as he entered the room he saw Bill C., his body lying across the floor, his head in the oven.

He tried to do what he could but it was too late . . . many hours too late, the police said when they arrived.

The suicide was discovered on a Monday evening. Tuesday the regular meeting was held, as indeed it was on every Tuesday night throughout October.

In November Bill had to make a trip to the Midwest in connection with the brokerage job he was trying to nail down. Although nothing came of his efforts concerning the job—another depression had hit the country in the fall of '37—the trip gave him an opportunity to visit Dr. Bob in Akron. Bill had been sober almost three years, Bob two and a half, and this, they figured, should be ample time for them to see where they were and even make some sort of informal progress report.

There had been failures galore. Literally hundreds of drunks had been approached by their two groups and some had sobered up for a brief period but then slipped away. They were both conscious of their failures as they settled down in Bob's living room and began comparing notes. But as the afternoon wore on and they continued going over lists, counting noses, they found themselves facing a staggering fact. In all, in Ohio and in New York, they knew forty alcoholics who were sober and were staying sober, and of this number at least twenty had been completely dry for more than a year. Moreover, every single one of them had been diagnosed a hopeless case.

As they sat, each with a paper in hand, checking and re-checking the score, a strange thing happened; they both fell silent. This was more than a game they were playing, more than a little casual bookkeeping to be used for a report. There were forty names representing forty men whose lives had been changed, who actually were alive tonight because of what had started in this very room. The chain reaction they had dreamed about—one alcoholic carrying the word to another—was a reality. It had moved onward, outward from them.

It is perhaps remarkable that their first response, before the excitement and the tremendous lift took over, was exactly the same. They were filled with a sense of wonder, of something akin to awe at this mysterious force they had helped set in motion.

But no sense of awe could stop these two for very long. Their humility before what God had wrought was profound and for a time they remained silent, but they were Vermonters, two hard-rock Yankee pragmatists. They might have been instruments, channels through which a higher power had started to work, but for them that afternoon, it was only a start.

Forty was a startling figure, but it was also an infinitesimal fraction. The number of alcoholics in the world had to be reckoned in the millions. And when they began to talk again that afternoon, they knew what they must do and that it would require a fundamental and sweeping change in their thinking and their whole approach. If they were even to begin to pass on their proven know-how to the millions who still suffered, they must never again think of themselves as a small and secret society.

For two and a half years their little word-of-mouth program had worked, and worked magnificently, but they could hardly expect every active alcoholic to make his way to Akron, Ohio, or Clinton Street in Brooklyn.

And yet they also realized that any decision about new approaches or new methods of spreading their knowledge was not a thing they could take alone. Any changes such as they were beginning to contemplate would require not only the approval but the support of the entire fellowship. Without wasting any time, Bob got on the phone to arrange a special meeting of the Akron group.

In the interval before the meeting—it was only a matter of a few days—Bill had a thousand ideas. The stalled motor of his imagination had started to turn again; the old power drive was coming back, full force.

Not since his nights in Stewart's cafeteria, when he'd first envisioned a world-wide movement, had he felt so alive or so in charge of himself. Now his imagination was working in conjunction with that rational, investigative side of his mind which had been trained to assess and evaluate all sorts of situations and enterprises.

In order to spread the word and reach out to drunks they might never meet personally, they would first of all need quantities of printed matter—books, pamphlets. Bill saw that these might serve a twofold purpose; they would tell the group's stories and at the same time they could clarify and keep straight its method of working. And they both knew this would be a great step forward, because as long as they remained dependent on word of mouth, there was a danger that everything they had developed might become garbled. Fine folks though recovered alkies were, they were not always what would be termed mature personalities, and there was nothing to prevent one of their more unstable members from intentionally or unintentionally distorting the program beyond recognition.

Also there was work to be done in hospitals. Perhaps they should have their own drying-out establishments, since most hospitals took a dim view of drunks, refusing even to recognize alcoholism as an illness. But if they had their own places, if they had their own staffs . . .

Of course, such dreams would have to be subsidized, but Bill had not the slightest doubt that now that they had the facts, the proof that their methods worked, they'd be able to raise thousands, millions even. Listening to his plans, Dr. Bob was more than a sounding board. He was—he would continue to be— a very necessary balance. He liked the idea of a book and saw it as a valuable way of codifying their beliefs, but as to running hospitals, having their own staffs and raising millions of dollars, he had his doubts.

Sitting in Annie Smith's kitchen, they discussed the pros and cons of each proposition, and by the night of the meeting Bill had his arguments well lined up. He felt in good form that night and was raring to go. Actually he hoped he'd meet a little opposition, because any argument would come like the scent of gunpowder to an old war horse. He was going to show them, show them all.

There were eighteen members present and the meeting began promptly at eight o'clock. They were still talking at midnight. After Bob had made a few remarks and Bill had launched into his plan, he had a curious sensation as he stood looking down at the row of stolid faces studying him that somehow this evening was going to be a repeat of the night in Brooklyn when he'd reported his offer from Towns. But as he went on, warming to his subject, it became clear that there were two marked differences: first, that night at Clinton Street he had been arguing, at least in part, for his own position, whereas now his full concentration was on their responsibility to the world of alcoholics and how best to reach them. And second, the men gathered before him now were anything but inarticulate. As soon as he stopped they started in on him. And not one of them lacked words. They went at him and his suggestions from every conceivable angle, and at first there seemed no unanimity in their arguments; they disagreed heartily with him and with each other.

Bill had more than once tried to analyze the camaraderie, the special bond he felt in such a group, but as he listened to those eighteen men expressing their views he was overwhelmed by the electricity that was being generated. There could be no mistaking who they were. These were his people, men who had wanted double everything, and now they were fighting for principles that they believed in, that had, they were convinced, saved their lives. The sheer animal energy of a recovered drunk was almost frightening, but at the same time it was wildly stimulating. Bill knew that if only this force could somehow be

269

channeled, it could accomplish anything, everything he had mentioned and more.

It was quite a meeting. Every suggestion was challenged, every idea thoroughly examined. Going into the hospital business they said would be regarded as—and, considering who they were, would soon become—a commercial racket, and what, they demanded, would this do to the spirit of the group and their principle of carrying the message to other drunks with no strings and no money attached?

Bill's point that word of mouth was not only too slow and too limited a way of carrying the message, but that it might also lead to the program's being twisted out of shape, seemed to make sense. But some could see no reason for having a book or even a pamphlet. After all, they pointed out, Christ's apostles had done all right without any printed matter. And as for raising money and subsidizing missionaries, they were convinced it would spell the end of the fellowship.

It was a long night and arguments grew loud and heated, but always, and this was apparent with each man who spoke, their concentration was focused on just one thing: on finding the best way to get the word across to drunks who wanted help. In the end—and it was well after midnight before they broke up—Bob and Bill found they'd been more persuasive than they'd known. The proposals were put to a vote and by a majority of two Bill was authorized to go ahead with his plan, return to New York and, if he felt it necessary, start raising money.

Something had been let loose in the world, a force that no one at the time could fully understand. To some it was dangerous and extremely frightening.

All of them had questions. What would the changes mean to them as individuals? As they grew and reached out along such grandiose lines, would they be able to stick together, would they cling to the simple, sturdy raft that had brought them to safety? The one thing that could wreck all they had built up would be their alcoholic power drives, those ballooning egos that had so recently been deflated. Would they soar up again, burst and finally blow everything apart, or could they somehow be held in check?

As a few of the Akron group who had been at the meeting saw Bill off at the station, they were admittedly deeply concerned. It was there, before Bill stepped on the train, that Dr. Bob put his hand on Bill's arm and said just one thing. "For God's sake, Billy, keep it simple."

3

The minority who voted against Bill's plan had good reason to be alarmed. There was a very real threat hanging over the entire project now. And they knew the threat lay in the direct connection between Bill's tremendous drive and alcohol itself. Without his passion to succeed there could have been no growth; the fellowship would have remained a secret society which doubtless would have dissolved in time as so many other fine endeavors had dissolved. Yet in the winter of '37 those who were most concerned knew that everything was being put in one man's hands and that this man was a drunk.

Recently there had been few signs of Bill's old obsession to excel and become number one, but these were canny alcoholics he was working with, and they knew that because an obsession may have nodded off it is not necessarily dead or even permanently asleep. What if, as he started out to conquer new worlds, he found himself thwarted? What if the tensions grew and he reached for a drink? What if Bill Wilson got drunk? It was in his power slowly and prudently to build a solid structure, or utterly to destroy the lifeline they had been clinging to. It is not surprising that some of those on the sidelines held their breath as they watched.

How much of this Bill understood—or rather at what depth he realized it—they could only guess. Not long before his trip west, something had happened which many hoped might serve as an example. They were trying to raise money for Clinton Street and Ebby had gone to Albany. Nobody knew what had happened there, but when he returned he was drunk and he had been drunk off and on ever since, Ebby, who had been Bill's sponsor, his rock. Ebby, who had first brought him the message. And Bill had tried to learn from this the lonely lesson that one may still have faith in a message, if not always in the messenger.

Fortunately when he got back from Akron he was not alone. The Clinton Street group, to his amazement, fell right in with his proposals. Then, too, there was Fitz M., who was often in town that winter and always ready to lend his quiet support. And there was Hank P., the greatest high-pressure salesman Bill had ever known. Hank always took fire from any idea Bill had. If a world-wide movement was going to take millions of dollars to launch, no problem: they'd raise millions.

The two of them immediately set to work approaching every rich man and every charitable foundation in Manhattan. But quite early on they discovered that the wealthy can have remarkably deaf ears. The Red Cross or the Cancer Fund had got there first, and although many professed their sympathy, they saw no real reason to help drunks, who after all had brought their problems on themselves. Perhaps if Bill or Hank could come up with a method of preventing alcoholism, they might be interested.

After six weeks of such talk and not one cent raised, Bill began to see that what they were proposing might never be a popular cause. He was more baffled than dejected when he stopped by one afternoon to talk to his brother-in-law, Dr. Strong.

After listening to Bill's diatribe about the rich, Leonard recalled a girl he'd gone to school with, a niece of Willard Richard-

273

son, who worked for and was a great friend of John D. Rockefeller, Jr. He wasn't sure if Richardson would remember him, but at least it was worth a try. He put through a call.

Richardson did indeed remember Leonard, and an appointment was set up for the following morning at the Rockefeller offices in Radio City. Richardson, who was in charge of all John D., Jr.'s, philanthropies, was a reserved elderly man, his twinkling eyes set in a thin, sensitive face. When he'd heard Bill's story, he admitted that he was very impressed and he asked if they might get together again at a meeting with a few more friends of Mr. Rockefeller. He also suggested that if Bill cared to, he might bring along a few of his recovered drunks. Bill said he would, they agreed upon a date and shook hands, and Bill raced home to put through a call to Dr. Bob.

It was just before the second meeting, held on a starry evening late in December on the fifty-sixth floor of the RCA Building, that Bill understood the meaning of the phrase "riding a pink cloud." Dr. Bob was with him—he had come east with several stalwarts from the Akron group; so were Hank, Fitz, Ned P., a new man, and Dr. Silkworth. The Rockefeller contingent was made up of Richardson, Frank Amos, A. LeRoy Chipman, who looked after the family's vast real estate empire, and Albert Scott, chairman of the board of trustees of the Riverside Church. As Bill lowered himself into a warm leather chair, he was told that John D., Jr., had just vacated that very chair. At last he was close, incredibly close, to the really big money.

The meeting was conducted along the lines of those in Brooklyn. After a few of them had told their stories there was a period of questions and answers. It was clear that the Rockefeller gentlemen had been genuinely moved by what they'd heard and they wanted to know what they could do to help.

The moment had come. Bill explained that they needed capital to go forward, expand and take their work out to others. But at this point Albert Scott asked if there wouldn't be a risk in this procedure. Wouldn't money spoil things? What they'd been hearing, he said, was like first-century Christianity, where one person carried the word to the next. Wouldn't holding property, the problems of managing professional workers, investing capital confuse and possibly jeopardize the essence of what they had?

Echoes of the old Akron arguments. But Bill and Bob were prepared. These risks were nowhere near so great, they explained, as the risk of standing still and allowing thousands to die because the groups were unable to reach them. And this the gentlemen understood.

In the end they all agreed that it was something that would certainly appeal tremendously to Mr. Rockefeller. There was no doubt in the room about that. Frank Amos, they decided, should make a trip to Akron, conduct an investigation and then prepare a report as soon as possible.

Amos was in Akron within the week. He interviewed members of the group and various associates of Dr. Bob; he examined real estate sites as possible locations for hospitals, and the report he prepared, from the point of view of the fellowship, was magnificent. Their project, he felt, deserved Mr. Rockefeller's complete support and he suggested an initial grant of fifty thousand dollars to be turned over to Bill and Bob.

Willard Richardson added his approval to the report and immediately passed it on to Mr. Rockefeller. And they had been right. Rockefeller was impressed. He saw the parallel with early Christianity and along with this he spotted a combination of medicine and religion that appealed to all his charitable inclinations. He said so in no uncertain terms. However, he was so taken by the potential of such an organization that he wanted to be very careful to do nothing that could in any way harm it. And money, he was sure, was the one thing that might eventually undermine their efforts.

About this he was adamant. When Richardson explained that Wilson and Smith were in dire financial straits, he yielded somewhat and said that he'd be willing to place a check for five thousand dollars in the treasury of the Riverside Church for their personal use, but he didn't want to be asked for any more. He was convinced that if ever a movement must be self-supporting, it was this one.

It was a shock. This time they had seemed so close.

Yet curiously Bill did not regard it as a setback. He'd drawn a new confidence from the response of the Rockefeller men, and somehow he accepted everything that was happening now as a personal challenge.

Five thousand might not be the fifty thousand he had been counting on, but it was something. (Three thousand had to go at once to pay off the mortgage on Dr. Bob's house and they decided that each of them would take thirty dollars a week from the balance as long as the money held out.) Bill knew it would give them a breathing spell in which to gather their forces and renew their attack on other foundations.

Perhaps it was the sort of adverse situation in which Bill always functioned at his best. He felt the same sense of adventure he'd had on the motorcycle trip with Lois. Once again he was setting out on a quest, an enterprise where there were no precedents to guide him. And again, when in later years he remembered this time, he was to think of it in cinematic terms: certain scenes stood out vividly while others faded away in a great montage of frantic activity, and everything that happened always took place at a wildly accelerated pace. It seemed incredible, preposterous, that he had done so much and against such odds.

There were differences, though. For one, Bill was no longer a loner. Without his knowing it was happening, his life had been taken over by the habits, the needs, the emotions of others, until now it seemed he had no personal destiny. There was only a collective destiny for them all. This naturally brought new anxieties, the anxieties of a frontiersman leading his train of wagons across a desert, knowing there are no signposts and that the only compass he has has never been tested. Also there was not the slightest question this time about the rightness of his mission. His total commitment was somewhat disturbing to many of those who stood aside; such dogged intensity of purpose is not always easy to watch.

All spring and into the summer he and Hank continued canvassing the rich, writing letters, freely using the names of their friends from the Rockefeller group, doing everything conceivable to solicit money. They consulted with Richardson frequently, but the results of their efforts were exactly the same. Though the rich remained polite, they could see no reason to invest in an outfit that was neither medical nor educational. Why bother to scrape up the leavings of society?

Finally Bill came to understand that what they needed was a foundation of their own. If they were registered as a tax-free organization, people would look more kindly on them, and if they had a board made up of nonalcoholics as well as alcoholics, it might create more confidence. Dr. Strong, Richardson, Amos and Chipman all agreed to serve as trustees, but at the start this seemed only to create legal problems: attorneys had to be consulted because no one could define a nonalcoholic. That question never was resolved satisfactorily.

Still they went on and in April the Alcoholic Foundation was established. They held meetings each month, though they had little to do at these sessions except commiserate with one another about their lack of funds. Dreams of hospitals and paid workers had to be left in abeyance, but there was nothing to stop them from moving ahead with the projected book. So every morning, in the little office in Newark, Bill began dictating to Hank's secretary, Ruth Hock.

There was remarkable timing in Bill's starting to write exactly when he did. It was as though it threw an inner switch that had been waiting to be thrown for years. He'd been sober for some time, but he was still close enough to the raw emotions and suffering, the self-loathing, the terrors, to be able to call them up and present the ugly facts of the obsession that had ruled his life and that finally had placed him beyond any human help. In 1938 he was in direct touch with all the simple truths that had been guiding him since his first meeting with Dr. Bob.

The difficulties of stating these truths were immense. He didn't want to pretend to answer the riddles of alcoholism, or even to diagnose the causes. He did want, however, to cut through the vast bog of ignorance and misunderstanding surrounding the illness, to answer questions specifically and, if possible, to establish an immediate identification with alcoholics who were still drinking. He knew a phony emotional appeal could never do this. The message that would catch and hold the interest of a drunk had to have depth and weight. It had to be honest. He understood that the truth he was trying to pass on, the insight that might create a new set of conceptions and cause a psychic change in the alcoholic reader had to be grounded in a power far greater than himself.

A professional writer would have run from such an assignment, but Bill sat down at his desk in Newark each morning and talked simply, honestly, unashamedly, using the language of religion where it applied. With no hesitation he described his surrender at Towns Hospital and the miraculous communion he'd sensed with Bob, as well as the tools they'd tried to use in their new way of life. He did not bother about style. The result was a plain prose, the tone and timbre of which was as true as the sound of the wind whistling through his Vermont trees, as straightforward as talk in a general store.

In no time he had the first two chapters finished and Ruth Hock typed them up. There would be problems ahead, big ones, but these early chapters held the strength and the exuberance of a man who has discovered something on his own. Nothing is more readable.

To some, much that Bill W. wrote sounded stereotyped, but to those who needed to hear it, it *felt* like life. And, coming as it did from another drunk, they could trust it, take hope and begin to live again.

278

As chapters were completed, copies were made and passed along for comment to the trustees and to various members of the group—and everyone had a comment. At the September meeting of the board, Frank Amos had suggested that it might be helpful if Bill showed a copy to his friend Gene Exman, the editor of religious books at Harper & Brothers. When Bill did, Exman's reaction was astonishing. After reading two chapters, he asked Bill if he thought he could write an entire book in that style. Bill was sure he could, and when he explained his ideas and his intention of including some two dozen personal stories from other recovered alkies, Exman said that Harper's would be interested in publishing such a book. He told Bill he was prepared to offer $1,500 as an advance against royalties.

It was a beautiful day for Bill W.

There is some argument about who first began to question the Harper offer. The happy news spread quickly through the fellowship and it is not known whether it was Hank or Bill himself who initially had some doubts. Certainly by the time the two met a few days later in Hank's backyard they both were expressing misgivings. If this book was to be their basic text and if the fellowship was to grow as they hoped, it didn't seem right that their main asset should be owned by outsiders. Besides, Bill would have to earn out the $1,500 advance before receiving any further royalties, and if the book was a success and sold as Harper's must believe it would, then thousands of inquiries might start pouring in and they'd have no money to cope with the situation.

Hank had done a little investigating. He'd contacted the Cornwall Press and had learned from them that such a book as they were planning could be printed for about thirty-five cents a copy, and could sell for, say, $3.50. Even if they had to give bookstores a discount, their net had to be tremendous, and Hank couldn't understand why all that should go to Harper's. Obviously they should form a stock company, sell shares and raise the money to publish their book themselves.

Bill was sure that the trustees would never go along with this. And he was right. When he presented Hank's plan they bombarded him with all the obvious arguments: authors were never successful at publishing their own work; he should be grateful that an old and reliable firm that understood the complexities of the business wanted his book. He must certainly accept the Harper offer.

These arguments carried no weight with Hank P. Since the foundation had not and could not come up with any money to back them, what they had to say struck him as academic. Not wanting to go against his old friends on the board, but at the same time responding to Hank's excitement, Bill called again on Gene Exman to explain his dilemma. To his amazement Exman agreed that an organization such as theirs should control its own literature; he understood perfectly and wished Bill the greatest success.

When Bill saw Hank next, the walls of the little office in Newark were covered with charts and diagrams, all showing the estimated profits on sales of a hundred thousand or five hundred thousand books that could be manufactured for thirty-five cents per copy and sell for a whopping $3.50. Encouraged as he was by his interview with Exman, some of Hank's talk nevertheless seemed wild to Bill. Yet he was finally convinced that no matter what happened, the proceeds of the book were bound to be enough to allow a few of them to become full-time workers; possibly they'd even be able to set up some sort of headquarters for the fellowship. That afternoon the two stopped in a stationery store and bought a pad of blank stock certificates.

Across the top of each certificate they wrote "Works Publishing Inc. par value $25." Since they were sure this book was to be only the first of many publications, it seemed a fitting title.

As they filled in the certificates, Bill was also convinced that since Hank knew every angle of supersalesmanship and he himself in his days on the Street had been no slouch, and considering all the magnificent aspects of what they were peddling, there was no way they could fail.

But they failed. They descended on their group of recovered drunks—Hank with a hard sell, Bill following just behind to smooth out ruffled feelings—and they got nowhere. They approached everyone who'd attended a meeting, every rich man they knew, and they did not sell a single share of stock. Why, they were asked, should anyone invest in a book that hadn't even been written?

Within a few weeks it was obvious that their dream was dying. They needed some kind of inspiration and Hank P. was the man for inspirations. Their timid customers had to believe the book would sell, and a book had to have one thing in order to sell—publicity, a huge spread in some national magazine.

The next day Hank and Bill were in Pleasantville, New York, talking to a managing editor of *Reader's Digest*. Like others before him, the editor had to agree their story was unique. He admitted he was impressed and, yes, the *Digest* might well be interested in publishing an article about their movement. And the article could come out at the same time the book appeared.

Back in Brooklyn, there was an immediate change in attitude. If a company like Harper's believed in them, if *Reader's Digest*, with its gigantic circulation, was giving them a spread, this might after all be something worth investing in. But these were ex-drunks Bill was talking to and they would invest in their own way. Some bought one share outright, some bought on an installment plan, five dollars down and five a month. But the point was they were buying. So were others, friends, acquaintances and members of the board, in somewhat larger blocks. Their biggest subscriber put in three hundred dollars and in the next months they managed to raise over four thousand, enough to keep Bill, Hank and Ruth going.

The fall and winter raced by, the busiest and one of the most productive times in Bill's life. His days were spent in Newark writing, his evenings at meetings, reading aloud what he'd written, defending it, sometimes rewriting it. The group at this point appeared evenly divided between conservatives and liberals. The conservatives, led by Fitz, felt that since the movement was based on Christian doctrine, they should say so flat out. The liberals, led by Hank and Jim B., another salesman, who'd recently joined them, were willing to let Bill speak of certain spiritual concepts, even to use the word "God" if he must, but they wanted a strongly psychological emphasis. Then, too, there were the radicals, Bill's old friends the atheists and the agnostics, who backed Hank and Jim. Bill listened to everyone, because even then he knew that the book had somehow to speak for all of them.

And so it went, strong but warm-hearted arguing, until they reached Chapter Five. That was where Bill wanted to explain exactly how they worked. Ever since he and Bob had tried to shape a program, their ideas had been based on Oxford Group principles: first admitting they were powerless over alcohol, then making a moral inventory, confessing their shortcomings to another, making amends whenever possible, and finally praying for the power to carry out these concepts and to help other drunks. This had been their word-of-mouth program. But now, putting it on paper, Bill felt a need to pin it down in specific steps, so that there could be no questions in the reader's mind, no possible loopholes through which the rationalizing alcoholic could wiggle away.

One night, late in December, stretched out on his bed at Clinton Street, he set to work trying to be explicit, to break down the program into smaller pieces and, if possible, broaden and deepen the spiritual implications of their ideas. When he had finished, he counted the steps he had outlined; there were twelve in all. For some reason this struck him as a significant number, and he added the steps to the opening section of Chapter Five.*

* See page 372.

372

He was frankly pleased with what he had written, and was in no way prepared for the violent reaction when he read his twelve steps to the group a few nights later. The conservatives were delighted; they bought them exactly as written; but the liberals were appalled and said so. As a body they seemed suddenly to backtrack and take up a solid position beside the radicals. There was far too much God talk in the steps. And why twelve steps? They'd been doing all right on five or six. If he wanted to talk about the spiritual, okay, but religion, never! It would only scare drunks away, and besides, the missions did the God bit and everyone knew missions always failed with alcoholics.

There seemed no way these opposing views could be reconciled. Since Bill had written what he believed in and since he *knew*, as few men have ever known, that it worked, had worked for him and could work for others, he started off defying the group and defending every word. Also, since the remainder of the book was to be based on the steps, some agreement on the matter had to be reached.

As the fights raged on—and these arguments lasted much longer than that first night; some were still at it weeks later—after joining the battle, stating his opinion as firmly as he could and sensing all the old excitement of combat, something—Bill couldn't have said what—made him decide to change his attack, to be still, sit back and listen. It was the canniest decision he ever made.

Several elements may have kept these evenings from getting out of control and becoming totally destructive. Lois had a way of turning up at opportune moments with fresh pots of coffee and reminding them that, after all, everything didn't have to be settled that night. But most important was the shift in Bill's approach. In recent years he'd developed a way of slouching down in a chair, his legs stretched before him, his head cocked quizzically, listening with one eyebrow slightly raised, and somehow in this relaxed posture he gave an impression of shrewd affability, of a man who was a little more aware than the others of what was going on and was possibly just a little wiser too. In the end it may have been this seeming confidence that calmed them down, his apparent belief that if the speakers were allowed to continue as long as they wanted, they'd talk themselves out, change their minds or at least reach some sort of compromise.

And that finally was what he saw happening, a compromise. Not a compromise in the sense of either side's surrender, but in something being created that blended the finest qualities of the opposing views.

First was the idea that they should always label their steps a *Suggested* Program of Recovery. Bill called this one a ten strike. They all agreed that no drunk would rebel at a mere suggestion.

The next point—and this turned out to be providential—was that whenever the word "God" was used in their literature, it should be followed by the phrase "as we understand Him." Bill saw that those italicized words would not only widen the gateway so that all drunks could pass through, regardless of their belief or lack of belief. In time they might also force many men to come to terms with what they understood God to be, with what it was in their lives that they truly believed in.

With these points agreed on, the steps were approved. They became a part of Chapter Five and before long were to be looked upon as the foundation stone of the fellowship.

Meanwhile batches of case histories were beginning to arrive from Ohio. Dr. Bob, perhaps wisely, had not explained too much to the Akron and Cleveland members about Bill's promotional schemes in New York, so they had not been involved in the hectic buying and selling of stock, but they worked hard turning out their stories. In the past year Bob had sobered up an ex-newspaperman, and he may have helped with the writing. Whatever the cause, the Ohio stories all had that special ring about them which only comes when an individual is speaking from his own experience; their truth was irrefutable and irresistible, exactly what the book needed.

The New York group was much slower and the case histories they finally handed in were long-winded and often wildly repetitious. Hank and Bill tried editing them, cutting, polishing, occasionally rewriting, and that was a grave mistake; drunk or sober, an alcoholic feels a pride in his own story that should not be tampered with. However, spirits were high, and without too many crushed feelings they worked on, discussing, debating every paragraph—often Bill felt himself more an umpire than an author—and the final chapters began to pile up.

In mid-January they finished the book with only a few last details to be seen to before handing it over to the printers. Not wanting the text to have medical errors or material that might upset the clergy, they considered ordering several prepublication copies to pass around for comments. This, too, had to be argued about, since it would take more time and, even more important, money. And everyone knew there was little left in the treasury. But they finally decided to play it safe, have their manuscript mimeographed and distributed to various doctors and ministers for criticism.

Another detail was a title, and at the start this threatened to become a controversy equaled only by the battle of the Steps. Since breaking with the Oxford Group, the New Yorkers had been referring to themselves as a "nameless bunch of alcoholics," and from this had come the phrase "alcoholics anonymous." No one knows who first used it. Bill thought it catchy and an appropriate title for the book, but the others disagreed heartily. "The Way Out" seemed the favorite, although literally hundreds of titles were discussed. At one point Bill considered "The Bill W. Movement"—the ego had not been totally deflated—but he was quickly talked out of that.

Akron favored "Alcoholics Anonymous," New York "The Way Out." Another burning issue, another impasse, and one that was resolved only when Bill sent a wire to Fitz in Maryland asking him to go to Washington and find out how many "Way Out"s were registered at the Library of Congress. Fitz's reply informed them that there were already twelve books entitled "The Way Out" and, as far as he could discover, no "Alcoholics Anonymous." That did it. No drunk was going to risk being the thirteenth anything. The book had its title, the fellowship had a name.

The first reactions to the mimeographed copies had begun coming in and they were heartening. Dr. Harry Emerson Fosdick was completely satisfied with the book, and so were other ministers, medical men and psychiatrists. But, as someone pointed out, all these responses came from Protestants. Curiously, since alcoholism was often referred to as an Irish Catholic disease, there had been not a single Catholic member of the Clinton Street group in its first two years. In early January, however, a young redhead, Morgan R., had started hanging around. He was an ex-adman, recently released from Rockland asylum. He seemed sober enough, and he was definitely a Catholic. Furthermore, Morgan had a friend on the Catholic Committee on Publications for the New York Archdiocese.

Morgan was instantly commissioned to deliver a clean mimeographed copy to the committee, and the group waited, not knowing how the Church would judge a book that dealt in detail with release from booze through spiritual means yet made no mention of Catholicism.

They need not have worried. In the entire book the committee found only one sentence they wanted changed. Bill had said at the end of his first chapter, "Many of us have found heaven right here on this good old earth." The committee suggested that he might change "heaven" to "utopia," since, after all, the Church was promising folks something a little better later on.

The suggestion was taken.

Within a matter of days, Hank, Ruth and Bill delivered the manuscript to the Cornwall Press and although, by the most optimistic count, they had no more than one hundred members in January 1939, they were so carried away by these early responses that they placed an order for a first printing of five thousand copies. Edward Blackwell, the president of Cornwall, was a little aghast at their offer of only five hundred dollars as a down payment, but he finally nodded—he admittedly had never known men like them—and agreed to play along and start the presses rolling.

Now it was a certainty. As soon as the *Reader's Digest* article appeared they'd have five thousand books in the shops. Hank and Bill immediately headed for Pleasantville to confer with the managing editor.

As they were ushered into the handsome *Digest* offices, Hank, rubbing his hands together, started the conversation with, "Well, sir, we're set. When do we shoot?"

The poor baffled man could only ask, "Shoot what?" Then—and the two watched it happen—he remembered who they were, remembered telling them the *Digest* might be interested in a piece on their society, and remembered too that he had forgotten to tell them that when he had brought the matter up with his editorial board they'd thought there would be no interest in alcoholism, that the subject might prove too controversial. He was genuinely sorry, but . . .

There had been blows before, but none like this.

All their stock had been sold, all the money raised, including a loan from Charlie Towns and one from Fitz's sister—and all on the expectation of the publicity they'd receive when the book appeared, on their promise that this would happen. What could they say? How explain to a man who's been handing over five dollars a week?

Some of those Bill talked with were kind and understanding. Many were not.

As "publication day" neared there was an occasional bright spot, but in the end even these were meaningless. Fosdick wrote a beautiful review which was reprinted in religious publications; *The New York Times* reviewed them; but there were no books in the stores. Twenty-eight free copies had to be sent to the members who'd contributed stories, forty-nine to those who'd bought stock; the remainder stayed piled up in a warehouse. What was to become of those copies presented a terrifying prospect since they had no money to make the slightest additional payment on the printer's bill.

In April 1939 there seemed no money anywhere. Back in the fall, when hopes were high, Bill had talked Lois into giving up her job, so now, four and a half years sober, he wasn't even a man with a wife who worked. Then, to compound the situation, the week the book was published they learned that the bank to which they'd been giving twenty dollars a month against the mortgage had found a buyer for 182 Clinton Street. They were told they had to be out by the first of May.

If ever there was a moment for a miracle, a resounding one, this was it. And again it was Hank P. who came up with, if not exactly a miracle, at least a solution that would change the situation overnight. Hank had been talking with their new man, the redheaded Morgan, and had discovered that he was a friend of Gabriel Heatter. Heatter, as everyone in America knew, was the M.C. of *We, the People,* a fantastically popular radio show that went in heavily for short interviews of a heart-rending nature. Hank's plan was to get Morgan on *We, the People,* have him describe his fall, his salvation through AA, and then, on a national hookup, put in a plug for the book.

But this wasn't all. Hank had decided that doctors were the public they should aim for. He wanted to launch a mail-order campaign, send out cards, inundate the medical profession with announcements about the broadcast and the book, *Alcoholics Anonymous.* And they'd attach an order form to every card. This would require considerable money, but Hank was a fast worker; he and Bill signed some promissory notes and, through a couple of affluent new members, raised the cash for the printing. Heatter agreed to interview Morgan, a date was set, and twenty thousand cards went out, one to every physician east of the Mississippi.

At this point—they'd been stung too often—someone came up

with the question, what if Morgan got drunk? After all, he'd been with them only a short time.

There was obviously one way to handle that. Hank found another new member, another solvent one, who happened to belong to the Downtown Athletic Club and was willing to foot the bill for two adjoining rooms. Morgan was checked into the club while various older members worked shifts guarding him, never letting him out of their sight.

Morgan didn't care for the idea, but what could he do? He stayed in his room and on the night of the broadcast he was cold sober. And he was brilliant. In New York and out in Ohio members sat glued to their sets. They were moved by Morgan's story, but they knew their troubles were over. As soon as the orders began coming in, carloads of books would start rolling across the country. Out of their sufferings and struggles a best seller had been born.

Hank and Bill had rented a post office box at Grand Central to take care of the order blanks, but they made themselves wait three days before they made their trip down Lexington Avenue and into the post office, accompanied by Ruth, who brought along a sizable suitcase to handle the replies.

Bill was the first to look into the box, and as he looked he had a slight sinking feeling in his stomach. But Hank immediately pushed him aside. Hank knew about these things. What the hell, they always kept the big mail pouches with mail orders out back; a clerk would deliver them.

The clerk delivered them, twelve replies. Most of the cards kidded the whole idea, and most of them seemed to have been written by doctors who, from their handwriting, obviously had had a couple too many. Out of twenty thousand mailings there were two orders for copies of *Alcoholics Anonymous*.

4

There are times in a man's life when all the waves of his history seem to be joining, building to some terrifying crest. In the spring of '39 Bill could feel such a time approaching.

When he stood on Clinton Street and watched their possessions being carried out and packed into a van, he didn't have the money even to pay the movers. All their furniture, including many of Dr. Burnham's finest pieces, was being put in hock to a storage company.

Various members helped as they could, but Bill's net assets at this point were a summer camp Horace C. lent him out in Jersey, a car borrowed from another member, a defunct book company and a storage bill. When later someone asked how he and Lois had got through the next two years, Bill explained, "We were invited out to dinner a lot."

With Clinton Street gone, the New York group met for a while in Bert T.'s tailoring establishment on Fifth Avenue, then in a rented parlor in Steinway Hall. Meanwhile the Jersey groups were beginning to branch out with meetings each week in South Orange, and there was always hopeful news coming in from Ohio. There was no question but that things were moving, AA was growing, but it was all taking place at a much slower pace than Bill had dreamed it would. Now, whenever he'd see a copy of the book, it was a rebuke. The idea of thousands of copies waiting unwanted in Blackwell's warehouse was embarrassing, one more example of Billy Wilson failing again.

Of course, there were moments, incidents which in themselves were encouraging. Every week it seemed he'd meet a new man who would tell him his life had been saved by AA and he was starting out a brand-new person. But after talking with these men, he would be obsessed by the thought of the hundreds of thousands of others they were not reaching, and now had no way of reaching, and the need to find a way plagued him always.

In the fall, when the weather grew too raw for summer camp living, Bob V. and his wife, Mag, offered the Wilsons two large rooms in Monsey, New York. The excitement in Monsey that winter was that the head of Rockland State Hospital, Dr. Russell Blaisdell, who for months had been allowing AA members to visit the wards, had been so impressed with their work that he'd decided to let certain alcoholic inmates attend meetings outside the asylum. Each week busloads of patients were being driven to meetings in Manhattan and New Jersey.

Everywhere there were signs of growth, everywhere these little incidents to be grateful for. In September an article appeared in *Liberty* magazine and although at first they'd been dubious about it—it was called "Alcoholics and God"—*Liberty* received over eight hundred pieces of mail, which they forwarded to AA. And Bill was grateful. A few books began moving from the warehouse, a few more pins began to appear on the office map, showing the locations of possible new recruits. His days were filled answering letters, explaining their work, and this, along with his concern for every drunk he met, kept him from sinking into a slough of depression. Still, as active as he was keeping, something was wrong—not in the program; in himself. But he could not pin it down.

About the same time as the *Liberty* piece, the *Cleveland Plain Dealer* carried a series of articles in the center of the editorial page, one appearing each day for a week. The impact of such coverage was primarily in Ohio—the Cleveland group jumped from a dozen members to over a hundred in the course of a month—but there were also repercussions in the East.

By the end of '39 Hank's business had completely collapsed, and they were forced to move into a tiny one-room office at 17 William Street in Newark. Through it all Ruth Hock had stuck with them, often taking a few shares of old Works Publishing stock in place of a salary check. One morning Ruth found in the mail a newspaper clipping containing a three-line prayer. It had been torn from an unidentified paper and sent in by an anonymous member. She read it and was instantly struck by how much AA thinking could be compressed into three short lines. On her own, Ruth had the prayer printed on cards, and without asking anyone, she began slipping a card into each piece of mail that went out from the Newark office.

> God, grant me the serenity to accept the things I cannot change,
> Courage to change the things I can,
> And the wisdom to know the difference.

And in this way the Serenity Prayer became part of the AA canon, its phrases part of the alcoholic lingo.

Every minority, certainly every small, tightly knit group, develops its own language—and its own humor. AA was no exception. To outsiders who attended meetings—these were referred to as "civilians," or sometimes as "earth people"—the members' laughter was not only baffling, it was often shocking, a kind of gallows humor. But to the drunks it was curiously therapeutic. When a sick and shaking man, who has been living alone with his secret guilts, suddenly finds himself roaring with laughter at his own behavior, that man is beginning to grasp some small degree of perspective. And when this happens in a room full of other guilty drunks, he is no longer alone.

In a way, sharing a special "in" language had the same effect. And their language was special, a combination of back-alley barroom jargon and the purest spirituality. Much of the latter came from the program itself and the wording of the Steps. (Whenever they paid a visit to a potential member, they were making a "Twelfth Step call" or were "Twelfth Stepping.") But there was a sound reason for the raunchy reality of their talk. It was almost as though some men consciously used four-letter words in one sentence, knowing that in the next they could then use love, tenderness, humility and even serenity, things they were beginning to understand as basically human, which their drinking had kept them from even thinking about.

Another reason for the frankness was that it helped keep them focused on their real enemy—booze. Booze, and what booze had done to them and what it could do again, was too lethal a subject to dress up in fancy phrases or disguise as a part of gracious living. These men didn't speak about "getting high" or "a little tiddly." They didn't let themselves go in for illusions of sipping a few cocktails on a penthouse terrace. They remembered the dry heaves, mornings with their heads resting on a toilet bowl. They were talking about something that had to do with staying alive or with their dying.

All of it, the crazy macabre laughter, the private language (new members were "pigeons"; men who still had money when they surrendered were "high bottom drunks"; those who'd hit the Bowery and had nothing were "low bottom"), their brutal frankness about their drinking, all of it served to create a sense of being with their own kind, the feeling Bill W. had been seeking all his life. And few things were more encouraging, or gave Bill's spirits more of a lift, than when he'd hear a new man speaking, and instead of using the words "they," or "you people," he would say "we." That man was in.

That man was one of them, and Bill knew he himself would be less than honest if he didn't admit that some of these little incidents were among the happiest of his life. What was it, then, that was keeping him from being satisfied, that indeed was filling him with queer, urgent dissatisfaction?

It was more than his frustration at not being able to reach all those they wanted to help. In no time he became convinced that his unrest was a strangely personal problem, one that had nothing to do with the program or his group, and ironically, at this point in Bill's life there seemed no one he could share it with.

He didn't, he knew, want to look at part of it, for part of it had to do with his feeling of belonging and yet at the same time being isolated. So much that was happening now—all the wondrous news about the growth out West—seemed to be happening offstage. It was related to him but only in a secondhand way. He had no direct connection with what was going on in a group in Cleveland, Ohio.

This was what he had wanted, what he had worked for. He was the one who'd envisioned the chain reaction. Could it be he had not realized how removed he would feel from some of the links in his chain?

Perhaps no man would care to examine these questions, yet they would not go away, and with them he was now beginning to feel an awkwardness and a kind of shame because of what he knew must be his lack of gratitude, because so often he seemed "off the program."

Throughout that whole winter there was a growing contradiction between the easygoing, confident role he was playing and what he truly felt about himself.

There had been no word from Mr. Rockefeller in three years, but at a trustees' meeting early in 1940 Richardson informed the board that the old gentleman had been keeping an eye on AA and, wanting to help in some way, had decided to give them a dinner.

It was to be quite a dinner, at the Union Club on Park Avenue. Bill was to arrange the speakers and invite whatever members he wished. Mr. Rockefeller already had made up a tentative guest list, which appeared to include every prominent name in the New York financial world. Bill saw at a glance that the combined wealth of the guests would add up—literally—to billions of dollars.

It turned out to be quite a night for the drunks too. February 8, 1940. All of them were done up in black ties and stiff shirts, most of which had been borrowed or hired for the occasion. Dr. Fosdick agreed to speak for religion, Dr. Foster Kennedy, who had defended them in the *A.M.A. Journal,* spoke for medicine, Bob and Bill for AA.

At the start of the evening, a few of the seventy-five assembled financiers seemed a trifle leery, fearing the whole thing might be another of Mr. R.'s prohibition efforts, but Bill had astutely seen to it that at least one AA member was at every table. Over the first course, an elderly, bewhiskered banker sitting beside Morgan R. asked which bank or which institution he was connected with, and Morgan answered that at present he had no connection with any institution, but he added happily that he had recently been released from Rockland State.

Due to illness, Mr. Rockefeller was not able to attend, but his young son Nelson explained his father's great interest in AA and introduced the speakers graciously. Bill, for once, did not dwell at any length on his own recovery, deciding that Dr. Bob could take care of their drunk stories. Instead Bill talked about the growth of the fellowship in the past year, about the new meetings in Chicago, in Washington, Detroit and many other cities.

He told, for example, how the message had first been carried to Philadelphia by an itinerant salesman, Jim B., how Jim had run into another alkie, who'd somehow sobered himself up after reading the *Liberty* article, and how the two of them had collected some others and begun meeting in homes; he told how Larry J. of the Cleveland contingent had had to make a trip to Texas and had carried the word with him, and in this way a Houston group had started.

He told about their first "mail-order group" out in Arkansas.

295

A loner there had straightened himself out after reading the book, and now, through the book and through letters to and from the Newark office, he'd been off the juice for six months, and a small group was already starting to hold meetings in Little Rock. Across the nation, they figured, there must be almost two thousand recovered drunks, and Bill tried to describe, in the time he'd been allotted, the genesis of as many groups as he could.

When he'd finished—and he was an experienced enough speaker by then to be able to judge an audience's reaction—he knew that he had captured not only the interest of his listeners, but their deep concern, and as they threw the meeting open to quesions and answers, for a few minutes Bill sat back on the dais, knowing he'd never felt more confident, more quietly assured, and gazed down at the sea of opulent faces looking up at him.

While the others fielded the questions—and they did this extremely well—he allowed himself to muse for one brief moment about the strange tricks destiny can play. Why, he wondered, why had they had to wait so long for this night? Why had God, through the agency of John D. Rockefeller, Jr., wanted to test him so? Had there been some lesson he had had to learn from the waiting, the deprivation?

It didn't matter—he half smiled as he rose to answer a question —it had happened. They had arrived now. He nodded to Mr. Wendell Willkie, who sat nearby. Whatever God and John D. had had in mind, it was all right. Their waiting was over.

When the last question had been asked and answered, Nelson Rockefeller thanked the guests for attending, and for witnessing with him what his family believed was the birth of an important movement. Then he reiterated his father's faith in AA, and his belief that its power lay in the fact that the message was always carried from one man to the next without any thought of financial income or reward. For this reason, he concluded, his father was convinced that AA must always be self-supporting.

296

All they needed from the public and from men such as were gathered here was their confidence and their good will.

And with that, the guests broke into loud applause, and Bill sat watching as they slowly pushed back their chairs and started to rise.

After a few hearty handshakes, a few friendly slaps on the back and a great many cheery good-bys, he watched as the whole billion dollars' worth walked out of the paneled dining room, out of his life.

It took a while to understand that evening, especially why Mr. Rockefeller had gone to such lengths, but it took longer for Bill to understand his own reactions.

In time the dinner would become a landmark in AA history, a turning point that could have a decisive effect on their attitude toward outside contributions and eventually would lead them to adopt their policy of corporate poverty. But this was in the future. In February 1940, Bill was still a man with a wife to support, no job, no roots and no prospects of establishing any. They moved from Monsey into Morgan's apartment on Fifty-fifth Street, then on to a small place in Greenwich Village. Yet even more disturbing than the gypsy life he and Lois were forced to live was what Bill could sense was happening to himself, as a person and as an AA member.

For one moment at the Union Club, he'd imagined, and only half jokingly, that during his years of waiting God had been testing him. Now he saw that he must begin to take things into his own hands. The dinner was almost, but not quite, his last contact with the world of high finance. Mr. Rockefeller sent out a letter to several hundred of his friends and acquaintances, once again proclaiming his faith and this time saying that he personally was contributing one thousand dollars to AA—undoubtedly a hint that they could do likewise. He also mailed out a few hundred copies of the book *Alcoholics Anonymous*.

297

(These Mr. R. bought at discount, paying one dollar a copy.) If his friends caught the hint, they probably balanced their incomes against Mr. Rockefeller's and decided to contribute accordingly. One international banker sent in a check for ten dollars.

There'd been no newsmen at the Union Club, but a statement was issued a few days later and the wire coverage was extensive. Some of the accounts were on the wild side—the *Daily News* carried the headline "John D. Dines Tosspots"—but on the whole the AA story was presented simply and with dignity. Mail inquiries increased, more pins appeared on the map, and to Bill the clippings that came in from all sections of America made very pleasant—and sometimes quite heady—reading. Maybe news releases would be the way. Maybe a series of sensational stories . . .

Hank P., their grand promoter, of course agreed with this idea instantly. They should get going at once with a barrage of arresting, shocking stories.

If things were bad for Bill, they were even worse for Hank. His business was gone and his personal life in turmoil. He was being sued for divorce and was now being forced to accept what he considered a degrading job out in western New Jersey. His plan, he explained to Bill one afternoon, was to take the book business and his secretary, Ruth Hock, along with him. When Ruth refused to go and Bill pointed out that Works Publishing had to stay in the New York area so they could be near their mailing address, Hank became totally irrational, flailing out at everyone and everything, especially at Bill.

It developed that Hank had asked Ruth to marry him, and when she had said no, he'd put all the blame on Bill. A few weeks later, at a meeting of stockholders, Hank was unable to give any kind of accounting. He'd been in charge of the financial side of the publishing project, yet he apparently had no record of the moneys that had been paid in or out. When questioned about this, he grew resentful, and despite anything Bill could say to calm him, Hank began inventing a series of tales about his office being robbed and his records disappearing. It was at this meeting that Dr. Silkworth, for the first time, saw signs of what he considered paranoia, and warned Bill that Hank might become dangerous.

For Bill, one of the worst parts of this whole experience was his inability to help Hank or in any way halt the steady, ruthless progression of an emotional state that could lead only to destruction.

When Ebby had got drunk he had been in Albany. Bill had not seen him, so what actually caused Ebby's slip was always somewhat mysterious. With Hank, every step was being mapped out. It was as clear as a graph on a fever chart. After four years on the program, after talking about, writing about and truly understanding what jealousy, pride and anger could do to an alcoholic, Hank was withdrawing while they watched into a private world of hostility, cynicism and resentment. Bill could see the tensions mounting every day, until he finally knew that no man could go on this way without having to reach out for some release.

By the time Bill and Ruth had located an office on Vesey Street in Manhattan and started moving their files out of the little Newark cubicle, Hank had become unapproachable to every member of the group. Soon rumors began that Hank P. was drinking, and one night Bill found him, his first pigeon, drunk and in a murderous mood.

It was a shock to all the members. But for some there was also the personal sadness of knowing they had been powerless to stop Hank, of having suspected that once the classic pattern had started, it had to run its course, and then discovering that they had been dead right.

And to a few, Bill's reaction, indeed all of Bill's behavior for the next six months, was almost as alarming, because that summer Bill, too, was launched on a course they knew no one could check.

Hank had got drunk in April and that same month the Rollie

H. story broke in the papers. Rollie, a nationally famous ball-player, had sobered up with the Cleveland group, and on his own had called in the press and given them every detail. This was the first big-name breaking of anonymity AA had known, and the furor it kicked up was monumental, not only in Ohio, but across the country. The story of Rollie's "miraculous recovery," complete with his full name and photograph, became a front-page item everywhere.

In New York, irate members turned to Bill demanding disciplinary action. But Bill's response was totally unexpected. He defended Rollie. He asked if they had considered how many alcoholics might read about him and decide to do as he had done. If this might not be a blessing in disguise. One night he asked an open meeting how they expected to reach out to others if they insisted upon remaining so secretive.

Inwardly Bill's questions were of a different nature. Ever since the Rockefeller release he had been smitten by the excitements of big-time publicity. Now, considering that a single member, a ballplayer out in Cleveland, could get such coverage, he began to wonder what might happen if the cofounder of AA, if he, Bill Wilson, were to start talking . . .

Within a matter of weeks Bill was on the road, giving out interviews and pictures. A group would ask him to speak, he'd get in touch with the chairman, who'd tip off a local reporter, then, after the meeting, they'd talk, and the next morning—if the war news didn't preempt him—he would find his picture splashed across page one, often with a rousing account of the number of hopeless drunks he had saved. It was work Bill W. thoroughly enjoyed, and in the beginning a great many groups went along with him. But only in the beginning.

Naturally—and inevitably, as he would learn—there were loud objections. "Who does he think he is?" "What the hell is he pulling?" and "what about Dr. Bob?" He wasn't the only super-star, and soon others were trying to get into the act. And as always, AAs were not shy about expressing their opinions. Nor was Bill. He could still rationalize his every action. This was America, he pointed out, and there was a little thing called free speech here. All organizations, all countries, were being run by big-name leaders now. Secrecy might be all right for others, but the public had a right to know who AA's founders were.

With that one phrase, "all right for others," Bill began to think of himself as an exception.

Instead of quieting anyone, his answers only fed the contention. Bickering continued in some groups long after Bill had visited them, and soon he began to hear about serious fights among old-timers. One of these started in Cleveland. Hank P. had turned up there and, latching on to a few malcontents, he circulated a story about Bill's close connection with the Rockefellers, how Bill had always been a promoter, and how the book business was becoming a huge racket. In time Hank moved on to Akron, but apparently Dr. Bob and Anne Smith had nothing to do with him and believed none of his stories.

At the start even the dissension held a kind of excitement for Bill. In the arguments that went on after meetings, there was very little of the comfortable, relaxed Bill Wilson, sitting back, helping two opposing sides reach a viable compromise; he was the aggressive protagonist returning to the arena, determined to win and force through his own point. Also, he was accomplishing what he had set out to do.

He'd accepted Rollie's challenge and was proving that he could command as much publicity as a ballplayer. With his old zest for combat, the Burr and Burton boy was showing them, showing them all. And besides, no one could deny that in some towns his promotional schemes were getting results. More drunks were turning up at meetings after his story appeared.

Bill welcomed the arguments, welcomed the attention, and if anyone pointed out a parallel with Hank P., he didn't look at it.

One night—and he remembered this because it was the first time he'd heard the words—an old-timer told him that he might indeed be the cofounder, they might owe their lives to him, but he'd better watch himself because he was sure as hell acting like a man on a *dry drunk*.

This warning did not stop him, but he knew there was truth in it, and it gave him pause. For there were times now, many of them, when he felt himself driven exactly as he had been when he was drinking, only without the stimulus of booze to support and propel him onward. Then, too, there were other times—usually at night when he was alone—when he would remember the yearnings, the hunger, the constant reaching out and wanting more, always more. These had been part of him even before the drinking had taken over. On shipboard, in Winchester Cathedral, alone in the Brooklyn house, he had been seeking, craving some other dimension of consciousness. Now, sober five years, the same passion was with him, the same wanting, but now it seemed his hunger was for a state of being he had once had and had let slip away somehow, without knowing how it happened. And with this awareness he was left with the old sense of having failed again.

And again, as in his drinking days, not being able to place it, finding no answers, only a vague, indeterminate sense of loss, he knew it was better to keep moving, keep going with the tide.

Two remarkable people had entered Bill's life the year before. Marty M. was one of the first females to sober up in AA. An attractive, intelligent young woman with tremendous charm, she possessed a drive which Bill immediately spotted as equal to his own. In time Marty was to have an important influence on the development of the fellowship. In time, too, she and Bill would have their battles and, ironically, over the very thing that was causing so much infighting now—the matter of anonymity. For Marty was to become one of the great pioneers in the field of alcoholism education, but at this point she was primarily one of AA's spectacular recoveries.

A patient at Blythewood Sanitarium in Connecticut, she'd attended a Clinton Street meeting, had instantly caught the message and returned to her hospital to spread the good word among the other alcoholic inmates. She'd had a little trouble, had spent some time with Bill and Lois in Monsey, and by 1940 they were fast friends, drawn together by their mutual need to learn, grow and move ahead in their new way of life.

Through Marty, Bill had been introduced to Dr. Harry Tiebout, the chief psychiatrist at Blythewood Sanitarium. In the late '30s and early '40s, American psychiatry was just moving out of its adolescent stage, but there was still heated debate among the Freudians, the Jungians and the Adlerians. The remarkable thing about Harry Tiebout was that he seemed completely receptive to any truth from any school, especially if it could shed light on the treatment of alcoholism. He had been frankly astonished by the change he'd noticed in his alcoholic patients after a brief exposure to AA. Not only did they stop drinking, but in many of his most obstinate cases, those who had put up the greatest resistance to all psychiatric approaches, he discovered a brand-new attitude, a genuine desire to cooperate and accept help. Utterly baffled at first, yet seeing the same thing repeated over and over, Harry Tiebout began in 1939 what was to become his lifelong absorption, a thorough scientific investigation into the techniques and principles of Alcoholics Anonymous.

He and Bill had liked each other at once, and Bill had decided soon after their first meeting that if ever his own problems grew insupportable, Tiebout was a doctor he could turn to.

In his early days at Towns, Bill and Silkworth had often discussed the question of the alcoholic and therapy, and they had agreed it was usually wise for a man to have a prolonged stretch of sobriety—and in Bill's terms, of course, this meant getting his spiritual life in order—before delving into the whirlpools of his psychic disorders. Bill still believed this. He had seen too many men who had considered themselves hopelessly fouled up suddenly straighten out in AA. In fact, he was so convinced that the answers lay in the program, it was to be another four years before he himself would seek professional help.

In the fall of 1940 he continued along the lines he had been following all summer, addressing meetings, talking to new members, constantly carrying the message to larger audiences, yet at the same time sensing that he personally was slipping further and further away from the rewards, the true meaning of the program.

Apart from knowing he had Tiebout to turn to, there were several other important factors that kept Bill from going overboard during this dry drunk period. Unlike Hank P., he always, in spite of fights and harsh accusations, had kept in close touch with his group.

The New York members had been growing increasingly restive lately about having to move from place to place, and had been searching for some kind of permanent meeting spot. In February, Bert T. and Horace C. discovered, and guaranteed the rent on, an extraordinary little building at 334½ West 24th Street. This had been built as a stable behind two brick houses, but in recent years it had been leased to the Illustrators Club, who had done quite a job of redecorating, paneling certain areas and roofing a long, narrow alley that led to the street.

In many respects it was an ideal location for the first AA clubhouse, with a meeting room on the ground floor and a general room and two tiny bedrooms upstairs. Bill and Lois eventually moved into one of these and the other bedroom was occupied by Tom C., an ancient fireman they'd got out of Rockland State, who, after a great deal of haggling, agreed to serve as janitor. Old Tom kept the place moderately clean and was always on hand to bounce drunks who grew too obstreperous. From the day the club opened, months before he actually lived there, Twenty-fourth Street had become the warm center of Bill W.'s life.

It was Clinton Street 1935, only more so. There were always

visitors, people driving in from Westchester or Connecticut, winos shuffling in from the Salvation Army down the street, or out-of-towners far from the safety of their group, who needed the security of this crazy, solid oasis in the city. These were men from every rung of Mark's social ladder, who never conceivably would have drunk together, never would have gone to the same bars, yet here they were in one room, helping each other keep sober. Whatever hour Bill wandered in, there was the feel of a meeting. In a sense they were all members of an exclusive club, and only they understood what dues they had had to pay to get there.

Soon there were a great many more regular meetings, and while these were going on, Lois and a group of wives began to meet upstairs and discuss their own problems, their methods of adjusting to their new way of life. Some believe that this was the actual start of what was to become AA's family groups. Then, too, it was here that AA began a series of closed meetings, originally aimed at the instruction of newcomers, which were always to be attended by admitted alcoholics only. Above all, it was the vitality of the place that kept pulling Bill back, that mysterious inner exuberance of men who knew they had been given a second chance.

Strangely—and many people commented on this—their new outlooks were often reflected in their physical beings. It was as if alcohol had imposed a layer of fat over their faces and, as they recovered, their whole appearance was changing. Individual character began to emerge, you could see bone structure again, and a kind of strength of personality you never expected.

The clubhouse was a rare and special place, and some of its quality had to rub off on Bill. That summer and fall, Twenty-fourth Street served as ballast, and in retrospect he was able to see that he had probably needed the club and the ex-drunks more than they had needed him. For it was at this time that he was beginning to sense that both his famous drive and his wildly active schedule were a release mechanism for his pent-up

305

fury—fury at himself, at his world and at his failure to transform AA from a small society into the big-time operation he knew it must be.

His depression, his deep dissatisfaction, was beginning to color everything; even his AA talks were taking on a flavor of self-pity and self-dramatization. After one such talk in Baltimore, when he had moved in heavily on the horrors and the terrifying isolation of the alcoholic, a young clergyman came up to him at the close of the meeting. He thanked Bill and then went on to say that one thing he did not understand was why Bill put such emphasis on his great misfortune. It seemed to the young man that it was indeed these very experiences, terrible as they were, which in the end had humbled Bill so completely that his eyes and his heart had been opened, and had led directly to the wondrous experience of AA. His misfortune had, in a very real sense, become his good fortune. "You AAs," he said, "are certainly a privileged people."

These remarks from a man he would never see again had a profound and frightening effect on Bill. He'd known that something was wrong, desperately wrong, but he had tried to override it. He'd told himself that he was a leader, the man others turned to for answers. Now he forced himself to stop, to look and, as he had suggested in the Fourth Step, to take a fearless moral inventory.

This took the form of a series of questions about his trip to Baltimore, and his true motives for going there. And he did not like what he saw. Had he gone to share with his fellow alcoholics? Had he any real sense of gratitude for what had happened in the past or for his privileged opportunity to work with others? Or did he—and this was not easy to answer—did he honestly think he needed others now? Hadn't he, in fact, become their teacher, their preacher, the one others depended on?

Had he changed so completely—was it possible?—that he was now seeing himself not only as the cofounder but as a great moral leader?

306

As he battled with these questions, alone, late at night—and not just once, but on many nights—and with what seemed their all too obvious answers, he again examined his famous drive, and he saw that it served to cover his failures, his impatience and his eternal frustration at not being able to move things as he knew they must be moved. In turn, this stock-taking led to a depression which, in its prolonged intensity, was worse than any he had experienced since Towns Hospital. And with the depression there was a sense of guilt because he could feel this way, he who had been given so much, whom others looked up to. This, in time, led to a new and hideous fear. What if he should break, if he, Bill W., should crack up as he had seen other men crack . . . ?

He had no answer and saw no way of finding one. Then one wintry night, when he was by himself in the tiny bedroom at the club—Lois was off somewhere—an extraordinary thing happened to Bill.

Someone said to Bill once—and he was sure it was a well-known quotation, though he was never able to track it down—"Life gives us moments, and for these moments we give our lives."

And to this Bill added that for some reason life never seemed to provide a warning that such a moment might be approaching. He was on his bed in the tiny bedroom at the club, as low in spirits as he ever remembered being. Actually, he was wondering if the pain in his middle could be an ulcer. A storm was beating on the tin roof overhead. It was quite late when he heard the doorbell ringing through the empty club, and old Tom announced that there was a bum from St. Louis asking to see him.

Before he could protest, he heard heavy footsteps on the stairs, and a little man, dripping wet and leaning on a cane, limped into the room and sat himself down on a chair across from the bed. He introduced himself as Father Ed of the Jesuit Order, and for the first time Bill noticed his clerical collar. He had

307

made a pilgrimage, he explained, just to talk to Bill. Then he said, " 'I thank my God upon every remembrance of you,' " and he smiled. "Philippians one: three." As he went on, at first talking about his work with alcoholics out West, Bill found himself looking into the most remarkable pair of blue eyes he'd ever seen, peering out at him from beneath a soaking lock of pure white hair.

He'd originally become interested in AA, Father Ed said, through studying the Twelve Steps in which he found parallels to the Exercises of St. Ignatius, the spiritual discipline of his Jesuit Order, and when Bill confessed he'd not known this, he appeared utterly delighted. Then the curious little man went on and on, and as he did, Bill could feel his body relaxing, his spirits rising. Gradually he realized that this man sitting across from him was radiating a kind of grace that was filling the room with a strange, indefinable sense of presence. Primarily, Father Ed wanted to talk about the paradox of AA, the "regeneration," he called it, the strength arising out of total defeat and weakness, the loss of one's old life as a condition for achieving a new one. And Bill nodded, and agreed with everything he said, and soon found . . . but Bill never really had any words for what he found that night.

It happened. That was all. And there was no way to explain it, any more than there had been a way to explain what had happened when he'd looked into Ebby's eyes and had understood, or what had happened at Towns Hospital when suddenly he had found peace. He didn't question Father Ed, he had no judgment of him, any more than a man would have questioned or judged the word of God.

As a matter of fact, it was the word of God they were talking about through most of the night. In time, Bill told him that he no longer understood God, that he had lost what once he had understood so clearly. And Father Ed told him that he would never understand, that our idea of God would always be lacking, "for to understand, to comprehend God, is to be equal to God." But, he added, our concept could grow, could deepen, and he spoke of the responsibility referred to in the Eleventh Step: "to improve our conscious contact."

Bill was soon talking about all the Steps, and especially the Fifth, with this gimpy little priest who with no warning had limped in out of the storm. In fact, he found he was actually taking his Fifth Step, admitting to another human being "the exact nature of our wrongs." He told Father Ed about his anger, his impatience, his mounting dissatisfactions. But nothing discouraged Father Ed. He quoted Matthew: "Blessed are they which do hunger and thirst." The saints, he said, were always distinguished by their yearnings, their restlessness, their thirst.

When Bill asked if there was never to be any satisfaction, the old man snapped back, "Never. Never any." There was only a kind of divine dissatisfaction that would keep him going, reaching out always.

Bill had made a decision, Father Ed reminded him, to turn his life and his will over to the care of God, and having done this, he was not now to sit in judgment on how he or the world was proceeding. He had only to keep the channels open— and be grateful, of course; it was not up to him to decide how fast or how slowly AA developed. He had only to accept. For whether the two of them liked it or not, the world was undoubtedly proceeding as it should, in God's good time.

And as he listened, Bill accepted and believed every word the old man said.

Next they were speaking of conversion and faith. Conversion, Father Ed said, did not mean arriving. And again he quoted Bill's words back at him: No one among them had been able to maintain anything like a perfect adherence to these principles. . . . AAs were not saints. . . . The point was that they were willing to grow along spiritual lines. . . . They claimed spiritual progress rather than spiritual perfection.

As to faith, which Father Ed referred to as the greatest of our undeveloped resources, he said that it would come, it had to come, and he reminded Bill that faith was hard, as hard and as easy as sobriety.

Sitting on a straight wooden chair not six feet from him, this Jesuit, this little man he had never seen before, explained these mysteries to Bill as no other man could have explained them. He was the only person Bill had ever met who was so sure of himself and so comfortable in his relationship with his deity that he could speak of Him lightly, even with a kind of naughty, family humor.

Ready to leave, he pulled his crippled body up and, leaning precariously on his heavy stick, he thrust his head forward and looked straight into Bill's eyes. And he told him that the two of them in that little room were among the blessed of all time, for they were here, living now. Out of those who had gone before, and all those not yet born, they had been elected to stand up now and speak their piece. There was a force in Bill that was all his own, that had never been on this earth before, and if he did anything to mar it, or block it, it would never exist anywhere again.

Then he hobbled over to the door, looked back, and as a parting shot said that if ever Bill grew impatient, or angry at God's way of doing things, if ever he forgot to be grateful for being alive right here and now, he, Father Ed Dowling, would make a trip all the way from St. Louis to wallop him over the head with his good Irish stick.

Bill's relationship with Father Ed was to prove unlike any other in his life. But he was soon given a chance to see that the outcome of their first meeting, the truths he had learned, were not unlike those which many members had been learning for themselves.

In the winter of 1940, a reporter from the *Saturday Evening*

Post, Jack Alexander, was assigned to investigate and perhaps do a story about AA. In showing Alexander around, Bill had the opportunity to visit or, in some cases, revisit a great many groups. And as he talked to older members he began to understand that his experiences of the past year were far from unique.

There seemed to be a pattern which many men had had to follow. In the beginning a man turned to AA quite simply because he knew he would die if he didn't, and at the start he depended on the fellowship, the philosophy—the spiritual principles, if you like—to stop his drinking. Then, in case after case, as things straightened out in his life he tended once more to depend on himself and seek his happiness through his own powers and desire for acclaim. Finally—and here the stories all differed slightly—through some incident, some sharp reversal perhaps, their eyes were opened still wider, and they learned a new lesson; they returned, and as if entering a new level of feeling, they could truly accept AA's teaching.

For Bill, it seemed a new lesson, but there was also a feeling of getting back to something he had always known, believed in, yet somehow had allowed himself to lose sight of in the business of growing. Now he was discovering it to be true and valuable, exactly as he first had felt it to be.

And as they said out in Akron, for Bill W. it was just in the nick of time.

Jack Alexander was an experienced, even cynical reporter. He'd had many doubts about doing a story on a society of recovered drunks. But in visiting groups, interviewing and getting to know the members, he was won over completely. The article he wrote was a magnificent piece of journalism; the *Post* accepted it and it appeared in March 1941.

With the publication of the *Saturday Evening Post* story, the world of AA—and of Bill W.—was changed utterly and irreversibly. The floodgates opened. Instead of a trickle of mail, the inquiries and the desperate pleas for help began pouring in by the thousands. There seemed no possible way that the little group of nameless drunks could cope with the situation or handle the demands being made on them.

For better or worse, in the year 1941 Alcoholics Anonymous was established as an American institution.

5

There was excitement throughout the fellowship at the prospect of such unprecedented growth.

Their pioneering days were over, but Bill knew that in many areas they would still be flying blind. Also—and this was true not only of the conservative element, who'd always shown concern at any expansion plans, but among some newcomers as well —he sensed a fear, and an awesome uncertainty about what would happen to AA. Fresh groups were springing up with such fantastic speed they knew there'd be no way of controlling them.

They had proved that drunks could stay sober, but they were far from sure that such large numbers of erratic personalities could meet, form groups and then proceed to work together in harmony. Of necessity, because of the very nature of the alcoholic character, there would be problems of leadership, of money, of individuals striving for power—and wouldn't these cause tensions and fights in the new groups that had no one with experience to guide them? Would they even stay sober? And mightn't the fights increase and create schisms that could one day split the fellowship apart?

It would be years before Bill would have answers to these questions, but within days of the *Post* story's hitting the stands, he and Ruth Hock knew what they were in for. As they plowed through the avalanche of telegrams and letters and tried at the same time to cope with the endless calls at the office—some of which were hilariously funny, others stark and tragic—they saw they were facing a situation they could never handle alone. Each letter, each plea for help, had to be answered personally with a warm and understanding word. Any sort of form letter would deny their whole premise and betray their basic belief.

Finally Bill sent out a call for members, for anyone who was sober and could type, or anyone who had a typewriter or even a wife who could type. And in no time the old Twenty-fourth Street clubhouse was transformed into an emergency head-quarters. Yet even with this battery of volunteers, some of whom worked with Lois around the clock, they made only a tiny dent. The flood of mail never seemed to reach a peak, never showed any signs of slowing down. The prodigious chain reaction Bill had envisioned had become a fact; nothing would stop it.

It was self-perpetuating and self-multiplying. They'd answer a letter, send along a copy of the book, and if there was another potential recruit in the same town as their correspondent or even in the same general vicinity, these two were urged to get in touch with one another. Or, as happened many times, a member whose business took him on the road, even though he might have no background in the program and his own sobriety might seem tenuous, would be sent off with a list of people to look up. Then, within a few weeks, they'd hear that a new AA group had been formed. And the new group needed advice. The new group had problems. They had growing pains, and all pains, all problems, were instantly referred to New York, which meant that they became Bill Wilson's responsibility.

Obviously he needed full-time, paid assistants. But being AA, this brought up two bugaboos: money and the old question of professionalism.

It was an absurd situation and one that took on an alarming urgency as more and more members understood what was at

314

stake. Not only did the thousands of new prospects * have to be answered; some method had to be devised to unify AA. If it could hold together, everything would be right; if it fell apart—which at times it showed every sign of doing—all would be lost, after this brief flurry there would be chaos, they would disband and pass from the scene.

It is not surprising, therefore, that many old-timers came to view the goings on at Vesey Street with alarm. It was not that they were afraid Bill would get drunk—they'd followed him through too many catastrophes—but there was the question of what his new role might do to him. For these men knew that in the last few years Bill's peculiar pride had been tested by everything imaginable except success. Now they watched him becoming the captivating center of all that was happening, a leader sending out his messages to an ever-widening domain.

There was, however, one thing that no one fully appreciated, and that was the change in Bill W. The events of the past months had left a curious imprint which made him singularly ready for this particular role.

Immediately after the Rockefeller dinner, he'd gone off on his dry drunk spree. Saying to hell with anonymity, he'd rationalized and justified everything, determined that he himself could shape and run the show. While this was happening, out of the turmoil and dissension he caused, he had slid into his blackest depression. He had met Harry Tiebout and had considered therapy with him, but before he began pursuing any outside help, Father Ed Dowling had entered his life.

That had been in the winter of 1940–41, just before the deluge. Bill said there was no way of describing what Father Ed did for him, the doors he flung open before him; after absorbing the impact of their first encounter, he awakened to a new reality, a

---

* In the year 1941, membership jumped from fifteen hundred to eight thousand, which meant that they probably dealt with another ten or fifteen thousand who looked in the door, turned around and went out. In time Bill was to learn that two-thirds of these would one day return.

totally altered view of himself and his place in the world. And with this he felt he was entering into a new relationship with AA.

And he was right. It was new to him. But there was one aspect of this relationship that was ancient and almost mystical. It was the relationship that on occasion may exist between a man and the thing he has created. It can be sensed between a painter and his canvas, when night after night he will return to stand before his work and possibly, after a time, will reach out to touch the easel on which his painting rests. Beginning in 1941, Bill W. was tied to AA by strands of loyalty and a kind of loving most men never know.

Until now his energies had been primarily involved with his own growth and with the interplay of certain individuals upon his life and that of the organization he had dreamed up. He still cared, at times he still cared passionately about many individuals, but the focus of his life shifted. Now his chief concern was for large groups of drunks—for AA as a whole—and for finding the structure by which they could function as a unified entity.

More and more in his talks and his writings he used the metaphor of men clinging to a life raft; they would either stick together, or surely they would die separately. And, not surprisingly, while searching for an overall structure, he found himself working in close relation with more individuals than at any other point in his life—and what individuals they were! Some very strange camels wandered under their tent. But Bill was not only ready for the problems; in many ways he was uniquely suited to the role he was being asked to play.

Fortunately, at this time of growth, the financial situation was somewhat relieved. There were still incredible problems in the little office on Vesey Street, but the book was beginning to sell, and living conditions were definitely improving for Bill and Lois.

Through a series of coincidences, a Mrs. Griffith had turned up at one of their meetings. She was an acquaintance of a newcomer Bill had been able to help. A woman of some means , she was also a woman wildly interested in houses. Building new ones and fixing up old ones was her "thing," and she was frankly appalled at the notion of Bill and Lois living on at Twenty-fourth Street. They would be suffocated in the crush, she insisted, and what was more, she knew the perfect place for them, a large, rambling house in Westchester she had built for a friend, but which the friend hadn't liked for some reason. It was a preposterous idea. There was no money; indeed, they were way behind in the payments on their storage bill. But one afternoon, while visiting Bur S. in Chappaqua, they drove over to have a look at Mrs. Griffith's house.

Bill liked it on sight, and after they'd broken in through a rear window and he had seen the great living room with its huge stone fireplace, the kitchen and three bedrooms on the ground floor, the long hall and master bedroom upstairs, he loved it, wanted it and knew there had to be some way of getting it. To Lois it seemed impossible. But Lois had underestimated Mrs. Griffith. Mrs. Griffith wanted the Wilsons in her house and was willing to let them have it for $6,500, with no money down, if they could pay her forty dollars a month. Bill figured they'd be saving twenty a month by getting their furniture out of storage, so all they would need would be another twenty per month.

In the spring of 1941 they moved into their Bedford Hills home, and named it, in the fashion of the day and in this case quite fittingly, Stepping Stones. It was not a settled time anyplace on earth, but in 1941 Bill and Lois, after twenty-three years of marriage, got their first taste of that special security that comes from having a house of one's own.

As he took the commuter train into the city each morning, Bill became absorbed in the grim headlines. The Low Countries had been shattered, France had fallen the year before, and now the papers were filled with accounts of the invasion of Russia. All the horror and hatred he had had to recognize in himself back in his drinking days seemed to be unleashed across the world.

There was still a strong spirit of isolationism in the country, and Americans appeared stunned and confused, but although the actual killing was still confined to Europe, with each morning's paper Bill felt an ominous sense of prelude. The possibility of America moving into another war was no longer unthinkable.

At the office he tried, and tried successfully most of the time, to become equally absorbed in the problems of AA—and there was no letup with those. Groups continued to mushroom everywhere, and each group produced its own bewildered questions about procedure, membership, public relations, etc.

Also, to his astonishment, the New York office had begun corresponding with a number of AA loners—men who had been able to make it on their own. These represented a kind of miracle to Bill, for in a way they denied what he'd always thought of as the basic premise: that the message could be transmitted only through close person-to-person relationships. There was proof now that it could be passed on through the mails, because here was a sailor writing during a long night watch, frankly admitting his fears of what might happen when he hit port and the rest of his crew headed for a bar; here were farmers and ranchers living at too great a distance from any city to contact a group, drunks, "hopeless alcoholics," who'd read an article or had been given a name—AA or Bill W.—and were somehow staying sober and writing for advice and encouragement.

Nevertheless, as Bill never let himself forget, it wasn't the office mail that was spreading the message. It was the band of tireless recovered alkies who went on day after day and carried the word out to others. The number of these stalwarts in the early 1940s was incalculable, but several, perhaps because of their unorthodox methods, were always close to Bill's heart. One of these was Irwin M.

Irwin was a supersalesman of Venetian blinds. A 250-pounder, he possessed a personality, an energy and a gusto as monumental as his build. AA was his religion, and because of a certain fanaticism in his approach, there was some hesitation in the beginning about giving him a list of prospects to contact. But since his territory covered Atlanta, Jacksonville and New Orleans, as well as

318

Birmingham and Indianapolis, and since there was a file filled with the names of Southerners who'd so far had no contact with AA, they knew they couldn't be choosy. They gave Irwin the list and sent him off.

Reports started coming in within weeks. Irwin had been incorrigible. With his whirlwind technique, he tracked down drunks in homes, taverns and offices, and once he'd got his hooks into them he never let go. When he had to move on to another town, he spent his nights shut up in a hotel room writing letters to all his converts, admonishing and praising them. Across the southland, new groups began to spring up in the wake of Irwin M., and if sometimes the questions of these newcomers indicated a confusion between AA and the Holy Rollers, it couldn't be helped. Bill hated to think what his atheist and agnostic friends would say if they saw these letters, but there was no denying they were coming from drunks who were sober. The South had been conquered again and much of the credit had to go to Irwin M. and others like him.*

Each week new pins appeared on the office map—a few were beginning to reach up into Canada—and with each new pin the need for a group directory, for proper office help and the money to pay for it became more apparent.

Finally Bill hit upon a scheme. He and Dr. Bob had agreed there could never be dues or fees for AA membership, but there seemed no reason why groups could not voluntarily make contributions to headquarters—say one dollar per member per year.

It was a simple plan that would impose no hardship on anyone, yet might provide enough cash to ease the pressure at Vesey Street and ensure a more efficient operation. Bill presented his idea to the trustees, who approved. They sent Bert T. to Chicago and Cleveland, and Horace C. down to Philadelphia, Baltimore

---

* From the beginning the Southern drunks presented special problems. For example, a group in Richmond, Virginia, believed in holding regular meetings, in getting away from their wives and talking things over, but they saw no reason not to drink beer at their meetings. It took time and the dedicated work of one John W. to bring them around.

and Washington, to sound out groups and promote the plan. Apparently these two did a fine job of explaining that the contributions would represent a special fund that would be supervised by the trustees and earmarked "for office use only." Naturally, there were arguments, but Bert and Horace had gone out armed with a batch of letters that had been received at the office. After reading some of the more heartrending, they would ask their audiences if they thought such pleas could be ignored and simply dropped in a wastebasket. Most of the groups endorsed the plan wholeheartedly, but of course there were objections and as always the objectors grew vociferous.

Their responses should have been expected. Since the start and throughout AA's history, the attitude of drunks toward money has always baffled outsiders. Fortunately, Bill's memory and his examination of some of his own behavior gave him a certain insight. One afternoon while Bill and Lois were still living at the club, he'd found himself in conversation with a long-time member who had had a slip. The man was in poor shape and clearly had no money. And although Bill knew the chances were a hundred to one that any cash the old boy might get his hands on would be spent on a bottle, Bill slipped him a five-dollar bill—he simply could not help it—and wished him well. That night at a meeting, just before the hat was passed, the secretary made a special pitch for money. They were behind in the rent, they needed a new coffeepot and several other important items, and he asked the group to try to be generous when the hat came by. Bill understood the situation and reached into his pocket for a coin, but when he took the coin out he saw it was a fifty-cent piece. He immediately put his fifty cents back and brought out a dime, which he dropped in the hat. Then it struck him. That afternoon, face to face with a drunk, he'd been big-hearted, loving, generous, but when it was a question of contributing to something as impersonal as rent—well, that was another matter.

He'd given five dollars to make another drunk—and himself—feel good, one dime to support his group. It was a chastening memory and one that made him somewhat hesitant to criticize those who were a little slow in contributing to a headquarters fund.

Gradually, though, in late '41 and early '42, group contributions began to trickle in, not so much as he had hoped, but enough to enable them to take on two full-time, paid assistants. Unfortunately, just at this point, a disturbing and potentially very dangerous situation began to develop in Celeveland.

The phenomenal growth of groups in the Cleveland area was unlike the development of AA anywhere else in the country. With the publication of the *Plain Dealer* articles back in '39, there'd been a veritable cloudburst of drunks in Cleveland, and ever since, new alkies had continued to pour into their meetings. They'd done a remarkable job and had solved many problems in ways that would in time become models for other groups. (For example, it was in Cleveland that the idea of individual sponsorship for new members began.) But it had not always been peaceful. They grew noisily in Cleveland and often with immense friction. Groups broke apart and the fighting was bitter. Yet this, too, was often beneficial, because within a few months each segment would become as big as the original group. Still the struggle for power and prestige among several of the early founders sometimes got out of hand, and there was always a question of how to quiet wars among conflicting brethren.

Then, too, the rumors about the New York office and the grand rackets Bill was promoting, which Hank P. had ignited during his visits, had never been totally doused. Now they all flared up again, to incredible heights. At Vesey Street they began to hear reports of several Cleveland groups wanting to secede and break off all connection with Bill W.'s brand of AA. Some of the stories, ridiculous though they sounded, were not easy to listen to.

Bill had constantly to remind himself that these did not always spring from malcontents, nor were they all the politically motivated schemes of a few individuals who wanted to take over and run their own show. There was a strong and serious group who were genuinely distressed by what they regarded as an attempt to commercialize AA. Men and women who'd been sober many years, who'd followed the plain principles of first-century Christianity, now felt threatened and wanted to make some protest against the changes, against what they regarded as a debasement of their deepest beliefs. What AA needed, they insisted, was not more money, more organization or a great central headquarters, but more dedicated Twelve Step work.

Finally the charges of commercialism grew so out of proportion that Dr. Bob and Bill decided to go out to a dinner in Cleveland. It was a melancholy occasion for a gathering of recovered drunks. When the meal was over, the chairmen of various Cleveland groups ushered the two into a hotel parlor. There they were met by an interrogating committee, a lawyer and a certified public accountant, and the stories all came out. Someone had talked to a trustee in New York, and he knew for a fact that the previous year Bill and Bob had divided sixty-four thousand dollars (Bill never understood how they hit on that figure). Someone else knew of Bill's close relationship with the Rockefellers (he was said to have been seen quite often coming out of John D., Jr.'s, bank).

The whole episode was a shock to Bill and to Bob, but they listened, they heard them out, and then Bill spoke. He'd come to Cleveland prepared, and he had brought with him a certified audit of all AA financial affairs from the very beginning.

It showed that although Dr. Bob was supposed to receive a royalty on the book, he had got none—everything had gone back into AA work. He still received a stipend of thirty dollars a week from the fund John D. Rockefeller, Jr., had started, but that was all. Bill had been getting the same thirty, and in addition, for the past year he'd been drawing twenty-five a week from the book company. In other words, his total income was fifty-five dollars a week. The committee's accountant studied the statement, then read it aloud and testified to its accuracy.

322

It was not a happy time. The committee apologized. Some were genuinely chagrined: they had only wanted to get the record straight, and they would do all they could to squelch the insidious rumors—but this never really happened.

It was an ugly and painful episode, and Bill did not pretend to hide the pain.

When he returned from Cleveland, Bill was determined that henceforth all AA financial dealings, whatever their nature, must be recorded in the simplest, clearest way, and that their books always would be available for any group's examination. He was also more convinced than ever that the fellowship must somehow, someday, become totally self-supporting. To accomplish this would take many years, and would finally be brought about only through the dedicated efforts of several alcoholic and non-alcoholic members of the board.

Meanwhile, mail continued to pour into the office and the worries and the dilemmas of the groups seemed endless. Steering committees quarreled, groups split apart, long-winded orators held forth, completely monopolizing meetings, and there were horrendous difficulties with panhandlers and "fallen women." In some areas, self-appointed gurus began selling AA therapy to newcomers for cash; on occasion entire groups got drunk, thereby wrecking whatever good will they had built up in their communities.

Clearly they were facing problems of two kinds: those that might be called organizational, and those that sprang from personality traits. Bill could usually spot the latter as the old alcoholic desire for power and domination, even for a bit of glory. But in AA these passions were more dangerous than in other societies, because they always surfaced in presumed defense of a noble cause and the hostilities they engendered could be disguised as righteous indignation. Bill and Ruth Hock coped as they could. Answering all letters, they became AA's chief retailers of experience—passing on the wisdom of older groups to those just forming, pointing out that most of their traumas had been met before and somehow overcome.

In time, out of this mass of correspondence, this wealth of experience, Bill began to detect certain patterns, difficulties that seemed common to many areas and reappeared over and over. And he began to wonder if there couldn't be some statement of principles, some form of what he referred to vaguely as a "code of traditions." There seemed a genuine need for some great, unifying, overarching set of truths that could apply to all groups all the time, and that might indeed serve them in their growth much as the Steps provided guidelines for individuals.

Whatever form these traditions might eventually take, he knew they could be offered only as suggestions. No governing body in New York City was going to dictate to AAs. They might take advice, but orders, never. They were independent alcoholics, every one of them, and they were clinging to their inalienable rights—even their right to be wrong. The only authority they would, or should, recognize was what they called their group conscience.

Bill understood this, yet at the same time he could think of no other society, no nation, church group or political party that did not have some sort of rules, that was not able to exert some form of discipline over its members and thereby enforce obedience to regulations. All nations, it seemed to him, all societies, had to be governed; in fact, the authority to govern and direct was the essence—it was almost a definition—of organization. Yet Bill knew in his heart that AA was, and would continue to be, the exception to this.

As he wrestled with these questions and gradually came to realize that there was no ultimate control even over membership —a few groups had tried to expel members but the expelled fellow had invariably come back, protesting that his life was at stake, that AA had no right to take it from him, and in every case the backslider had been returned to the fold—as he was studying all this and trying to formulate a code of traditions whereby AA might hold together, he saw the world around him being torn apart. Weighed against the horrors of the war, the problems of Bill W. and his society of recovering alcoholics had to appear shamefully petty, or as they would have said in East Dorset, of no real account. But that was the climate of the world in which AA was born, and in which Bill worked to create its traditions.

Within months of the Wilsons' moving to Bedford Hills, in the same year that the *Post* story appeared and their fantastic growth began, the Japanese Air Force attacked Pearl Harbor and overnight a nation that had been divided was suddenly united. Bill immediately applied for a commission in Military Intelligence. Looking back at this application in the perspective of years, it seems a brave and an infinitely touching document. On an attached sheet of paper he listed all the short-lived positions he had held since the close of World War I and then all the corporations he had investigated, even little Penick and Ford. Only in a final paragraph did he state that in the depression years he became interested in the cure of chronic alcoholism and mention AA. Finally, as if in an attempt to impress the army brass, he boasted that the fellowship had been endorsed by several periodicals.

One can only guess at what his innermost feelings were when he learned that he, a patriot, a Vermonter, a veteran of the First World War, wasn't even acceptable to his country as an old retread. Bill said only, "It was hard." But there can be no doubt about the result of this rejection. If earlier Bill's relationship to AA had been that of a father to a son, or an artist to his creation, in 1942 it became more that of a young lover and his girl. During the 1940s, there was not the smallest segment of AA that he did not know, study and love. And he drew from this new relationship a joy and a sense of security that he had never before experienced. The love affair was to last for fourteen years and in a way it was more intense and more fulfilling than any he had ever known.

6

Men who worked beside Bill in this period have said that in his private life Bill Wilson could make mistakes, horrendous ones, but as far as AA was concerned he was never wrong. This is not true. Bill made mistakes with AA, but again, like the lover, he instinctively sensed the error, tried never to make the same one again, and thus, in the end, he and his love were somehow strengthened.

Also it must be remembered that all this was happening at a point in his life when he was completely free to give himself over to his infatuation. He had a home, a wife who adored him and whom he could trust. Furthermore, although he had many staunch admirers and there were always hundreds of AAs with whom he could share any problem, at this time he was relieved of the burdens of a close friendship. Throughout his life there had been a series of intimate friends, and the fact that there was none now was not intentional on anyone's part; they'd simply moved into other areas. Mark Whalon was in Vermont, and Bill saw him only on occasional visits to East Dorset. Ebby was in and out of his life, Hank P. lost in his own sick world, and Fitz M. deeply involved with his family down in Maryland. There was nothing and no one to stand between Bill and his absorption. His eyes were fixed on what he believed to be the greatness of AA and he held before him always his vision of what it could become.

A measure of this absorption was his reluctance to leave the office at night despite his love for Lois and their life in Bedford Hills. There might be one more letter to answer or one more drunk might wander in who had to talk with someone, and the evening hours were always the best time for talk.

This was a development, he learned later, that many AA couples faced. When a man has begun to live again, when he is filled with all the potentials of his rebirth and sees them reflected in a fellowship that is constantly moving, reaching out, it is not always easy to share the excitement with a spouse who, no matter how devoted, has not changed in the same ways. The spouse's view has to be colored by what one was, not merely by what one is and will be. Some hopes of the recovered alcoholic are too intoxicating to share.

But of course it wasn't all heady, high hopes. Bill was still the pragmatist. His head may have been often in the stars, but his feet were planted in an office where day by day he was struggling to organize a group of unpredictable drunks.

The outside world and even some members of the board viewed these efforts with interest, if not always with understanding. For it seemed to them that Bill was attempting to create a new form of society and he was trying to do this with the most unstable of materials. What was more, he was increasingly convinced that they could operate such an enterprise with no laws and no regulations. AA headquarters had no power to issue a single directive to any member and make it stick.

Any two or three alcoholics who gathered together for sobriety could call themselves an AA group. This meant that the most unmoral, antisocial, the most critical, antireligious or even anti-each other, rampant individuals could collect a few kindred spirits and announce that they were an AA group—and they were, if *they* thought so. To many this seemed carrying the principle of independence to such absurd lengths that it was more than socialism, it was anarchy.

At this time there was a story going the rounds about a group that had posted a sign in its clubhouse: "Anything goes here, except you mustn't smoke opium in the elevator." It was a story that amused Bill W., though not the trustees.

Still Bill persisted: they could only make suggestions. Almost every letter that went out to a group—and this practice has continued throughout AA's history—carried with it some such phrase as "Of course you are at liberty to handle this matter any way you choose, but the bulk of our experience does seem to suggest . . ." To Bill it was indeed remarkable how often these examples of experience were followed and how many times his advice was taken.

But the nonalcoholics remained skeptical. To the psychiatrically oriented, all this liberty was an example of the alcoholic's refusal to grow up and accept responsibilities. To them it was only a matter of time before such adolescent egos would blow up and totally wreck what had been created. Yet as the years passed they had to admit that something was holding AA together.

For Bill, this "something"—and often it was as indefinable as that—had to do with the surprising willingness of the individual to place the welfare of his fellows above his own desires. AA was not a course of behavior that could be regulated. It was an attitude of mind and of heart, and at times it seemed so essentially spiritual in nature that he could not analyze it. But he was certain that this "something" existed, and at times when he considered it, it appeared to fall into two parts.

He knew that within every recovered drunk there were two built-in authorities which the outside world could never understand. In the life of each member there still lurked a very real tyrant who was far more ruthless than a Hitler, and his name was booze. He was always with them, *cunning, baffling, powerful.* And every member had learned about his weapons.

To Bill there could be no more forceful restraint than this.

Yet fear was not enough; it had chastened only a few. It took something more to bind these anarchists together. And here Bill was entering an area for which he knew he'd not yet found the proper words. For himself he had no hesitancy in referring to an inner voice, but in talking with others he would say higher power, life force, or any words the listener might be comfortable with. But by whatever name they cared to use, it was this that brought about those moments of insight which drew members closer to their fellow drunks—and possibly to their creator. It was this that had brought forth the kind of loving Father Ed spoke of, which outsiders sensed but could not share.

Individual alcoholics would never need directives from any human authority—most of them understood their recovery was a case of do or die—but the groups and their troubled relationships with certain members, with other groups and with the world around them were another matter. And finding guidelines for them was not to be easy.

In the early forties, when Bill undertook this task, it seemed to him they were facing several grave issues: the financial situation, the number of breaks in anonymity that were occurring across the country and, in time, the question of what would become of the fellowship if anything should happen to the handful of old-timers who were trying to mediate and solve group problems. But as the seeds of what were to grow into the Twelve Traditions were planted and gradually began to take on shape and substance—first in letters to outlying groups, then in a few short pieces Bill wrote—it became clear that he was formulating a declaration of principles that would touch on many subjects: on group autonomy, requirements for membership, on singleness of purpose and professionalism in AA.

As had been the case with the Steps and the book *Alcoholics Anonymous*, each Tradition was arrived at the hard way, from lessons learned in dealing with groups and Bill's own involvement in their hassles. (For example, whenever he discussed

329

professionalism, Bill told of his temptation to work for Towns Hospital, and how the wisdom of a group conscience had finally made him turn down the offer.) His arguments were disarming because they were based on irrefutable personal experience.

The first ten Traditions focused on the internal workings of groups, the last two on their position with respect to the outside world. Good public relations, Bill knew, would always be essential to growth; over half the membership, he figured, had originally been drawn to AA by some favorable coverage in the media. But underlying all the traditions, the very foundation out of which they grew, was the idea of anonymity.

In Bill's thinking, anonymity also seemed to fall into two parts —the practical and the spiritual. About its practical side he had no doubts. More than any man he knew, he'd been driven by a passion for personal acclaim, and whenever he spoke about breaking anonymity, his talk was peppered with incidents from his own history, especially from his conspicuous dry drunk period. Perhaps it was this that made him understand the temptation in others. Those who'd been obscure so long could now tell their stories and find instant stardom; in a way it seemed to give a hard-edged identity to the drunk's damaged sense of himself.

In the beginning the whole notion of being anonymous had come from fear. They felt they had to hide from public mistrust and contempt. Also, at that time, some were fearful that they wouldn't be able to handle the number of appeals for help that would come pouring in when the book was published. They needed the protection of anonymity. The newcomer needed it —no man wanted his boss, possibly not even his friends, to know he was joining a group of lowly alcoholics—and the groups needed it to protect themselves from members who might go shooting off on wild publicity binges of their own.

These binges still occurred. Occasionally a character would come along who seemed sent by fate to test them, because his behavior would touch upon and go counter to every one of their principles. There was such a clown in Florida. He was sober, there was no arguing that point; he was a devout AAer. But he'd decided to fix up the program and do a little rewriting of the Steps. What was more, he wanted to go public and in time managed to line up a radio network and a sponsor—a famous insurance company.

Bill's correspondence about this was voluminous. The man insisted that his message was inspired; it was true he was being paid, but AA had no right to stop him; there was such a thing as free speech here—and there was something very familiar about these words. Bill answered that he was indeed free to speak, but AA was also free. He then contacted the network and told them that if their program went on as scheduled, he could promise them they would receive letters from every member of every group across America, and these would not be the sort of letters a sponsor would care to read. The program was finally canceled, and no harm done, but the incident represented one of the rare times Bill W. felt called upon to utilize the formidable clout of AA.

Not all breaches were this clear-cut, but Bill usually could explain that any break on a public level was dangerous—as in the case of a few prominent figures in Hollywood. He saw that it might temporarily appear to be a good thing for AA and for an actor's career, but he also knew that staying sober presented enough problems without adding to it the awesome responsibility —and the tensions that would inevitably go with it—of realizing, if one should slip, what the ensuing publicity might do to the fellowship. That seemed an additional burden no recovering drunk should have to take on.

A few cases, however, appeared to fall into a gray area, and were not so easy to resolve. Bill's old friend from the Monsey days, Marty M., became a prime example of one such case. Since coming to her first meeting, Marty had been giving her time, her mind, her incredible energies, indeed her entire life, to educating the public about alcoholism. She had attended the Yale School of Alcohol Studies, had become a close associate of the top scientists in the field, and due to her considerable talents as both a speaker and a writer, public understanding of the illness was increasing. The heavy curtain under which alcoholics had been living was being lifted a trifle, and because of her work AA was getting more members.

But this brought up questions. If Marty was free to tell her story, using herself as an example of recovery, and using her full name when addressing the public, what about others? What about the AA messiah who wanted to bring out a magazine—which in truth was nothing but a tract for the return of prohibition? He could say his work was educational too. Or what of the member who'd tied up with a liquor trade association—they recognized a good thing—who wanted to use his cautionary tale as part of an "educational" campaign? How could they say no to him?

Of course, money problems entered in here. Marty had a very legitimate reason for wanting to raise funds for what she envisioned as a national council on alcoholism, but others across the country also needed cash for AA clubs, hospitals, publications, etc., and using the AA name to raise money only caused confusion in the public's mind. As if to compound the problem, this was happening at the same time Bill had determined that the fellowship must be self-supporting.

Marty—in Bill's words, "to her eternal credit"—finally recognized the confusion she was causing and tried to resume her anonymity. In the future she would use her full name in connection with her outside or professional work, but at meetings and in all matters related to AA she would be simply Marty M.

There seem never to have been gray areas or the same kind of confusions in Bill's thinking about the spiritual side of anonymity. But as with the mysterious ingredient that he knew was holding AA together, he had not fully understood it; he had not yet found a vocabulary to describe the spiritual reasons for remaining anonymous.

For one thing, he didn't know if what he was feeling applied to

332

others, or if it was something that spoke only to him, to his condition. Still he never questioned its importance in his life. When he thought of it, but even more when he practiced it, when he was not selling, not the cofounder, but just a drunk talking to and recognizing himself in another human being, then, always, he felt himself drawing closer to some indefinable force. Then he was truly living in the now, then he had placed himself in some area of being that was outside the clash of opposites, approval versus disapproval, past versus future. Conscious simply of the person he was with, he would become aware only of the moment, the immensity and movement of the moment. Sometimes when this happened it was almost as if distant chords of music had begun to sound, but he could never say what struck them.

Words can only belittle and reduce certain truths—and Bill felt at these times he was nearing a great truth. When he had had similar "spiritual experiences" as a young man and had felt on the verge of grasping a message or moving into some higher state of consciousness, he had never talked about it; indeed, he'd felt a responsibility to shield it, so that it would not be lost or twisted out of shape until he'd fully understood its meaning.

So for several years he went on and wrote and spoke of anonymity only in terms of sacrifice, of protection for others, and the feeling of genuine humility it could evoke—all of which were true, even though for him they were not the whole truth. And for years he went on following, trying to understand, a mysterious power he sensed was there, a part of his concept of anonymity. Though he could not quite comprehend its meaning, he continued to respond with a kind of inner excitement to the something he felt was implicit in the idea, and this excitement constantly beckoned him on.

In 1945 someone suggested that the Traditions should be codified and sent out to groups for their reactions. In order to keep up with the demands being made on its services, the office had moved to larger quarters, at 415 Lexington Avenue. Ruth

333

Hock had left to get married, her position had been taken over by a new AA member, Bobbie B., and there had been other changes. There were often translators in the office to handle inquiries from foreign countries, more paid assistants in the mailing and shipping departments, and among the special services they were trying to provide was the publication of a monthly magazine, *The Grapevine*. After some discussion this seemed a suitable forum in which to present the Twelve Traditions.

At about the same time there were two other major developments. One had to do solely with Bill's personal life. The other—his notion of forming a board of representatives from various sections of the country to take over the running of the fellowship—probably had more to do with ensuring AA's future than any idea Bill ever had. The plan was to undergo many changes and it would be years before it reached fruition, but it is remarkable that he started working on it at this early date.

The development in Bill's private life was the result of a decision to begin a series of regular sessions with Dr. Harry Tiebout. This was a move he'd been considering for some time, yet to the members who learned of it, it was curiously disturbing. To begin with, it seemed out of character.

For many Bill W. had become their spiritual mentor. He'd written the Steps, and his lucid and loving assessment of problems, more than anything, had been holding them together. It seemed inconceivable that their Bill, who'd been released from his obsession, had not by the same means been freed from every other difficulty and defeat. Seeing him at meetings, or lolling around the office, relaxed yet always in control, always radiantly alive and still so ardent for new experiences, they simply did not want to believe that this man could on occasion be crippled by depressions and so utterly depleted by his own efforts to decipher their causes that he finally would have to turn to an outsider for help. But this was the fact. Beginning in the summer of '44, twice a week Bill drove the fifteen miles from his home in Bedford Hills to Tiebout's office in Greenwich, Connecticut.

There was always a degree of luck, Bill said, or perhaps he conceded there might be a bit of guidance involved, when a patient finds the right analyst. Tiebout knew his colleagues were leery of so-called "emotional cures." Relying on the mind and the analytic process to uncover the causes of emotional stresses and strains, they presumed that when the destructive emotions had been ferreted out and freed, positive, healthy emotions would automatically appear to take their place. But after working with numerous alcoholics who'd stopped drinking through AA, Tiebout thought it just as logical to assume that emotions could be changed by emotions (or as they said in AA, by new spiritual values). Then when the change had occurred, Tiebout believed that the mind could be put to work firming up the new emotions as a part of the patient's personality structure.

Over and over he mentioned in his lectures his AA patients and their new feelings, their new responses to therapy and to all of life after they had experienced an emotional change in the fellowship. In his papers he often quoted Bill—always referring to him as Mr. X.—and especially Bill's account of his night at Towns Hospital, in which he described what had happened as "a great synthesizing experience, in which everything became clear . . . as though a cloud had lifted and everything took on an indescribable illumination." Tiebout may have questioned and explored the roots of the alcoholic obsession, but he never doubted an alcoholic's ability to change emotionally, or the validity of Mr. X.'s spiritual experience.

For Bill, going to Tiebout represented a tremendous venture in open-mindedness. In an essay he was to write some years later about the Sixth Step (in which the alcoholic becomes ready to have his "defects of character" removed), Bill speaks of this as the point that separates the men from the boys. Intellectually he had always realized the importance of this. In *Alcoholics Anonymous*, he'd declared that the AA way of life demanded rigorous honesty with one's self, and he begged all newcomers to be fearless and thorough from the start, pointing out the perils that lay ahead for those who tried to hang on to their old ideas. The results for them would be nil, he said, until they became willing to let go absolutely.

From the start they had spoken of the program as a program of action, but for those who had grown and had achieved some degree of emotional sobriety, action meant more than dashing about and frantically carrying the message to others. It meant taking action on the inner man, on his values and his deepest sensibilities. Of the twelve suggested Steps, only three made any mention of other people; the remaining nine dealt solely with the recovering drunk's inner life.

In this department the results of Bill's attempts at "rigorous honesty" had not been nil. He knew he was not the same man he had been in '35, but if he was still being immobilized by spells of depression, if he was still burdened by ancient guilts—of the sort which he knew in other cases had started in childhood and so were often the last to go—then he was still a man hanging on to "old ideas" and possibly even displaying the typical alcoholic's desire to go on nursing and clinging to his guilts. But however Bill viewed his problem, at this point, just before his fiftieth birthday, and with all the ego-flattering prestige of being considered a spiritual leader, to stop, take a look, and admit he needed professional help was more than open-mindedness; it was an act of courage.

It would be guesswork to speculate about what finally sent Bill to Tiebout, or about his feelings during their sessions, but it is clear that the impact these two men had, one upon the other, was profound and lasting. This is apparent in their writings. In the papers Tiebout presented after '45, there are many signs of his deeper understanding of conversion as a psychological phenomenon and of the role surrender can play in the recovery from alcoholism.

In an address Bill delivered before the American Psychiatric Association in Montreal, he spoke of his months in therapy as "removing certain festering neurotic roots . . . and hence my depressions." But Tiebout's influence can be felt in the pieces Bill did for *The Grapevine* and in his next two books even more than in his talks to professional groups. The doctor had not only given him insights into the unconscious drives that had been pushing him around, but he had in a way shored up many truths that Bill had uncovered almost instinctively while working with other drunks. He saw now—although he kept himself free from psychiatric jargon and continued to write in his simple kitchen-table style—that what the alcoholic had to surrender was his inflated ego, those traits of his personality which he'd carried along from early childhood into his adult life. With the drinking drunk these were always easy to spot: the old feeling of omnipotence, an inability to tolerate frustration, and his excessive drives.

In discussing this inner child who lived on in everyone, but was so obvious in the alkie, and whom Bill realized he had better recognize and come to terms with, Tiebout quoted a phrase of Freud's. And for Bill, remembering himself standing in a bar, king of all he surveyed, living just for the day, expecting, indeed demanding, that his will prevail, these words seemed the perfect description of that kid in the cellar who could still rear up and take control, whom Freud had labeled "His Majesty the Baby."

Unlike most patients in therapy, Bill's spiritual underpinnings were secure. He knew his goals. And fortunately—and here again there may have been a bit of guidance as well as luck—while he was working on these problems Bill was in no way isolated. He was still deeply involved in all the activities of the office. And also, ever since that stormy night at the old Twenty-fourth Street clubhouse, he'd remained in close contact with Father Ed Dowling.

Soon after they met, Father Ed had presented Bill with a copy of the Prayer of St. Francis. And during this period it was never far from Bill's thoughts. Just saying it over, or repeating a particular phrase: ". . . that where there is despair, I may bring hope, that where there are shadows I may bring light . . ." or "Grant that

I may seek rather to comfort than to be comforted, to understand than to be understood, to love than to be loved . . . for it is in self-forgetting that one finds . . ." somehow simply remembering these words would serve to clear the channels that were so easily choked up with fears and misunderstandings, and he would be able to return once again, even in moments of stress, to his real search.

In a way, he said, he sometimes felt he was a lay brother to Father Ed, and Father Ed, he knew, was a lay brother to God. The two men corresponded constantly, and they saw each other whenever the little Jesuit was in the East, or when a trip took Bill anywhere near St. Louis.

He was beginning to travel more now, and more extensively, talking to groups in California and throughout the West, selling the Traditions and putting out feelers for group reactions to his board of representatives idea.

The reaction to the Traditions was definitely mixed. Groups that had had troubles welcomed them immediately; others wanted their own regulations. Some of the more intellectual members in the East insisted they were nothing more than a projection of Bill W.'s own private hopes and fears for the fellowship, and, like everything in AA, each tradition had to be debated and argued about endlessly before a group would vote its approval.

Bill W. was still a star attraction, still a charming, dynamic speaker, and he addressed crowded meetings everywhere. These days it was not only the size of the audiences that impressed him. For the first time he was noticing a marked change in the character of the groups. In their early days, meetings had been made up almost entirely of low bottom drunks, the grim and hopeless ones. Now younger men were coming in, and quite a few women too, people who still had jobs, money, even social position. This was sometimes disturbing to the old hard-liners, who looked down on these fresh faces and wondered how the hell they could be alcoholics: they hadn't suffered enough. But Bill and the groups themselves gradually came to realize that these new members had hit their own emotional bottoms, and that it was no longer necessary for a man to experience every possible kind of hell in order to admit that he was licked.

On the whole, his audiences were attentive and most respectful, but occasionally when he'd launch into one of his pet subjects —the organization of the New York headquarters, or the need for service boards to handle special meetings in institutions, or take care of foreign groups—he would notice a certain apathy settling in, a few of the old-timers even nodding off. This attitude was sometimes reflected in his mail:

"Dear Bill, we'd love to have you come and speak. Please tell us about where you used to hide your bottles and all about that big hot-flash spiritual experience. But for God's sake, please don't talk anymore about those damn Traditions."

In 1947, there was a piece of news from the Akron groups that threw everything—all of Bill's thinking—into a new dimension. Dr. Bob had been stricken with what they understood would probably be his terminal illness. And, in what seemed no time at all and was actually only a few years, Anne Smith died.

True, the Smiths were older than he, and Bill tried to make himself focus on this, but it did no good. Anne's death and Dr. Bob's illness were a terrible reminder that life was narrowing down, closing in, and there was the inescapable fact that if it could happen to them, it could happen to him.

The old order was changing, and the abrupt realization of this filled Bill with new apprehensions, not for himself, but for AA. Also it made him see that he must start moving ahead—and quickly—with his idea for a board of representatives or, as he was calling it, his conference plan.

Until now, the only link between the members of what was becoming a fellowship with world-wide services and AA itself had been Dr. Bob, Bill W. and the secretaries who sent out the letters. Outside New York City, no one even knew the names of the trustees, yet if something happened to Bill and Bob, the running of AA would be in the hands of these men, who—fine and noble characters though they might be—were strangers to the drunks. It wasn't that the members lacked confidence in them; they did not know them, they had no reason for confidence. And Bill saw that any misstep on the part of the trustees might wreck the whole setup and wreck it permanently. Without the support of the groups (and this had to be far more than financial support; AA was totally dependent on their moral support) all their services to new groups, to loners, their work in hospitals and prisons could evaporate in no time.

He had talked about it before, and he had written innumerable memoranda on the subject, but now he began to see they could be facing a completely untenable situation—a board of trustees who in reality were a tiny isolated island in the midst of a huge fellowship that was spreading out across several continents. In Bill's view there was only one solution: a conference board of men elected by the drunks themselves in all sections of the country who could represent the groups, who would meet once a year, inspect headquarters, and to whom the trustees would be accountable.

Once having worked out details as to how such a board might function, Bill was open to suggestions or any sensible modification, but he was not prepared for delays or for any opposition. And there was opposition. There were persistent objections from trustees, who explained that such a venture would be wildly expensive. Furthermore—and even worse—it could plunge AA into all sorts of disruptive political activities when conference delegates were chosen. Politics was one thing they had always managed to stay clear of. They begged Bill to put the idea aside and try to relax.

But for all the progress he'd made with Tiebout, for all Father Ed's beautiful guidance, relaxing when he met resistance was not something that came easily to Bill. As the arguments grew more extreme, the atmosphere in the office became more tense, and some of the exchanges at board meetings grew pretty acrimoni-

340

ous. Bill, however, continued firing off memos. One of these ended in a burst of invective. After pointing out that as things stood now, the trustees had all the authority and no responsibility to anyone, not even to Dr. Bob and himself, he then reached back to his Brooklyn Law days, and announced that he'd made an extensive study of trusts, and his study had turned up nothing more than a long and melancholy history of malfeasance and misfeasance of boards of trustees.

But he was getting nowhere in New York, and Bill decided to go out to the grass roots and explain his plan to the groups. Learning of this, several board members grew alarmed about the trouble he might cause and began to wonder if they shouldn't contact some of the old-timers in Ohio to see if there wasn't some way to stop Bill W. But again they need not have worried, again the thing they did not understand was that no matter how stubborn or how convinced Bill might be of the rightness of his cause, at heart he was still a recovering drunk who wanted to be with and share his experiences with other drunks. When he stood on a platform, hands jammed in his pockets, slouching forward yet still towering above the lectern someone had set up, and quietly addressed a group, or explained himself over a mug of coffee in one of their after-meeting meetings, he might veer off onto one of his pet concerns, but he clearly was a man who cared primarily about the drunks getting sober and growing in their sobriety.

After one of these trips—and there were a great many in '48, '49, even into '50, all of them made ostensibly to explain the conference plan—Bill returned to New York with some truly startling information.

At first he didn't know how to report what he had found. It was a bonanza, it was a gift from God, a ten strike. It was also a bit of serendipity in that it was something of great value he had come across without ever looking for it. For what Bill had discovered was the beginning of AA family groups.

In town after town he'd been hearing about the wives of members holding meetings on their own, sometimes in little groups of

341

three or four, sometimes in quite sizable gatherings, and meeting not to discuss their husbands' problems but to find ways whereby they themselves might better understand and use the program. Occasionally they'd meet in a room adjacent to the regular meeting, or a handful might get together in a station wagon parked outside while the AAs met inside.

Perhaps he could have anticipated it. It was a logical and inevitable offshoot of all he'd been working for, but the point was that it was there, and Topsy-like, independent of anyone's guidance, it had just grown. Some of the groups had written New York, and Bobbie B. had registered them under a special heading, but Bill had had no idea of their number, or of their purpose.

In the beginning, when many older members thought of wives meeting—if they'd thought of it at all—they had considered the idea a little suspect, a sort of gossip club probably, or possibly a ladies' aid society that could take care of coffee and cake. But now he had seen them in action. These wives or, in some cases, husbands of drunks were also victims of alcoholism. Their lives had been twisted out of shape, but the remarkable thing was that they were willing and honest enough to look at this fact. And, as with AA, they were discovering they were not alone, that there were certain patterns that seemed to run through many of their stories. And again, as in AA, it seemed they could share their problems only with another wife or husband who'd been through the same thing.

When their spouses were drinking they too had been filled with bitterness and self-pity. Often a marriage that had started out on such a high, so alive with young hopes, had gradually deteriorated into the relationship of a wayward boy and his protective, possessive mother. Then when the drunk sobered up and the great honeymoon with AA began, to everyone's shock these problems still weren't solved. Often they were worse. There was a new jealousy and often a very deep hurt that strangers had done the job they'd tried but had been unable to accomplish. Sometimes the emotional outbursts after AA were more devastating than before, and of course these scenes could impose cruel scars on any children involved.

But the important thing—to Bill, the glorious thing—was that so many of them, all on their own, had had the courage to look at these facts and see that changes must be made—and the changes must be in themselves. It was this, and not their husbands' failings, they were meeting to discuss in little rooms, in kitchens and parking lots all across the country.

What they needed at this point was very much what AA had needed in '35—confidence, some sense of organization and possibly someone to oversee their activities and give them a means of contacting one another, a sort of central clearing house.

When Bill got back after discovering this new development, Lois was right there as always, waiting at the station.

There is some disagreement about Lois's first reaction. Bill remembered that she understood the whole situation at once and leaped at the idea of trying to help. Lois's memory is slightly different. She had a home in the country, she loved it, loved puttering in her gardens. She also had every reason to believe she had done her work. Only gradually, she recalls, as she began to recognize the tremendous need for family groups, did she decide she really had no choice. She would have to do what she could to organize and unify these groups.

But once the decision was reached, she began to move, and all of Dr. Burnham's daughter's amazing vitality was put to work.*

The response to the Traditions had been much more affirmative than Bill had first realized. Perhaps the groups had needed time to digest them. There had been articles about them in *The Grapevine,* they had been discussed in detail at open and closed

---

* An account of the family groups, which soon took on the name of Alanon, cannot be summarized in a book that is trying to tell the story of Bill W. The genesis, the development and the incredible courage of this offshoot of AA cries out for a book of its own. Bill often said there were few things in his life that gave him more joy and that Alanon remained always lodged in a special corner of his heart.

meetings, and by July 1950, when they were presented at an international convention in Cleveland, they were thoroughly understood.

There were some three thousand members at the convention, and on a hot summer afternoon, in a roaring shout of approval, the Twelve Traditions were adopted unanimously as a platform. They all believed they had found the means whereby AA could go on, function and hold together.

Several weeks later Bill paid a visit to Akron, knowing Dr. Bob was to undergo an operation in a few days. Both men realized that this might be their last session together.

They talked of many things that afternoon, and they remembered many things. They laughed and shook their heads as they went over the vast number of incongruous characters who had joined them since those summer nights when they had sat so often in the same little parlor on Ardmore Avenue. Bill recalled one afternoon at the office when he had talked for hours with an Indian princess who had sat cross-legged on the floor beside his desk, dressed in a thin sari and with a bright ruby glowing in the center of her forehead. She had been a very sick alcoholic but had heard about AA, had sobered up, then traveled to New York to learn more and carry the good word back to her country. Unfortunately, no one had told the princess about New York weather and she'd had to stop at Macy's to buy a huge tweed jacket, which she wore buttoned up over her sari. That same evening Bill and the princess attended a meeting, where hats and coats were being checked at the door by a young man who introduced himself as Joe. Bill had thought Joe a newcomer, but when he asked he learned that Joe had been around for many months and was doing fine. He was from Chicago, a former member of Al Capone's gang, and everyone was delighted with the progress he was making.

The cofounders could have gone on for days exchanging such stories, but there was one thing Bill knew he had to bring up. It might be an awkward subject to discuss with a man whose own future was indefinite, but the future of AA and what was to happen to it when the two of them were gone depended on the conference plan. Bob knew about the dangers, the politicking that might go on in various districts when they had to choose delegates, but he agreed that a board representing the drunks could guarantee the future. They could do for the overall services what the Traditions now were doing for AA unity. Perhaps, he said, they should try calling a conference, show them the offices, all the books, and let them decide how much responsibility they should take over. Dr. Bob was convinced that all decisions concerning AA should be made not by Bill or himself or by trustees, but by the drunks themselves.

When it grew late and Bill had to leave, Bob rose and saw him to the door, and for a time they stood together on the little front porch, then they shook hands. After Bill had moved down the steps and had taken several long strides down the sidewalk, he turned and looked back. Dr. Bob was still there, standing erect as always, but there wasn't much color in his cheeks, and his neat gray suit seemed much too big for him.

As Bill smiled, Bob lifted his arm in a combination salute and wave, then he winked. "Remember, Willie," he said. "Don't louse it up. Keep it simple."

Bill winked back at him, smiled again and hurried on. Dr. Bob Smith died November 16, 1950.

In trying to transmute the hard fact of Bob's dying into something he could accept, Bill's mind dwelt on many seemingly unconnected ideas.

They were Vermonters, but aside from that and all that implied, they were men of very different temperaments.

Forty years before, old Fayette Griffith had sat beside a boy in a buggy, and had tried to make him see that the things we have in common are stronger, more important than the things that separate us, and that the whole idea of democracy depended on this truth and on men's remembering it always. Bob Smith would

345

have known in his gut what Fayette was saying. Bill had known it the night he and Bob had met in the Seiberling gatehouse and all that summer in Akron, he had known it all through his early years, but Bob had never had to struggle to maintain and hold it.

He had had to struggle with other things; with his obsession always, and far more than Bill. There was never a two-day period, he told Bill once, when at some point he did not have a physical craving for booze. Still he'd gone on. He'd won. And thousands of others, men he had never met, never heard of, had won because of the way he had gone on. In his unpretentious way he'd fought his obsession, had joined forces with Sister Ignatia at St. Thomas Hospital in Akron, and with her helped open the doors of the first religious institution anywhere to welcome AAs. Together they tended over five thousand alcoholics, and Bob Smith never considered any fees for his medical services to a drunk.

There are those who have wondered why in their first years the Ohio groups got off to a more solid start than the Brooklyn and New York meetings, and some have suggested that the reason may lie in the fact that Bob was a physician, trained to accept men as they were, and to work with them as they were, whereas —and AA can thank its God for this too—Bill was always the promoter, the seeker, always reaching out into a new dimension. Even in his spiritual life with Father Ed, he found little of the comfort many derived from conventional religions. Bill's spiritual quest rode him, hounded him, haunted him. Yet he knew he could never give it up, because he sensed that it, with all its unanswered questions, was what was keeping him sober, keeping him going, and that somehow it was closely tied in with the source of power he had always been seeking.

And in that November of Bob Smith's dying, remembering the strange communion of their first meeting, remembering the closeness with other drunks, he knew he was still seeking, still trying to find the real meaning in, or just behind, his concept of anonym-

346

ity. But whatever his final answer might be, whatever the conclusion to the riddles, he knew that Bob Smith, in his quiet, simple daily living, was nearer the truth, closer to that secret power, and so, perhaps, closer to his creator than any man he had ever known.

Perhaps AA needed them both, the quiet doctor who kept his inner life simple, and Bill W., to whom nothing was ever simple.

7

On a hot July afternoon in 1955, Bill W. stood on the platform of the Kiel Auditorium in St. Louis and looked down at the endless rows of faces lined up before him. As he slowly straightened his back before speaking, his mind seemed to stand apart, and for an instant, with a strange and quiet lucidity, he could see that somehow—without his knowing it was happening—all his years had been leading him toward this platform, toward this moment and what he knew he would have to say.

There were five thousand members with their families and friends in the audience. For three days they had been meeting to celebrate the twentieth anniversary of the founding of Alcoholics Anonymous. Now, on their last day together, they had fallen silent; a peculiar tension could be felt in every part of the auditorium.

So far the speeches they'd been hearing had followed the general pattern of AA talks at open meetings; they'd revealed what the speakers had been like, what had happened to them, and what they were like now. On the first night Bill had talked of what he called the first of their three legacies: Recovery. The audience had hung on his every word.

His second talk had dealt with their second legacy: Unity. In

348

this Bill had included an account of AA's growth, and to illustrate his points he brought up stories of various groups and how they had begun: not only groups in the United States and Canada, but those he and Lois had visited in Scandinavia, Holland, France and the British Isles; stories about the wondrous, rationalizing French, who'd kept insisting that wine wasn't liquor and so it shouldn't count, and the secretive British, who took their anonymity so to heart in the beginning that they were often impossible to find.

The Oslo group, he had discovered to his delight, had been founded by a Norwegian coffee shop owner from Greenwich, Connecticut. This little man had been in America twenty years, living the life of a veritable derelict, but in 1947 he'd found AA and a new life. For the first time then, he wrote his family back in the old country, telling them all that had happened to him, and in a matter of weeks he received a letter from them. His brother was a hopeless alcoholic, about to lose his job on an Oslo newspaper and, they feared, about to lose his life. The coffee shop owner immediately sold his shop and bought a ticket for home. But the brother indeed seemed a hopeless case; he had no interest in hearing a translation of the Steps, or in any AA stories. Thoroughly discouraged, the coffee shop owner started canvassing local doctors and ministers, but found the same lack of interest everywhere. Finally he began making plans to return to Greenwich. On his last night in Oslo, his brother asked him to tell him again about his anonymous American friends—and this time it happened: it worked. Sober and back on his job, the brother started running a small ad in his newspaper. The wife of a sidewalk florist answered his ad, and he made his first Twelfth Step call. Soon there was another call, then a third and a fourth, and AA was established in Norway. Three years later, when Bill and Lois arrived at the airport in Oslo, a large delegation of sober AAs was waiting beyond the customs gate to welcome them. It was true that the delegation spoke no English, and Bill knew no

Norwegian, but it didn't matter. He soon learned that there were hundreds of members spread among many groups and that new groups were springing up all the time.

To some, these stories were the high points of the St. Louis convention. For others, there would be isolated incidents: the first time they saw the Lasker Award, the bronze Winged Victory that had been presented to AA on the recommendation of twelve thousand physicians of the American Public Health Association, or the simple sincerity of the telegram from the White House wishing them well. Others would never forget the contagious exuberance of Sam Shoemaker, seemingly not a day older and not a mite less enthusiastic about God and AA, or the sight of Dr. Emily, now eighty-five, as proud and handsome as ever, or the quiet nobility of Father Ed Dowling, oblivious to his painful lameness as he made his way across the stage and filled the vast auditorium with his special radiance and what Bill called his "touch of the eternal." Women as well as men would remember Lois standing beside Bill, her hair graying but her blue eyes dancing with a child's pure delight as she told about the family groups. There had been no more than sixty when Bill first discovered them; there were seven hundred in America now, and already groups were starting in ten foreign countries.

But most would remember Bill's recital of his struggles to establish a governing board, his old conference plan. Soon after Dr. Bob had died, the trustees had agreed to let him call a conference as an experiment. Now, four years later, it had moved far beyond the experimental stage. The destructive politicking over the choice of delegates, which so many had feared, never took place. Groups arranged assemblies, and these assemblies proceeded to elect their representative by written ballot on the basis of a two-thirds majority. If no one got two-thirds of the vote, the names of the candidates were then placed in a hat—in keeping with an old town meeting custom—and invariably an excellent delegate was selected in this way.

The first conference, held in New York in April of '51, had

been a truly heartening experience. There had been many old-timers among the delegates, but also quite a few men who'd been sober only five or six years. They arrived, made a thorough examination of headquarters, met the trustees and service staff. They examined the financial books with a microscope. In session after session there was heated but cordial debate, and in the end many knotty problems had been resolved. Also at this first conference it had been decided that the Alcoholic Foundation must be renamed. To drunks the word "foundation" implied charity, paternalism, even high finance, and the delegates wanted none of this; AA could assume responsibility for itself and pay its own way, so it was agreed—and again by a two-thirds vote—that the new name would be the General Service Board.

When their first conference ended and the delegates left to return to their groups, Bill knew that something momentous had happened, and as he went on with his report to the audience in St. Louis, it was clear that these first delegates had proved a point he and Dr. Bob had believed in for so long: the group conscience should be their sole authority.

No one in Kiel Auditorium on the last afternoon of that '55 convention would ever forget the sense of expectancy when Bill again stood before them and they waited for him to speak.

He seemed to have grown, to be somehow a little larger than life, a man who just naturally created memories. If Bill W. had engaged a Madison Avenue PR firm, one old-timer recalled, and if this firm had worked around the clock on his account, they could never have done for him what he without even trying did for himself that afternoon. There had always been a powerful affinity between Bill and the imagination of alcoholics, and now this could be felt in the farthest corners of Kiel Auditorium.

Even at a distance one got the impression of a tall, thin, completely relaxed man, yet with a tremendous inner energy; a personality that carried over big spaces—that indeed seemed to expand when confronted with bigness. A warm light played over his face as he squared his shoulders and then leaned slightly forward across the lectern like some old backwoods statesman who'd stopped by for a chat. He was imposing, yet friendly, radiant but homespun.

Some of course knew roughly what he would say. They knew a resolution was to be presented and that it would have to do with the General Service Board, with what was being called the third legacy, Service. But no one had been prepared for this moment, or for the fact that Bill would offer the resolution himself.

He was silent for only half a minute perhaps, but in that brief time, as he looked into the faces below him, he had a quick flash of understanding. He knew too that, like all the other flashes in his life, it would take longer to describe than to experience. These were his people, he realized; he was their leader. They were assembled here to honor him for something that had not really been his doing. But that was all right; he had no objections; some people would always want and believe they needed a leader. To them he had become a symbol. He was more than an administrator, more than a cofounder, or the author of the Steps. He was the custodian of their deepest beliefs and of that faith which somehow had created dignity and peace out of their unbelievable hells.

And in this same moment he also knew—as he had known once long ago as a raw recruit in the state militia—a sense of responsibility that went beyond any personal feelings or desires, and he understood that if ever, now or in the future, he allowed private concerns to mar or obscure this trust, he would not only be betraying these people, he would be failing himself.

As he cleared his throat before beginning to speak, he was struck by one other startling truth. These people before him were not children, their lives were no longer unmanageable. For twenty years he had tried to guide them, nurture them and establish a structure within which they could grow, but now AA had come of age.

The resolution that Bill then proposed was stated in the simplest terms. It declared that the time had come for the fellowship to take its affairs into its own hands and that the General Service Conference should now become the permanent successor to the founders.

The resolution was passed by the convention and the chairman, Bernard B. Smith—who more than any man had worked with Bill to see this plan brought to fruition—turned and offered the resolution to the delegates for their confirmation. They gave their consent by a show of hands.

Ber Smith made a few remarks, and then there was nothing more to do, except for Bill and Lois to find some way to say good-by.

As Lois spoke, thanking the convention, trying to express her feelings about what the afternoon had meant, Bill saw that she too was becoming a symbol, not only of the suffering the alcoholic's wife must endure, but of the courage and hope of families in AA.

When he moved back to the lectern and began to speak again, Bill knew he was feeling what many fathers must feel when their sons and daughters start to move on, make their own decisions and live their own lives. The well-meaning parent, he said, who tries to hang on to his authority and overstays his time is one who can do much damage, and he never wanted to see this happen in AA. He'd be around, happy to help out in pinches, but that would be all. In the natural course of events, when it was time for the old guard to be relieved, he believed it right and fitting for them to march off briskly to the strains of a good quick-step. Still, for a moment, and again like a parent whose son has come of age, he couldn't help wanting to turn the clock back and he couldn't resist a few last admonitions.

But—for Bill—it was a very short talk. When he finished, when he had grinned and waved at the crowd, who would not stop cheering, had helped his mother and Lois off the stage, he felt warm inside and good clean through.

Others noticed—and he was aware of it too—that all evening a little half smile kept playing across his lips. He knew now that AA was safe at last—even from him.

Bill W.'s life did not end in St. Louis. He'd said at the convention that he was entering his autumn years, the season for reflection. He guessed he'd do some writing and try to recapture a few of their experiences in a book, but he thought that primarily he should try to grow up a little more. As one of the teachers in AA's way of life, he'd seen many of the pupils giving better demonstrations than he, and perhaps it was time for him to try to catch up with them.

These were gentle thoughts, but a poor description of his next years. When he finally dismounted the tiger he had been riding for twenty years, Bill was an extremely young fifty-nine, a man of tremendous virility, with an adequate income, good health and a stock of unanswered questions. And he still possessed the curiosity of the schoolboy who'd wanted to learn everything there was to know about a boomerang.

A remarkable and quite sudden expansion of his interests took place. He had discovered that there were a great many subjects he'd been cut off from, and now—or so he believed—he was free to pursue them all. He had also announced publicly—and again he believed it at the time—that he was handing over his stewardship and would no longer be the AA handyman around the office. But, as someone pointed out, every recovered drunk Bill met and every AA project had been his personal concern. It was consequently not surprising that he maintained his office at headquarters and kept himself fully informed about all AA activities.

He had, however, one pet and perennial concern and that was the ratio of alcoholic to nonalcoholic members of the board. It was of paramount importance to him that the majority of trustees, if only a majority of one, be alcoholics. It became his cause, his own private war, and he was willing to risk anything, any relationships, to win a battle or even a small skirmish in this war.

He admired the nonalcoholic members. They were some of the

354

finest men in America, some of his closest friends, and all of them had devoted themselves to AA without stint. But on this one subject Bill W. was adamant. He was stubborn, bullheaded, any term they wanted to apply to him—and indeed through the years they used far harsher ones (he even applied them to himself)— but he could not yield. The thought of nondrunks having a final say in any decision stuck in his craw; it became his King Charles's head.

One of the more wounding skirmishes was with Dr. Strong, Dorothy's husband. Leonard had been in on the very inception of AA, one of the foundation's first board members; before that he had been Bill's doctor, his confidant, the one who had put him in the hospital, paid the bills and stood by him always. No man could have done more. But Leonard Strong was a physician, the son of a physician, and deep in his being was the medical man's belief that in the final analysis decisions had to be made by detached, uninvolved persons. It was over this very matter that Leonard felt, in 1954, that he must resign from the board. Happily, nothing could permanently affect the bond that existed between Bill and the Strongs.

Year after year, the subject of ratios would be brought up. Bill would argue tenaciously, but each time he'd be voted down. His reactions to these defeats were often severe—he couldn't help reading personal rejection into this difference of opinion—and he would be thrown into spells of depression that were difficult for those who knew him best to understand.

Also at these times he began to recognize many symptoms of his old dry drunk benders. AA had been born out of his experience, his pain, his drunkenness—and his rebirth. He and Bob Smith had created a microcosm of democracy in AA and the board must be made to see that the name on the mailbox was the people, or in this case, the alcoholics. His jaw would set in an old, familiar way, and his early litany would start ringing through his head: Someday, somehow, he'd show them, he'd show them all.

But that day was a long time coming. Not until 1966 was a

system worked out and finally agreed upon in which, by a method of rotation, the percentage of alcoholic trustees would always outnumber the nonalcoholics.

In other areas Bill did a much better job of adhering to his plan for his autumn years. For example, he did a tremendous amount of writing. In '54 he had completed his series of essays, *Twelve Steps and Twelve Traditions,* and although it did not sell as well as what AAs were calling the Big Book, it was reasonably successful. Immediately after St. Louis, he decided to write an account of the fellowship's first twenty-one years, based on the talks he delivered at the convention. This was published in 1957, under the title *Alcoholics Anonymous Comes of Age.* But despite the superb editing of his old friend Tom P., Bill's insistence on acknowledging every individual's contribution and every accolade AA had been paid kept it from being the straightforward history he'd intended. He seemed obsessed during this period with "setting the record straight" and he produced innumerable tape recordings, manuscripts and incomplete outlines entitled "High Points," "Main Events," etc.

His most important writing now, aside from the hundreds of letters (many of which were abridged and quoted in *The AA Way of Life,* published in 1967), were his articles for *The Grapevine.* In these pieces, Bill wrote with no literary pretensions, but they were so filled with humor, moral intelligence and fresh insights into the alcoholic's character that members bought them, kept them and read them over and over.

These were also years of travel, and not just short visits to Vermont to renew his relationship with Mark Whalon and keep in touch with the vast numbers of Griffith and Wilson cousins scattered across the state. He and Lois toured the Northwest, the Coast, all sections of America, and later made another trip to England.

Often when they'd set off, they would resolve to be just Mr. and Mrs. W. Wilson, but the word would get around: Bill W. was staying at the inn, and a delegation would turn up, wanting to talk, wanting advice or simply wanting to look at him. And Bill was honest about this: it was not displeasing. He might write about ego deflation, but His Majesty the Baby had never abdicated completely. Billy Wilson enjoyed being recognized.

In connection with this he often told a story about running into Joe Hirshhorn. One afternoon he and Lois were hurrying to catch a plane. He hadn't seen Joe in over thirty years; he'd read about him, of course, and about the great Hirshhorn art collection, but their paths had not crossed until they literally bumped into one another at La Guardia Airport. Both men were excited by meeting, pummeled one another on the back, and Joe, as effervescent as ever, wanted to know what the hell had been happening to Bill. A little taken aback, Bill said he thought everyone knew. He'd become the number-one drunk in America.

Joe nodded, but Bill could tell from the blank look in his eye he had no idea what Bill was talking about. "You know, Joe," he said, "AA."

"Oh . . ." and Joe's whole face brightened. He was delighted. Delighted! Because Bill Wilson was certainly one man who needed to find AA.

And with this, he rushed on to catch his plane, and Bill and Lois, a little crestfallen, hurried to theirs.

Once, at tiny Truck Bay in the Caribbean, they found themselves at the same club as Dr. and Mrs. J. Robert Oppenheimer. Bill and the great physicist took an instant liking to one another, and after several long walks together and many more long talks, "Oppie" became convinced that Bill should join him at the Institute for Advanced Study at Princeton. Bill's time could be his own, he promised, and he'd be free to pursue any subject that interested him. Oppenheimer was eager to have Bill there to oversee and evaluate some work that was being done on the possible chemical composition of neuroses—especially depression.

They were together only briefly, these two men from such totally different worlds, but perhaps they sensed certain similarities in outlook and in their approach to unsolved problems.

357

In the end, Bill did not accept Oppenheimer's proposal to work at Princeton, but his eyes were beginning to open to many new discoveries, new possibilities. While he had been concentrating his energies on arresting alcoholism through what he called spiritual means, many scientists had started looking into the interrelated social, psychological and biochemical aspects of the illness. Bill had an understanding of the social part, and he'd dipped more deeply than most men into the psychological aspects; now for the first time he began to explore the biochemical.

Shortly after his talks with Oppenheimer, two men who were to have a great influence on this work entered Bill's life: Dr. Abram Hoffer, of Saskatchewan, Canada, and Dr. Humphrey Osmond. For several years these two physicians had been involved in research with schizophrenics, and in the course of their studies they had tested hundreds of hospitalized alcoholics, who proved to be suffering from mild and previously undiagnosed forms of schizophrenia. Their findings were of great interest to Bill, and the simple vitamin therapy (B_3, niacin) they were using, with what seemed remarkable results, fascinated him. He could see in it possible answers not only for the schizo-alcoholics, but for many emotional and physical problems that plagued his recovering drunks.

The possibilities inherent in the Hoffer-Osmond findings impressed Bill as few things ever had, but at the time they met, the two doctors, with all their great knowledge, seemed to him at about the same stage as Ben Franklin when he first flew his kite in an electric storm. And listening to them talk, he felt very much as he had as a young man when he'd stumbled drunkenly into the General Electric laboratories in Schenectady. It was a private preview of the future.

In a way, these three represented an extraordinary team. Until they met, the research findings had been generally ignored by the medical profession despite two double-blind studies and the publication of several pamphlets and books. The doctors explained philosophically that widespread indifference, even occasional hostility, was often the response to new findings. Bill would find the history of medicine replete with such examples. But Bill could not share this philosophical approach: it held too many echoes of early attitudes toward AA. Clearly what they needed was organization, a unifying force, some sort of clearing house for their information. In these areas Bill W. had had some experience.

He immediately went to work for them and for the next six years this became his primary concern. In true Bill W. fashion, he was able to attract to the project eminent figures from a variety of medical fields, doctors from within AA and many who had no connection with the fellowship, and through these new friends, new doors and new avenues of perception were constantly opening before him. He oversaw the publication of brochures, organized seminars, and in the course of the next several years was responsible for disseminating great quantities of information about B_3.

It is perhaps too early to judge the ultimate value of these efforts. There are men who believe that in the long view, Bill's work with niacin therapy may prove one of the major contributions of his life. For the purposes of this narrative, it is Bill's attitude toward the work and its relationship to AA that is significant. During his time with Hoffer and Osmond he never at any point forgot the traditions of anonymity and of not endorsing outside causes. A reminder of this was carried in every brochure he prepared, along with the request that Bill's name not be mentioned in connection with the undertaking. He insisted that all correspondence concerning it should be addressed not to the office, but to his P.O. box in Bedford Hills. The fury of the early Ohio groups over his behavior and the misunderstanding of his visits to Tiebout were still alive in his memory. Despite his caution, some old-timers were appalled when they learned of his interest in "drugs," and he received several letters suggesting that

359

the district attorney's office might like to be informed that Bill W. was now practicing medicine—and without a license. But these he knew were exceptions, additional evidence of the strange camels who wandered under their tent.

Meanwhile his own AA story and his relationship with the groups were changing. Often after a day in the city or perhaps after an early supper with Lois, he would feel like driving to a nearby town and dropping in on a meeting. He'd arrive a little late, find a place at the back of the room, and over a cup of coffee—it was never very good coffee, but it was coffee and coffee meant AA—he would stretch out his long legs, relax and listen.

It was always wonderful. It had changed so little. The members might be better dressed, the talk on a slightly more intellectual plane than at Clinton Street, but there was the same earnest exuberance, broken by the same beautiful laughter, and always the same indescribable feeling of hope. Sitting back in his chair, unnoticed, he'd be struck again by the extraordinary thing that had come to pass, for the cure for the illness that had baffled men throughout history had finally been given not to the scientists or the ministers, nor to the learned of this earth, but to the outcasts, the lowliest of the sufferers. And as his eyes traveled around the room, he knew that these men and women, for all their good clothes, had each at one time been an unforgivable and unforgiving outcast, and the sight of them now filled him with something close to wonder. But then—and this usually happened just before the halfway break—he would be recognized and the atmosphere of the meeting would change in a subtle way. He would be called upon to make a few remarks—not as a member but as cofounder.

He knew what was expected of him in this role. If he spoke of his difficulties, his doubts and failings, they would be disconcerted. They wanted him to proclaim a message of faith and to do it with a consistency unaffected by any of the ups and downs of his own spiritual life. It seemed little enough to do, so he did it. But this may have been why he often found himself leaving meetings early with a vague feeling of unease. And as he drove home he would sometimes realize he was getting almost as tired of the person he was supposed to be as of the person he really was.

What he wanted to be, what he needed to be, was a member of AA, and this he had never been. One night, as he was heading the car into the garage, he thought of himself as a sort of minor Moses. He had led his people across the wilderness, but for some reason God had not wanted him to enter the promised land. Such high-flown thoughts could stop him, and sometimes, after parking the car for the night, he would stand and look up at the stars. No matter how he saw himself, it did seem a paradox that he, through the Steps, through his writing and talking, had been a channel through which others had found the truth he was still seeking.

He had tried, ever since leaving Towns Hospital; he had studied religions, the ancient ones as well as all the modern sects. And he knew even this had been a blessing for AA: the fact that he'd aligned himself with no one denomination left the door open for men of any faith. It seemed sometimes that what he'd been seeking was deeper and far simpler than anything the known religions offered, yet there was no denying that other drunks had found it, had been able to accept a church. Some nights he seemed the only one still seeking.

In the early sixties, the AA HQ, needing more space, took over the entire fourteenth floor of an old building on East Forty-fifth Street. Here Bill kept a plain but quite comfortable office. From a large window beside his desk he had a fine view of the United Nations building, with the river behind, and to the south he could see all the towering skyscrapers of lower Manhattan.

Here, on the few days of the week he was in the city, he

would sit receiving friends, or studying questions staff members had been worrying over, and invariably, by reaching back into his own experience, he'd come up with an answer that solved the problem quite simply. Or he might write letters to groups, to old members and new acquaintances, letters which numbered, literally, in the thousands. And in this office, on a January afternoon, he wrote what he knew was one of the major documents of his life.

Behind his desk stood a file cabinet, containing the outlines, "Main Events," "High Points," all the constant reminders of his desire to get the record straight, and it may have been his consciousness of them that prompted his letter to Dr. Carl Jung in Zurich.

He began by introducing himself and apologized for his long overdue expression of gratitude for the critical role Jung had played in the founding of AA. He reminded Dr. Jung of Jung's conversations with Roland H. in 1930, and then, in the simplest way, he related what had happened to Roland after he left Zurich: Roland's spiritual awakening, his meeting Ebby and carrying the message to him, and Ebby's carrying it to Bill. It was not a long letter but he got everything in: the chain reaction and some details of his own experience at Towns. And he ended with the statement that Jung's place in the affection and history of AA was like no other.

Within a week, Bill had a reply from Jung:

Dear Mr. W.

Your letter has been very welcome indeed.

I had no news from Roland H. anymore and often wondered what has been his fate. Our conversation which he has adequately reported to you had an aspect of which he did not know. The reason that I could not tell him everything was that those days I had to be exceedingly careful of what I said. I had found out that I was misunderstood in every possible way. Thus I was very careful when I talked to Roland H. But what I really thought about was the result of many experiences with men of his kind.

362

His craving for alcohol was the equivalent, on a low level, of the spiritual thirst of our being for wholeness, expressed in medieval language: the union with God.°

How could one formulate such an insight in a language that is not misunderstood in our days?

The only right and legitimate way to such an experience is that it happens to you in reality and it can only happen to you when you walk on a path which leads you to higher understanding. You might be led to that goal by an act of grace or through a personal and honest contact with friends, or through a higher education of the mind beyond the confines of mere rationalism. I see from your letter that Roland H. has chosen the second way, which was, under the circumstances, obviously the best one.

I am strongly convinced that the evil principle prevailing in this world leads the unrecognized spiritual need into perdition, if it is not counteracted either by real religious insight or by the protective wall of human community. An ordinary man, not protected by an action from above and isolated in society, cannot resist the power of evil, which is called very aptly the Devil. But the use of such words arouses so many mistakes that one can only keep aloof from them as much as possible.

These are the reasons why I could not give a full and sufficient explanation to Roland H., but I am risking it with you because I conclude from your very decent and honest letter that you have acquired a point of view above the misleading platitudes one usually hears about alcoholism.

You see, "alcohol" in Latin is "spiritus" and you use the same word for the highest religious experience as well as for the most depraving poison. The helpful formula therefore is: *spiritus contra spiritum*.

Thanking you again for your kind letter

I remain
Yours sincerely
C. G. Jung

° "As the hart panteth after the water brooks, so panteth my soul after thee, O God." (Psalms 42:1)

There is no way—Bill himself found no way—to express what this letter meant to him. It was a confirmation of all that he, with no formal training, no real guidance, through his own intuition had come to believe. It was that and more. It came at a moment in his life when he needed it, only a few weeks after the death in St. Louis of Father Ed Dowling, the man who more than any other had understood his search. ("The divine dissatisfaction, the beautiful unrest that would keep him going, reaching out always . . .")

Ever since his early AA days, when Bill had read Jung's *Modern Man in Search of a Soul,* he had looked on the great doctor as not wholly a theologian, nor a pure scientist, but as someone who seemed to stand with him in that strange no man's land that lay between. And now he had passed on the formula: *spiritus contra spiritum.*

Bill kept the Jung letter as a talisman. In time it was copied, read at meetings, reprinted in *The Grapevine,* but the original stayed in his top desk drawer and, sometimes, even though he knew it by heart, he would open the drawer, look down at the signature and reread a phrase.

In the last years of his life, which were also the last years of the 1960s, Bill developed the habit of coming into the city on Tuesdays. There was no particular reason to choose Tuesday—sometimes he'd attend meetings of the General Service Board, or of the editors of *The Grapevine*—it was simply a habit and old men, he was discovering, like habits.

Most of the time he stayed in his office, but occasionally he'd wander down the hall to study the pins on the world map. They estimated that there were four hundred thousand members now, but Bill didn't put much store in figures. He knew too many drunks who'd been sober for years yet no longer attended many meetings, and you had to be a signed-up member of a group to be counted in AA statistics. Still he figured it was probably more in the spirit of things to underestimate, and he had confidence in the pins on the map that indicated fifteen thousand groups in the United States and eighty-eight other countries.

In the afternoon there would be a stream of visitors into his office. Earnest young "hippies" seemed to enjoy talking to him and he enjoyed them; troubled women brought him their doubts and sorrows; AA sinners confessed their sins; the ambitious shared their ambitions. Even the oddballs seemed to get some comfort from swapping ideas with this gray-haired older man. And Bill had no delusions about getting older. The doctors were always after him to quit smoking, scaring him about incipient emphysema, and in the mirror he was catching glimpses of a bony-faced old Vermonter, as though nature in her quiet way was returning him, with age, to his origins.

When the office would close for the evening there were only occasional visitors, but Bill would stay on at his desk, looking out the great window as light left the sky. But the coming of night had never discouraged him, and the thoughts that rambled through his mind, he said, were mostly cheerful. He didn't mind getting older. It was a little like mountain climbing, an old Vermonter once told him: the higher you go, the more out of breath you are, and you're tireder too, but the view's a lot more extensive.

Maybe at long, long last he was beginning to relax. For one thing, the differences among people no longer appeared so important. And with this knowledge had come a wonderful sense of liberation. Sometimes, as he sat with his feet propped up on the windowsill, peering out at the city and at the same time looking back at the extraordinariness of his life, he would try to figure out not his spiritual beliefs, but his philosophy.

Aldous Huxley had called Bill the greatest social architect of the century—it was a nice thing to have said—but Bill sometimes wondered if the thing that he and Dr. Bob had tried to do was so new after all. Wasn't it what he had felt wth the old vets at Gettysburg? Wasn't it what Fayette had tried to drum into him about Lincoln and democracy? As his eyes traveled over the great façade of the United Nations building he sometimes wondered if the United States might not be the only country in the world based on a belief in man and man's ability to change—on a belief in conversion. What other country was so willing to admit they were wrong and then, like every recovering drunk, be willing to change? Prohibition had been wrong, so they had repealed it. In the twenties and thirties, America was totally isolationist. They'd gone to war and come out of it the world's greatest internationalists. Maybe—although Bill never pursued the thought—AA could only have been started by a couple of Yankees who believed in the revolutionary American notion that men could change themselves completely.

Occasionally he would rise, walk over to the file cabinet and run his fingers over the folders of outlines. Curiously, another thing that no longer seemed important was getting the whole story told. The history of the leaders didn't really matter. AA, after all, was a society that functioned pretty well without them, without any sanction from the top. It was the little man, the nameless drunk, who would and should always have the final say and on whom the future would depend.

He also questioned how the story could be told without the laughter and black humor that were impossible to put into words or convey to an outsider.

Still he knew he would like to leave a message, some word that those coming along in the future might stumble across and through which they could hear him saying, "I was here." And he knew his message would have to do with anonymity, because that was where the philosophy he could never formulate and the spiritual power he was always trying to understand seemed to join.

There were arguments now, and some of them sounded very sensible, that any anonymity in the program had outlived its usefulness. Alcoholism was recognized as a disease, they said, so why not admit you were in AA? A Western senator had been completely frank, had declared his membership and had won his election—a fine man who'd done much good. Movie stars and literary figures felt no shame in having been alkies, wanted to go on the air and advertise their recovery. They wanted to help others by doing so, and that was indeed praiseworthy, and yet . . .

And yet at the very root of his being Bill knew that this aspect of the program was more than a symbol of what the ego gives up and more than a shield for the fellowship. Surely there had been more the first time he had called on Bob. Neither of them knowing or caring who the other was, they had been free to speak directly, openly, about their needs, and because of this they had discovered each other not from without, but from within. And their case was not unique; it had happened to him too many times and to too many other thousands. Somehow —and he had no other words for it—he knew he was always more at home with his spirit when he was simply an anonymous drunk working with and sharing with another drunk.

It was a feeling that could not stand the strain of being woven into a creed, and maybe because he had always found it the hardest thing to describe, he had felt that it brought him closer to that secret power he had always been seeking. "For if you can name it," Father Ed had said, "it is not God." And in a way this had tied up with St. Matthew and "Take heed that ye do not your alms before men, to be seen of them: otherwise ye have no reward of your Father which is in heaven . . . thy Father which is in secret . . . which seeth in secret . . ."

In the end he knew he need not put it into a message, but he was sure it was something they should not give up lightly. Whatever more there was to be learned about it was perhaps already hinted at in their Steps.

As he sat looking out at the lights of the city, he realized that his feeling about himself and AA was very much the feeling of a boy who had stood on the mountaintop beside his father, gazing up at the stars, awed by the vast distances, not knowing if there was a meaning intended or presumed, overwhelmed by the mysteries, yet at the same time feeling safe and cared for, knowing his father was beside him. All his life since then, as a boy and as a grown man, he had been trying to force answers, to shape and improve people. Now he was beginning to think that from here on, all that might be asked of him was to relax, keep the channels open and, yes, to be a touch more loving.

He could share fragments of these thoughts with late visitors who stopped by the office, but how much of them he was able to hang on to in the last months we cannot know. We can only hope they were nearby as the threatened emphysema developed and his life was taken over by oxygen masks and around-the-clock nurses. It was not an easy dying.

He and Lois had gone to Bermuda in the spring of '70, trying to build up Bill's strength for the annual conference, but at the conference he was put to bed in his hotel room. In May and June they were with Dr. Ed Boyle of the Miami Heart Institute, trying to get Bill strong enough for a convention in July.

At the convention members had glimpses of Bill in a wheelchair on his way from the hotel to the hospital and then being brought back, and he appeared briefly in the auditorium. He stayed on in Florida into August, returned to Bedford Hills, and was in and out of hospitals all fall, the emphysema complicated by bouts of pneumonia.

Unable to attend the intergroup dinner in New York, he sent a short message, which Lois read. In it Bill quoted an Arabian greeting a member had sent him. "I salute you and thank you for your life." He spoke of the many blessings that had been bestowed upon the fellowship, and said that if he were asked which of these was most vital to AA, he'd say it was their "concept of anonymity." The message went on for a few more lines, then he saluted them again, and again thanked them for their lives.

By November there were nights of wild hallucinating followed by days of lucidity. His breathing continued to grow worse and in January it was decided he should return to the care of Dr.

Ed. A member chartered a plane and Bill was flown south. He died in Miami on January 24, 1971.

The news of Bill W.'s death was carried on the front page of *The New York Times.* Immediately picked up by the wire services, it spread—sometimes with an old photo of Bill clutching his fiddle—as a big news story around the world.

On Sunday afternoon February 14, memorial services were held in New York at St. John the Divine, in Washington at the National Cathedral, later at St. Martin's in the Field in London, and in the Chapel at Norwich University. In Santo Domingo and in hundreds of churches around the world, men of all faiths, of all nations and in many languages tried to find the meaning in what Bill had done. They read passages from the Big Book, the Twelve Steps and the Twelve Traditions, and in trying to locate the fitting word, they even reached back to Pericles, stating that the whole earth was the tomb of certain men, that "their story is not graven only in stone over their native earth, but lives on far away without visible symbol, woven into the stuff of other men's lives."

Some old-timers could almost hear Dr. Bob saying, "For God's sake, boy, keep it simple." But the thing that perhaps would have interested Bill was that behind the rolling cadence of the prayers and the hymns, behind the silent solemnity of the cathedral, the memory many people took with them was the sight of and the sound in the voices of AA members when they read their Serenity Prayer, or a few little lines from St. Francis ". . . that where there is despair, I may bring hope . . . where there is sadness, I may bring joy. . . ."

For no one seems to have felt it was a funeral. From everywhere, men reported it was more like an Easter service.

In New York it only seemed that every AA member was in or was trying to get into St. John the Divine. In Greenwich Village, one member, Joe B., who had been sober three years, unlocked the door of the tiny storefront they used for their regular Sunday meetings.

It was two o'clock, just the time he had planned to take the subway uptown to the cathedral, and he wasn't at all clear about why at the last minute he'd changed his mind about going and had decided to come around here instead. The world would not end if for one Sunday afternoon they skipped a meeting.

He left the door open and stepped into the little room. The place had a heavy, stale smell, which didn't surprise Joe. There had been a couple of real live ones at the Saturday-night meeting, genuine Bowery rummies. You couldn't have them, along with forty AAs, all of them smoking, spilling coffee and packed together in a room this size, without causing a smell. But it wouldn't take long to air it out and he set to work plugging in the coffeepot and unfolding the chairs that were stacked up against the wall.

He didn't know why he had wanted to go to the services. Joe wasn't a religious man; he didn't yet know what he thought about the "spiritual" side of the program. He was just curious, he guessed, to hear what they would say about Bill.

He'd met Bill only once. It was at the time they were all talking about *Time* magazine's wanting to put Bill's picture on the cover, and he had said no. Such humility, such self-effacement, had impressed everyone at the gathering, but Joe remembered Bill shaking his head, and he remembered he looked like a shrewd Yankee trader. For a quick moment their eyes had met, and Bill hadn't winked, but there was a sparkle like a wink in his eye when he said that he guessed his turning *Time* down would be remembered a lot longer than having his face spread over a magazine for a week.

Joe had thought him a very shrewd Yankee. And he knew that he owed him something. Still that didn't explain this afternoon or why he was here.

Over the little platform they had built for speakers there was a framed sign. He'd been seeing it at a lot of meetings lately. It hung beside the Steps.

> I am responsible.
> Whenever anyone, anywhere, reaches out for help,
> I want the hand of AA always to be there.
> And for that, I am responsible.

It was a good saying, and Joe approved, but—he looked up at the clock—it was nearly two-thirty now and no one had showed. No newcomer had needed his hand, not this afternoon. He walked slowly back to the coffeepot and began pouring himself a cup. He guessed he'd just lock up, go on, call his girl, maybe take in a movie.

He'd filled his cup and was looking around for a spoon when he heard the footstep. He turned, and there, standing in the doorway, was a man. He wasn't old, wasn't young. He wasn't poorly dressed and not well dressed, but his hands, even though they were clasping the front of his coat, were trembling in an uncontrollable way that Joe recognized. And there was something about his eyes.

"Come in," Joe said. But the man did not move. "Yeah . . ." Joe smiled. "This is the right place."

Then he held out his cup and the man took a slow, tentative step into the room.

"You look like you could use some coffee. . . ."

THE TWELVE STEPS

1. We admitted we were powerless over alcohol—that our lives had become unmanageable.
2. Came to believe that a Power greater than ourselves could restore us to sanity.
3. Made a decision to turn our will and our lives over to the care of God *as we understood Him.*
4. Made a searching and fearless moral inventory of ourselves.
5. Admitted to God, to ourselves, and to another human being the exact nature of our wrongs.
6. Were entirely ready to have God remove all these defects of character.
7. Humbly asked Him to remove our shortcomings.
8. Made a list of all persons we had harmed, and became willing to make amends to them all.
9. Made direct amends to such people wherever possible, except when to do so would injure them or others.
10. Continued to take personal inventory and when we were wrong promptly admitted it.
11. Sought through prayer and meditation to improve our conscious contact with God *as we understood Him,* praying only for knowledge of His will for us and the power to carry that out.
12. Having had a spiritual awakening as the result of these steps, we tried to carry this message to alcoholics and to practice these principles in all our affairs.

THE TWELVE TRADITIONS

1. Our common welfare should come first; personal recovery depends on AA unity.

2. For our group purpose there is but one ultimate authority —a loving God as He may express Himself in our group conscience. Our leaders are but trusted servants—they do not govern.

3. The only requirement for AA membership is a desire to stop drinking.

4. Each group should be autonomous except in matters affecting other groups or AA as a whole.

5. Each group has but one primary purpose—to carry its message to the alcoholic who still suffers.

6. An AA group ought never endorse, finance or lend the AA name to any related facility or outside enterprise, lest problems of money, property and prestige divert us from our primary purpose.

7. Every AA group ought to be fully self-supporting, declining outside contributions.

8. Alcoholics Anonymous should remain forever non-professional, but our service centers may employ special workers.

9. AA, as such, ought never be organized; but we may create service boards or committees directly responsible to those they serve.

10. Alcoholics Anonymous has no opinion on outside issues; hence the AA name ought never be drawn into public controversy.

11. Our public relations policy is based on attraction rather than promotion; we need always maintain personal anonymity at the level of press, radio and films.

12. Anonymity is the spiritual foundation of all our Traditions, ever reminding us to place principles before personalities.